Secrets
of
German Medieval Swordsmanship

Sigmund Ringeck's Commentaries
on Johannes Liechtenauer's Verse

Translated & Interpreted by
Christian Henry Tobler

Chivalry Bookshelf
http://www.chivalrybookshelf.com

Secrets of German Medieval Swordsmanship:
  Sigmund Ringeck's Commentaries on Johannes Liechtenauer's Verse
Translated & Interpreted by Christian Henry Tobler

Printed in Hong Kong
Book Design by Brian R. Price

Published by the Chivalry Bookshelf
ISBN: 1-891448-07-2
ISBN13: 978-1-891448-07-2

SUBJECTS
Martial Arts | History, Medieval German |
Literature, Medieval German

AUTHORS
Liechtenauer, Johannes (14th c.)
Ringeck, Sigmund (15th c.)
   Tobler, Christian Henry (1963 -)

Chivalry Bookshelf
http://www.chivalrybookshelf.com

Table of Contents

Acknowledgements

There are a number of individuals who helped to make this book possible and I hope that I don't neglect any of them here.

I've been fortunate to have photographers and other collaborators that are knowledgeable and passionate about this material. Andrew Bajorinas shot the photographs for the first four sections of the book, with Ben Schenkman acting as my training partner/victim. For the mounted guard pictures, Ben took a turn as photographer with Andrew posing on horseback. Logistical support for the photography sessions was provided by Maureen Chalmers, Cynthia Emmert, Russell Hanoman, and Susan Krasnoger. Order of Selohaar members Laura Burleson and Laurie Maxwell aided me, along with the aforementioned partners, in the interpretation of Ringeck's teachings, while Bonnie Kraft gave my introduction a critical read from an outsider's point of view.

One of the most pleasant experiences of writing this book has been the enthusiasm, friendship and support that I've received from all corners of the Western Martial Arts community. I'd like to thank those who have lent their hands or inspired me: Jörg Bellinghausen, Bob Charron, John Clements, David Cvet, Christian Fletcher, Stephen Hand, the truly invaluable Stephen Hick, Marlon Hoess-Boettger, Ian Johnson, Christoph Kaindel, Mark Rector, Jennifer Reed, Bart Walczak, and Grzegorz Zabinsky.

Special thanks go to Paul Kalinowski and his staff at Hillside Equestrian Meadows in Wolcott, Connecticut for the use of their horses. Hillside is a very special place, combining a 50 acre equestrian facility with a vocational training and rehabilitation program for individuals who have suffered brain injuries. It was an honour to work with these folks!

Last, but far from least, I'm indebted to my fine friends at *Chivalry Bookshelf*, Brian & Ann Price, and Gregory Mele - they believed in this work; through their hard work and commitment my words and ideas have found a home on paper.

Jörg Bellinghausen

If someone invents a time machine, and feels obliged to consult me for a possible destination, I will suggest southern Germany in the 15th century.

I suspect that when I make this request, they will want to know why I have made the choice. It won't be to see a land so familiar to me, as it looked five centuries ago; nor to prowl the halls of the great Swabian and Bavarian castles in a time when they were seats of power, not merely tourist atractions. It won't be to see the marvel of real knights--instead of modern stunt riders--jousting in tournament (although I'd certainly stop to watch). It wouldn't even be to pause to watch the construction of a magnificent Gothic cathedral, or to see people marvel at the first printed books. All of these are marvelous reasons, but I should like to call upon a "friend" I have never met: the German *schirmaister* (fighting instructor) Sigmund Ringeck.

Their next question will undoubtedly be to ask why a person from the 21st century would want to learn the ancient art of fencing.

The Western Martial Arts were every bit as sophisticated as their Asian counterparts. The German *Kunst des Fechtens* was a system incorporating both unarmed and armed combat, with and without armor, on foot and on horseback, using daggers, long and short swords, bucklers, shields, falchions, spears and poleaxes. Parallels to *koryu*--the traditional martial arts of the Japanese samurai--immediately come to mind. But unlike the latter, which have been carefully preserved, sometimes by only a small circle of adherents to the present day, the *Kunst des Fechtens* and almost all other European martial arts were discarded and finally forgotten. Europeans are pragmatists - and the more effective firearms became, the more skill with a sword became obsolete. Ultimately, in the early days of the last century, even dueling became a relic of bygone days, the art of fencing a competitive sport.

So why learn, or better, why *reconstruct* a fighting method more than 500 years old? There are many answers to that question, but the simplest, and perhaps best, is this: Just like old tales and stories, old songs and dances, the martial arts of our ancestors are a link to our history, they belong to our culture. Historical martial arts are much more than just a good workout. They are windows to our past. We learn not only how our forefathers fought, but also about the weapons they used, the clothing and armor they wore, the laws they followed, the values they held. We can try to catch a glimpse of the lives and mindsets of those that lived long ago, only to find that they were surprisingly similar to ours and yet very, very different. And we can also learn about ourselves. Wielding a sword in earnest fencing practice reveals a lot about the individual's character, as does the study process itself. A student must be patient and committed. They must expect to make errors, and more often than not, be prepared to start from scratch yet again. No amount of physical skill will carry a serious student through without this combination of resolutuion, drive, and humility.

Since there is no real master to study under, the modern practitioner must rely on the study and on the interpretation of the various *fechtbücher*, or fencing manuals.

But let's pause a moment and take a look at the situation in Germany in the late Middle Ages. In the 15th century, the map of what is now Germany looked quite different from what it looks like today. While large parts of it belonged to the Holy Roman Empire and were ruled by the emperor, in reality, it was more like a patchwork of different duchies and shires governed by local rulers, which frequently used war as a means of solving political differences.

The larger cities such as Cologne, Frankfurt and Nürnberg, wealthy through trade and often being a *Freie Reichsstadt* (Imperial City), responsible only to the emperor, often quarreled either with one another, or with the rulers of the territories surrounding them.

Warlike conflicts and violence were quite common in this day and age; there was a lot of need for the instruction the fencing masters offered.

Like craftsmen, the fencing masters were often commoners, organizing themselves into "brotherhoods," similar to the craftsmen's guilds. In 1487, the most powerful brotherhood, the *Marxbrüder*, or "Brotherhood of our virgin Mary and Saint Marcus," was given a letter of privilege by emperor Friedrich III granting the same rights as the a craftsmen's guild. Only after an apprenticeship under an acknowledged master, a period of traveling and further learning and passing several tests, a student was granted the title *Meister des langen Schwertes*. Only after that, was he allowed to teach fencing to other students. Little is known about the masters themselves, especially about the Nestor of the *Kunst des Fechtens*, Johannes Liechtenauer. Aside from the fact that he lived in the 14th century, that he very likely came from Swabia or Bavaria, and that he compiled his art from various systems he studied in his traveling years, we know nothing about him. Sadly, this holds true for almost all of the other masters.

Most of these late medieval fencing masters were freelancers, usually temporarily employed by a nobleman or by a city. They regarded other fencing masters as fierce professional competitors, and thus tried to keep "their" art secret. Because of this, most of the *fechtbücher* are deliberately written in a cryptic way. While later writers added glossa and commentaries to those texts, these are written in the jargon of the day. Words may change their meaning over the years, so even for a native speaker, these texts can be hard to understand.

The *fechtbücher* were not written as "how to" guides, but served as a memory reminder for a student who had trained directly under a specific master. This student would know how the fight developed before the particular situation, and what options he might have afterwards. Modern students –not having received personal instruction from the master himself- are bound to interpretation and speculation, which can be, and often are, wrong.

So, analyzing the illustrations or the text of a manual alone is hardly enough to fully understand a technique, let alone to perform it correctly. Only by careful and diligent study of many written and pictorial sources, primary and secondary, combined with serious, hands-on studies -in and out of armor, in various types of clothing and in various environments- one will eventually be able to develop an understanding of a technique.

Hopefully, this book is of assistance to the modern practitioner.

Christian Tobler has pursued the task of bringing Ringeck's manual on the art of the long sword to an English speaking audience with vigor, enthusiasm and diligence. Transcribing and translating both the verse of the grand master Johannes Liechtenauer, and Sigmund Ringeck's glossa and commentaries into understandable English, not to mention bringing those words to life in the reconstruction of actual techniques is a daunting task. I think he has handled it admirably. Having played a small part in the birth of this book, I wish Christian good fortune and success with this project, and hopefully we'll see more books on European martial arts on the bookshelves in the years to come.

But most of all, if all of these efforts would lead to Meister Sigmund nodding his head as we fence, correcting a bit here and there, but still able to recognize the techniques we use as the ones that were a part of his curriculum, then we will have achieved our goal.

If somebody invents a time machine, that is.

Jörg Bellinghausen
Königswinter, Germany
November 2001

Introduction

"In Saint George's name, here begins the art of fighting..."

- Ringeck's prologue

Germany in the 15th Century

Six hundred years ago, most of what we now know as Germany made up the greater part of the Holy Roman Empire, a conglomeration of principalities, duchies, and free cities that Voltaire would later decry as "neither Holy, nor Roman, nor an Empire." The Holy Roman Emperors considered themselves inheritors of the legacy of Charlemagne, who had viewed his state as the successor to Imperial Rome. They therefore claimed to be Christendom's supreme temporal power, just as the Pope was its supreme *spiritual* authority. In reality, the Emperor's authority was limited. Imperial suzerainty never held sway over England, or France, and influenced Eastern Europe only when backed by German military might;[1] and was often challenged or curtailed by forces within the Empire's borders as dukes, ecclesiastic princes, and the ever-changing alliances of nobles scrambled for power. As for the Empire's claim to the moniker *Holy*, the Imperial "honeymoon" with the Papacy had begun and ended with Charlemagne. While the Pope still crowned a new Emperor, the relationship between the Imperial Crown and the Holy See was at best stormy and at worst one of open conflict.

Internecine warfare within the Empire was commonplace. Civic leagues fought noble alliances, robber barons raided towns, and the nearly constant strife between parties supporting the Emperor and those supporting the Pope insured that armed conflict was never far off. Domestically, legal matters were often resolved with trials by combat, travelers needed to protect themselves from assailants on the Empire's roads, and town militias required training for the protection of their citizenry. In this culture the practice of arms was a necessary component in the lives of people in all strata of society. With so much need for skill in arms, the fencing masters of the day found their craft in high demand. There were apparently many of these masters within the Empire, some of whom enjoyed the patronage of great magnates. These masters-at-arms trained noble pupils and often their household troops. While we know little of how this training was conducted, we are fortunate in that some of these masters left us manuscripts recording some of their teachings.

Ringeck's Fechtbuch and the Liechtenauer Fighting Tradition

The late medieval fencing manual, or *fechtbüch* ("fight book"), that is now commonly known as 'Ringeck's Commentaries' is an untitled manuscript from the early to mid-15th century (c.1420-1440). It resides in the State Library of Saxony[2] in Dresden, Germany and is comprised of 127 leaves (254 pages) of Middle High German text without illustrations. The manuscript appears to have been re-bound at some point in its life, as two of the leaves are currently out of their proper order.[3] It is not known (and will likely remain so) whether the manuscript is an original or a copy of an earlier version.

---

[1] Both secular and monastic - the Teutonic Knights with their on-going crusades into Poland, Lithuania and Russia had brought much of north Eastern Europe into the Imperial sphere of power.

[2] Scanned images of the manuscript are available on the internet at the *Academy of European Medieval Martial Arts* website (www.aemma.org).

[3] Leaves 124 and 125 should actually be inserted between what are now leaves 47 and 48.

The longsword portion of the manuscript claims to be the work of "Sigmund Ringeck, at the time Fight Master of Albrecht, Count Palatine of the Rhine and Duke of Bavaria." Today, the whole manual is associated with the name *Ringeck*, but the name appears only this one time in the manuscript and in relation to only one section of the work. It is therefore unclear as to whether or not the Ringeck named in the long sword commentaries is the author of the entire manuscript. So when you read references in *this* book to the name Ringeck, be mindful that this means "Ringeck, *or whoever the author of this passage really is.*"

Ringeck's *fechtbuch* is, for the most part, a series of commentaries on the work of an earlier master: the great 14th century master of arms, Johannes Liechtenauer. What we know of Master Liechtenauer is limited: he was probably born in the 1320's in Liechtenau, Franconia, Germany. In his travels throughout the Holy Roman Empire and Eastern Europe he studied with many local masters of arms and absorbed their teachings, which he later incorporated into his own system of fighting. Liechtenauer's teachings include how to fight with the lance, sword, spear and dagger as well as instruction on *ringen*, the wrestling and grappling techniques. His combat techniques are divided into three basic types, based on the environment of the fight: *bloßfechten*, for fighting without any defensive armour, *harnischfechten*, for fighting in armour (*harness*) on foot, and *roßfechten*, for fighting on horseback.

The sophistication of Liechtenauer's methods is a compelling counter to the perception, common even among historians, that medieval fighting was crude and dependent upon brute strength. Liechtenauer advanced a fighting method based on controlling the initiative in all fighting encounters, and applies the principles of leverage, timing, and distance to gain and maintain that initiative. His teachings were apparently effective: their direct influence lasted for over 250 years, and their influence on German swordplay continued long after.

Liechtenauer's teachings were recorded in a series of cryptic verses. Called *merkeverse* - "teaching verse" - these phrases seemed to have been designed with two purposes in mind. First, they cloaked Liechtenauer's fighting tradition in secrecy, for the uninitiated could read little instruction from them. Second, they provided a series of mnemonics – reminders of the teachings once you'd already learned their actual meaning. If only the *merkeverse* had survived, these fighting methods would now be inscrutable.

Starting with the priest Hanko Döbringer in the late 14th century, the masters who studied Liechtenauer's method began to not only pass on the *merkeverse*, but also *glosa* (commentaries) that explained what the old master's obscure words meant. The *fechtbucher* of this period (the 14th through 17th centuries) often begin with a complete recitation of Liechtenauer's verse, followed by passages quoting specific *merkeverse* couplets together with the explanatory glosa.

Sigmund Ringeck's work follows this pattern, and his *fechtbuch* includes interpretive commentaries on Liechtenauer's arcane phrases, then provide example techniques. As Döbringer's glosa is a very high-level conceptual treatment of Liechtenauer's verses, Ringeck's commentaries may be the earliest known glosa[4] aimed at practical instruction in specific techniques.[5]

---

[4] There is still debate regarding which is the earlier work, Ringeck's manual, or that of Peter von Danzig (See footnote #9 p. xiv), whose 1452 work is very similar in its commentary. It all depends upon whether or not the c.1440 date is too early for the Ringeck manuscript. In any case, the two fechtbucher seem to be closely related: one may derive from the other, or a common antecedent might have influenced them both.

[5] This is not to suggest that Döbringer's work is not valuable. There are elements of *merkeverse*, as well as techniques, that appear only in his book and his conceptual view of the system is unique and informative, but specifically aimed at a student of the system.

The Philosophy of Liechtenauer's Fighting Art

The basic philosophy of Master Liechtenauer's system is summarized in three words: *Maintain the initiative!* Everything in his martial art is aimed at either maintaining or regaining the initiative in the fight; that is, at staying on the offensive so that your opponent must remain occupied with defending himself. Liechtenauer's teachings instruct in how to win fights, not how to avoid losing them. "He who goes after strikes, rejoices little in his art," the master says, admonishing us not to focus on warding off the enemy's offense but on attacking. Once you have the initiative, your assault on your foe should be relentless so that he can do nothing but defend. A man forced to deflect attacks over and over will ultimately be defeated. If your opponent attacks you first then you must use defensive techniques that also contain a counterattack - you must retake the initiative *from him*.

Liechtenauer devised numerous ways to control the initiative. These tactics can be summarized in some simple rules. As the specific techniques unfold throughout this book, keep these tactics in mind:

> *Attack first* - Seize the initiative by attacking the enemy before he can attack you. This attack should be relentless until the enemy is struck down, for he can not attack you if he is preoccupied with his own defense.

> *Defend yourself by counterattacking* - If you need to protect yourself from an attack by your opponent, use a technique that also counterattacks him.

> *Stay near the opponent's weapon* - Should you bind against your opponent's weapon, or lay hands upon him to grapple, you should try to work in such a way that you are never far from his weapon or person so that you can control and limit his actions.

> *Use strength against weakness and weakness against strength* – If your opponent weakly resists your offense, then overpower him and complete the attack. If he opposes you strongly, yield to his strength and attack from a different side or angle instead. Never use strength against strength, for this puts victory in the hands of brute strength, not skill.

The dynamics of maintaining initiative in a fight are ensconced in what Liechtenauer calls "*Vor und Nach*," or "Before and After." The Before is the offensive principle, where you attack your enemy *before* he can respond, while the After is the defensive principle where you must respond *after* your opponent attacks. However, the intent of the After is not simply to defend yourself, but to use methods that do so while bringing you back to an offensive posture - that is, to bring you back to the Before. This is expressed in the master's *merkeverse*: "Before and After, these two things, are to all skill a well-spring." This is the very core of Liechtenauer's art and it applies to everything we are about to study in Ringeck's manual.

An Overview of Ringeck's Manual

Five different sections comprise Ringeck's manuscript, each representing a type of combat: unarmoured combat with the long sword; fighting with sword and buckler; unarmoured wrestling; fighting in armour on foot; and fighting in armour on horseback. These sections appear in the above order, although there are a couple of oddities in the organization of the material as it appears in the manuscript.

Strangely, Ringeck does not include dagger fighting, despite the weapon being mentioned in Liechtenauer's prologue, quoted in Ringeck's book (presented here in Chapter 1). This seems a bizarre omission, as Liechtenauer names the dagger as one of the primary weapons in his system, and almost every other German fechtbuch includes dagger fighting. However, since we know so little about the origin of the manuscript itself,[6] we have no way of knowing whether or not Master Ringeck may have originally included dagger commentaries in his teachings.

---

[6] We don't know if the manuscript is an original or a scribe's copy of a copy, for instance.

Section I - The Knightly Art of the Long Sword

The first section, comprising roughly half of the manual, consists of Ringeck's commentary on Master Liechtenauer's "Knightly Art of the Long Sword" - the techniques for unarmoured long sword fighting. This weapon was double-edged and averaged 48 inches in total length, 36 inches of which was blade. The long sword of Ringeck's time could be wielded with one hand, but was usually held with both. The right hand held the grip just below the crossguard while the left hand held it closer to the pommel. It usually featured a blade that tapered to an acute point, admirably suited to thrusting, but also capable of delivering powerful cutting strokes.

The section begins with an exposition of Liechtenauer's *merkeverse* for the long sword, after which follows Ringeck's interpretation, which he does by explaining small sections of verse at a time. Footwork and tactical basics are described first. Next, Ringeck begins discussion of the seventeen *hauptstücke*, or "primary techniques." The first five techniques are specialized cutting blows, or strikes, that epitomize Liechtenauer's philosophy of the fight: these five strikes act as both a defense and a counterattack, often in one movement.

Following the five strikes are a discussion of the four primary guard or stances, various ways to break free from a crossing of the swords to attack again, grappling techniques that work in conjunction with the sword, and finally the techniques of *winding*. Winding is a hallmark of this system; it is a turning of one's sword while it is bound against an opponent's sword and allow one to regain leverage in the bind and to re-angle the sword so that the point can be brought into position to thrust. Lastly, Ringeck offers some techniques that aren't specifically discussed in Liechtenauer's teachings, but are *derived* from them. These include some additional guards and counter-techniques.[7]

A note to the reader
I'll now offer some rather unconventional advice. After you read the first couple of chapters on Liechtenauer's *merkeverse* and the tactical basics, skip ahead and read the chapter on *Vier Leger* - the "four guards" -then return to the *Zornhau*, and begin reading sequentially again. An understanding of the guards is critical to learning the rest of the system, for every action can be described in terms of moving from one guard to another. Additionally, Ringeck discusses the guards quite a bit before even explaining them! This is typical of the organization of thought in this manuscript - concepts are often given brief mention well in advance of their full explanation: you'll see winding as a part of other techniques long before you read about winding in its own chapter, for instance. As this can be confusing for modern readers, you should read the entire long sword section and *then read it again*, for many things will become clearer the second time around.

Pay close attention to how the same tactical concepts appear over and over again. In all cases, the intent of the techniques is to take the initiative from your opponent. This can be done by striking aside his attack and hitting him at the same time, by thrusting while opposing his blade, by using his timing against him, or by suddenly attacking another target after he has defended your first attack. In all of these techniques the idea is to use defensive techniques that are, or become, *offensive* ones.

Likewise, as mentioned above, all good techniques begin in one of the four guards, and end in another of the four. Thus, any thrust from below must come from a position similar to the guard *Pflug*, and any thrust from above, the guard *Ochs*. A vertical cut out of *vom Tag* will finish in *Alber*, while a cut from below out of *Alber* would naturally finish in *vom Tag*. A displacement out of one guard will naturally finish in another.

Understanding the interconnectedness of the system's core elements is the true key to learning; the individual techniques simply serve as reinforcements and applications of those principles.

---

[7] There is also a curious section of the manuscript that repeats Liechtenauer's long sword verse along with some commentary on the first couple of primary techniques. These may derive from another author than the rest of the manuscript - they are written in a different style and from a more conceptual point of view, rather than the practical rundown of techniques that figures in the other commentaries. I've included this section as an appendix at the end of this volume.

Section II - Sword and Buckler

Ringeck's techniques for fighting with sword and buckler, a small shield held by a single hand grip, follow next. They are interesting for several reasons. They have no Liechtenauer *merkeverse* associated with them. They are organized into six forms or "plays" that include enough material to easily recognize a miniature system within them. For me, the most interesting thing is how clearly they appear to have been extrapolated from Master Liechtenauer's long sword system. The six plays include the use of binding, winding, thrusting in opposition, and quickly moving to attack a different target once one has been defended.

The buckler techniques should feel familiar to anyone who has studied the long sword methods. They should also be familiar to those who have studied the earliest in the currently available corpus of *fechtbucher*, the so-called "Tower Manuscript," I.33, which is a late 13th or early 14th century German work depicting sword and buckler techniques exclusively.

Section III - Wrestling

"All fencing comes from wrestling,"[8] wrote Hanko Döbringer, a 14th century cleric and one of Master Liechtenauer's early exponents. Wrestling and grappling techniques formed the foundation of all medieval martial arts. The wrestling section of Ringeck's book takes up a large part of the manuscript, second only in size to the long sword teachings. It is comprised of three major subsections.

The first of these sub-sections, which begins with the heading "Here begins some good wrestling techniques and counter-techniques," contains several types of techniques including throws, joint locks, holds, ground fighting, and strikes. These various techniques appear in what seems to be a haphazard order. The second subsection, which starts with "Here begins *other* good wrestling techniques and counter-techniques," is a smorgasbord of twenty-three techniques, along with a handful of counter-techniques. All of these techniques are throws of various kinds. The last sub-section, beginning with the heading "Here begins the wrestling while closing," is comprised of thirteen techniques and a couple of counters for wrestling with someone as you approach them.

These three sub-sections all have headings that indicate the start of a new, tactical concept. They also have several techniques that overlap. It is tempting to think that they might represent three separate books that may have sprung from different sources. Certainly, the lack of any *merkeverse* makes it less likely that these wrestling techniques originate with Liechtenauer.

Section IV - Foot Combat in Armour

If your idea of combat between knights is two heavily armoured men swinging swords at each other as hard as they can, then be prepared for some surprises. The knights and men-at-arms of the 15th century wore plate armour with maille protecting their joints. This protection was so effective that the sword's edge became virtually useless in fighting a man so equipped. To work around this defensive advantage, virtually all of Ringeck's armoured foot combat techniques, or *harnischfechten*, are designed to use a weapon's point for thrusting into the gaps in the plate armour defenses.

The swordplay is performed at the half-sword, a way of holding the sword with one hand on the hilt and the other grasping the blade in the middle, to provide better control while delivering powerful thrusts. The sword can also be swung with both hands on the blade so that the hilt and pommel strike like an impact weapon such as a war hammer or pollaxe. Techniques for armoured spear fighting and specialized techniques for grappling with an armoured man are also included in this section. Ringeck once again comments on Master Liechtenauer's verse in this section, but this time there less exposition of the *merkeverse* than there was for the long sword teachings.

---

[8] Döbringer, Hanko, *Fechtbuch*, 86 recto.

Take note of how the basic concepts of long sword fighting appear here as well. The concepts of "Before" and "After" apply just as much to fighting in armour at the half-sword as they did with the long sword in street clothes. A number of the primary techniques for long sword fighting have specialized application here. Lastly, pay close attention to how the guards are described, particularly those for half-sword fighting - they are derived from the four primary guards that inform the teachings of the long sword.

Section V - Mounted Combat

Liechtenauer's teachings on combat on horseback, *roßfechten*, describe techniques for fighting with lances, swords, and wrestling on horseback. These techniques continue to leverage the basic concepts first expressed in the long sword teachings, and include methods for setting aside lance attacks while striking the other rider, methods for trapping the opponent's sword, and ways to throw your foe from his saddle. The sword must be wielded primarily with the right hand, while the left hand controls the horse's reins. Despite this, the basic lessons from the long sword teachings continue to apply. Even the familiar long sword system of four guards appears, albeit adapted significantly to suit the demands of sitting in the saddle.

As with the armoured foot combat, Liechtenauer's *merkeverse* appears alongside Ringeck's glosa but there is no prefatory exposition of the verse. Ringeck quotes a subset of Liechtenauer's mounted combat teachings, plus some additional verses known as *figures* that summarize concepts and techniques at the end of some passages of glosa. Although these 'auxiliary verses' seem to be written in Liechtenauer's style, we can't be sure of their authorship. Eight of these figures appear in Ringeck's book, but from other period manuals we can tell that there were apparently twenty-six of them in total.[9]

The mounted combat techniques are probably least likely to be practiced by most readers. However, I urge you to study them as they reveal once more the simplicity, elegance, and consistency of Liechtenauer's fighting art. And, hopefully, some of you may be motivated to further investigate them - there's much more work to be done before we can fully understand how these techniques work when coupled with accurately reconstructed medieval equestrian skills.

About the Project

The Translation and Interpretation
I was first exposed to Sigmund Ringeck's *fechtbuch* in 1999 when the Historical Armed Combat Association (HACA) made an English translation of part of it available on their website.[10] This translation was done by Mr. Jörg Bellinghausen, of Königswinter, Germany, and covered the first two-thirds of the long sword section. Jörg's work sparked a lot of discussion and debate on the HACA on-line forum and has been the source of a good deal of the interest that the medieval German *fechtbucher* now enjoy among Western Martial Arts enthusiasts.

Mr. Bellinghausen's work was based on another translation, from the medieval German of the manuscript into New High German, which was done by Mr. Christoph Kaindel of Vienna, Austria. Mr. Kaindel's work, which included most of the manuscript's content save for Liechtenauer's verse and the mounted combat material, in turn was based on a 1965 transcription of the original manuscript by the German academic linguist Martin Wierschin.

I had studied Mr. Bellinghausen's translation for roughly a year before I became so enthralled with Ringeck's book that I had to take a stab at translating more of it. I am not a native German speaker nor am I a professional linguist, so my first efforts in this endeavor were comical at best. But I kept at it and learned as I went, working first with the

---

[9] All twenty-six figures appear in Peter von Danzig's *fechtbuch* (1452), as well as the work of Hans Czynner and the early 16th Century work 'Goliath'. (Danzig: Rom. Biblioteca dell' Academica Nazionale dei Lincei e Corsiniana, Cod. 44 A 8 (Cod. 1449), 1452.); Czynner (Hans Cyznner, Graz, Universitätsbibliothek - MS.963 1538); Goliath, (Anonymous, Biblioteka Jagiellonski, Krakow - MS. Germ. Quart. 2020 1510-1520.)

[10] www.thehaca.com

remainder of Christoph Kaindel's translation as yet untouched by Jörg. At that point I had not even seen Wierschin's transcription and certainly not the manuscript itself, so I was as yet unaware that there was anything more to Ringeck than I had already seen.

When I finally did get to see the complete transcription I was surprised, and more than a little daunted, to find that there was an 'undiscovered country' filled with Liechtenauer's *merkeverse* and an entire section on mounted combat. Rather than bore the reader by explaining the labor in translating those parts of the manuscript from medieval German into English, I will pause to acknowledge some friends, without whom the task would have been impossible: Mr. Bellinghausen and Mr. Marlon Hoess-Boettger of Zurich, Switzerland.

This is not a literal translation of Ringeck's book, but a loose one whose aim is to convey the *sense* of his work. I have in places created subheadings where Ringeck has none, and I have made adjustments to the material's order of presentation because in some sections of the manuscript the organization of the material is very obvious, in others it is difficult to follow. For the long sword techniques I have preserved the order, as Ringeck follows Liechtenauer's *merkeverse* - it's important for the student to see that sequence because it is repeated in numerous other manuals. The wrestling section however, is another matter: In some cases I've made considerable changes in the order of presentation because there's little rhyme or reason to where the techniques appear in relation to each other.

In each section of this book, you will find Ringeck's commentaries and my own. I've devoted a lot of time and considerable space to technique interpretation. My foremost concern in writing these comments has been to convey the connections between the techniques so that the practitioner can understand how simple and integrated a fighting system this really is. For instance, the long sword techniques involve, at most, ten basic motions. The same stances and basic modes of attack appear over and over - it is only how they are strung together that varies from technique to technique. And these connections apply across the entire spectrum of fighting methods that appear in this work. Whether one is on foot or on horse, in armour or unarmoured, the same fundamentals apply.

The reader should note my use of the word *interpretation*, for that is what my comments are - one man's interpretation. I've no doubt that seasoned practitioners will take issue with some of them and equal confidence that translators more skillful than I will find room for improvement in that area. I welcome this, because debate forces all of us to learn. Our knowledge of medieval fighting arts is changing at a brisk pace and we must all, with humility, accept the fact that our current understanding must be improved upon and in many cases, completely superseded.

The Photographs

Photographic interpretations accompany almost every technique in this book. While my team and I have labored to show them with as much clarity as possible, the reader should be aware of some limitations. Photographs in a book cannot compete with video footage. Neither can ever be a substitute for first-hand instruction in a martial art. These pictures have all been posed, so there is only so much they can do to convey the dynamism evident when a technique is performed at speed. In fact, many of the techniques, particularly those that result in a thrust to the face, would be impossible to perform safely at full speed without considerable protective gear.

In the chapters dealing with mounted combat, I have had to content myself with presenting photographs for only the guards for using the lance and sword. There is considerable investment of time and training required to get to the point where *two* horses will tolerate a pair of armoured riders fighting each other with weapons at close range. This proved to be beyond our grasp with the time and resources my team had available. More work will need to be done to fully understand the dynamics of these techniques than the scope of this project allows. However, I hope the combination of the guard photographs and my commentary text will allow the reader to appreciate how integrated the techniques for fighting on horseback are with the rest of this fighting system.

Some words for the Martial Arts Practitioner

The techniques we will explore together are not just quaint curiosities from an old book. They constitute a very real, and very dangerous martial art - a medieval *Western* martial art. It is my expectation and wish that many readers will endeavor to work hands-on with these techniques. It is my hope that they will do so safely. Please take every possible precaution in working with these combat methods. Even with the best safety gear, a careless attitude can cause accidents that injure - or kill - a training partner. Many practitioners train today with wooden swords, known in our period of study as "wasters." If you train with these, be mindful that these are essentially sword-shaped baseball bats: if swung at speed against an unprotected head, they could kill. Use caution in learning the wrestling techniques contained in this book - you can easily dislocate joints, and break bones with them if you aren't careful. Always wear substantial protective gear when sparring and be especially sure to protect the head, neck, throat, hands, joints, and groin.

It is my most fervent hope that my readers will use this martial art responsibly in their lives. Martial arts practice provides exercise, sharpens the mind, and can teach us much about *ourselves*. Just as with any of the more familiar Eastern martial arts practiced today, this art has hand-to-hand combat techniques that can be used for self-defense. However, these same techniques can be just as easily *misused* and I will be bitterly disappointed if this happens. I believe Master Liechtenauer kept his teachings secret not only to safeguard his and his student's livelihoods, but also to keep them from falling into the wrong hands. So in helping to break this secrecy, I have bent the rules a bit and taken a chance on the honour and responsibility of my readership.

In Saint George's name, let us all therefore strive to learn and practice this art in safety, without malice, and in the spirit of Chivalry that so infused Master Sigmund Ringeck's age.

Christian Henry Tobler
Oxford, Connecticut, USA
November, 2001

Notes and Acknowledgments on

I wanted the photographs to reflect some feel for the historical period that Sigmund Ringeck lived in, and so decided that this book would present the techniques in period-style clothing and equipment. In the long sword and wrestling material, you'll find Ben and I in reproductions of 15th century doublets, woolen hose, and turn-shoes. In the sword and buckler section we've opted for sleeveless *pourpoints* in lieu of the doublets. The long swords we used are a matched pair made by **Del Tin Armi Antiche** in Italy. The shorter arming swords wielded in the sword and buckler photographs are also Del Tin products, while the bucklers themselves were purchased through **Museum Replicas Ltd.** of Conyers, Georgia.

The armours in this book are a bit late in look for Ringeck's time, with the average time period for them falling in around 1470. However, they reflect the overall level of protection that Ringeck's students would have had to expect to face: almost complete coverage of the body in plate armour with maille defending the gaps between the plates.

The armour harness that I wear throughout the armoured foot combat sections is a reproduction German Gothic armour made by **Christian Fletcher Medieval Military** of Nampa, Idaho. Its design was derived from several contemporary period armours. In the foot combat sequences, Ben wears arm and leg armour made by Mr. Fletcher, along with a *cuirass* (breast and backplate) made by Museum Replicas, based on a prototype by **Medieval Reproductions**, Peter Fuller of Calgary, Alberta, Canada. His *sallet* (helmet) and accompanying *bevor* (throat defense) is of Indian manufacture. In the mounted sequences, Andrew wears another harness built by Mr. Fletcher (one of his earliest full harness projects), save for the helmet, which is another Indian import. Both Andrew and Ben's harnesses are suggestive of the Northern Italian or Flemish export armours that found their way into so many parts of Europe in the second half of the 15th century.

I'm delighted to present so much of Mr. Fletcher's work in this book. He is one of those rare modern armourers that combines outstanding service with fine craftsmanship, and his skill level has always been on the increase throughout the years that I have done business with him. It's been an honour to be one of his patrons and it is no exaggeration to say that this book could not have been all that I wanted it to be without him.

The tent that serves as the backdrop for the armoured foot combat was purchased from **Revival Enterprises**, of Highland Village, Texas, and is a reproduction of a Burgundian pavilion of the 15th century. However, the gear used for the mounted pictures is modern Western tack - time and budget constraints didn't allow for the commissioning of a correct medieval saddle and bridle. Medieval saddles are constructed in quite different fashion than modern saddles, so I have no doubt that the correct gear plays a vital role in the proper execution of Ringeck's techniques during a real encounter.

about the author

Christian Henry Tobler was born in 1963 in Paterson, New Jersey. A graduate of the University of Bridgeport's computer engineering program, Mr. Tobler has worked as a software developer, product manager, and marketing specialist in the analytical instrumentation field. He is the Grand Master of the *Order of Selohaar*, an eclectic, mystic order of chivalry that he co-founded in 1979. A veteran of 15 years of tournament fighting, he is also an avid collector of reproduction arms and armour. Christian has been focussed on the study of medieval *fechtbücher* for the past several years and teaches a weekly class in medieval combat. Mr. Tobler lives in Oxford, Connecticut with his wife Maureen Chalmers and far too much armour for the size house that they live in.

The Order of Selohaar

The *Order of Selohaar* is an eclectic, mystic order of chivalry founded in 1979. The Order is "dedicated to the preservation of honor, nobility, arcane wisdom, and martial excellence." As a part of that mission its *fechtschule* (Fight School) has been meeting under Mr. Tobler's guidance to study the fighting manuals of the late Middle Ages. The group's focus has been the late medieval German *Kunst des Fechtens* - the art of fighting. *The Order of Selohaar* may be reached online at:

http://www.selohaar.org.

Subheader names the specific technique described on the page

Chapter Name

Original manuscript reference from which the technique is drawn

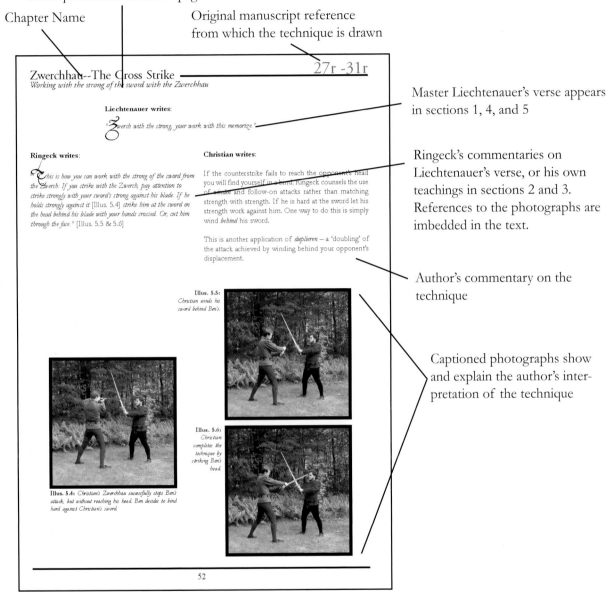

Master Liechtenauer's verse appears in sections 1, 4, and 5

Ringeck's commentaries on Liechtenauer's verse, or his own teachings in sections 2 and 3. References to the photographs are imbedded in the text.

Author's commentary on the technique

Captioned photographs show and explain the author's interpretation of the technique

I've chosen a multi-level approach to presenting information in this book. Each chapter begins with general commentary that provides a conceptual overview of the techniques contained therein. On the pages within the chapters, I've provided several different views of the techniques: Liechtenauer's mnemonic verse, Ringeck's commentary, my own interpretative commentary, and photographic interpretations of the fighting sequences. Each photograph is captioned and referenced in the Ringeck text. The practitioner thus has several different angles from which he can approach the techniques (presentation design by Brian R. Price). A sample page appears above.

For my wife Maureen Chalmers, and my parents Marilyn and Junius Tobler

Chapter 1
Master Liechtenauer's Verse

This is an exposition of Master Johannes Liechtenauer's instruction for the long sword. Known as "teaching verse" or *merkeverse*, its form seems to have been dictated by two functions. Liechtenauer and his students used it to obscure the teachings so that the unindoctrinated could not decipher it; passing the tradition through verse ensured a certain degree of secrecy. It also acted as a mnemonic. Evocative rhymes can serve as an admirable teaching and memorization tool. My students and I now use *merkeverse* actively in our training; while sometimes cryptic and obscure, once you have learned from Master Ringeck's *commentaries*, you will find Master Liechtenauer's *verse* a very useful mnemonic.

Translating the verse was a profound experience. As I read it, I felt that I was touching the heart of the Liechtenauer tradition for the first time. These words, with some modifications, formed the core of a fighting system for nearly three hundred years; an awe-inspiring testament to the efficacy of the arts we are about to explore. We will see the verse again and again as we make our way through the commentaries: Ringeck's format takes the original one section at a time and explains it so that we may understand the master's secret words.

Some notes on the translation of the verse

I've included two lines not included in the Ringeck's exposition of the Liechtenauer original. These are the third and fourth lines for the *Krumphau* (*"krump wer wol setzet, mitt schrytteen er vil hew letzet"*). As they appear in the commentaries that follow, and in every other major work that quotes the verse, I have concluded that they have been accidentally omitted here; I have therefore chosen to restore them to their proper place. There are also instances where the words as quoted in the complete exposition vary in some way with how they appear in the sections containing the commentaries. I've made some adjustments to reach a point where the verse makes the most sense and so that it is in agreement with its appearances in other German *fechtbücher*.

"*Here begins the Knightly Art of the Long Sword.*

"*In Saint George's name, here begins the art of fighting, written in verse by Johannes Liechtenauer, who was a great Master of the art, God have mercy on him. It begins first with the long sword, afterwards the spear and sword on horseback, and also the half sword in battle, all written down in what follows.*"

Jüngk ritter lere	Young knight learn,
gott lieb haben frowen ja eren	to love God and revere women,
so wechst dein ere	so that your honour grows.
vbe ritterschaft und lere	Practice knighthood and learn
kunst die dich ziert	the Art that dignifies you,
vnnd in kriegen zu eren hofiert	and brings you honour in wars.
ringet gutt fasset glefen	Wrestle well, and wield lance,
sper schwert vnnd messer manlich bederben	spear, sword and dagger manfully,
vnnd jn andern henden verdörben	whose use in others' hands is wasted.
haw dreyn vnnd hart dar rauschen treffen	Strike bravely and hard there! Rush to, strike
oder la farn das in die wysen	or miss. Those with wisdom
hassen den man sicht brysen	loath, the one forced to defend.[1]
daruff dich fasse	This you should grasp:
alle künst haben lenge vnd masse	All arts have length and measure.

Das ist ain gemain lere des langen schwerts	This is the general teaching of the long sword

Wilt du kunst schawen	If you want to behold the art,
sich link gen vnd recht mitt hawen	left against him and right while striking.
vnd linck mit rechtem	And left to right,
ist das du starck gerest fechten	is how you strongly want to fight.
wer nach gät hawen	He who goes after strikes,
der darff sich kunst wenig fröwen	rejoices little in his art.
haw nahent waß du wilt	To strike closing is what you wish,
kain wechßler kompt in dinen schilt	no change comes into your shield.
zu kopff zu lybe	To the head, to the body
die czecke nitt vermyde	the twitches do not shun.
mitt gantzen lybe	To fight with the entire body,
fechten waß du starck gerest tryben	is what you powerfully want to do.
hören waß da schlecht ist	Listen to what is wrong,
ficht nitt oben linck so du recht bist	do not fight above the left, if you are right;
vnd ob du linck bist, jm rechten och sere hinckest	and if you are left, on the right you limp as well.
vor vnd nach die zway ding	Before and After, these two things,
sind aller kunst ain vrspring	are to all skill a well-spring.
schwech vnd störck	Weak and Strong,
jn des daß wort damitt mörck	Indes – that word – always remember.
so magst du lörnen	So should you learn
mit künst erbetten vnd weren	with skill to work and defend.
erschrickstu geren	If you are scared willingly,
kain fechten nymer mer lern	no fencing should you learn.
fünff he? lere	Five strikes learn
von der rechten hand wider die were	from the right hand against the opposition.
dann wir geloben	Then we promise
in kunsten gern zu lonen	that your arts will be rewarded.

---

[1] *Martin Wierschin's glossary indicates that "brisen" means to be cramped or tied-up. He goes on to clarify that the opponent is pressed to defend himself.*

Das ist der texte

Zorn hawe krumpt were hawt schiller
mitt schettaler alber
versetzt nachraysen über lauff
haet setz durch wechsel zug durch laff
abschnitt hendrug henge wind mitt
blosem
schlach fach schich mitt stossenn

This is the text:

Zornhau, Krumphau, Zwerchhau, Schielhau,
with Scheitelhau, Alber;
Versetzen, Nachreisen, Überlaufen,
Absetzen, Durchwechseln, Zucken, Durchlaufen,
Abschneiden, Hände Drücken, Hangen, Winding to
the openings;
Strike, cut, with thrusting.

Der zorn haw

Wer dir ober hawet
zorn haw ort jm drawet
wirt er es gewar
nym oben ab an far
biß storckenn wider
wennde stich sicht er es nym es nider
daß eben mörcke
haw stich leger waich oder hörte
jndes vndd vor nach
ane hurt dein krieg sy nitt gach
weß der krieg remet
oben unden wirt er beschemet
in allen treffen
den maistern wilt du sy effen
in allen winden
hew stich schnitt lern finden
auch solt du mitt
brieffen hew stich oder schnitt

The Zornhau (The Strike of Wrath)

Who strikes at you from above,
threaten with the point of the Zornhau.
If he becomes aware of it,
take it away above and drive on.
Be stronger against:
turn, thrust. If he sees that, take it down.
Memorize this:
strike, thrust, position – soft or hard.
Indes and Before and After heed.
Your War should not be in haste.
Who tends to the War
above, gets ashamed below.
In all meetings with
the Masters, you want to imitate them.
In all winding
learn to find strikes, thrusts, and cuts.
Also should you test along
if you can strike, thrust, or cut.

Die vier blossen zu brechen

Vier blossen wisse
reme so schlectstu gewysse
an alle far
on zwifel wie er gebar
wilt du dich rechen
die vier blossen künstlichen brechen
oben duplier
vnden recht mutier
ich sage dir für war
sich schützt kain man an far
haust du recht vernommen
zu schläge mag er clain kummen

To Break the Four Openings

Four openings know,
aim: so you hit certainly,
upon all go
without regard for how he acts.
When you want to consider,
how to break the four openings with skill:
above Dupliere,
below well Mutiere.
I say to you truthfully:
he can not defend himself without danger;
if you have correctly learned,
to striking he will barely come.

Die Krumphau

Krump vff behende
wirff den ort vff die hende
krump wer wol setzet
mitt schrytteen er vil hew letzet
haw krump zu den flöchen
den maystern wiltu sy schwöchen
wenn er blitzt oben
so stand ab das will ich loben
krüme nitt kurtz hawe
durch wechsel do mitt schowe
krump wer dich irret
der edel krieg in verwirret
daß er nitt waist für war
wo er sy one far

The Krumphau (The Crooked Strike)

Krump with nimbleness,
throw the point to the hands.
Who Krumps to displace with a step,
he will strike last.
Strike Krump to the flats
of the Masters when you want to weaken them.
When he flashes from above,
then move away, that I will laud.
Strike the Krump short,
changing through show with this.
Who Krumps to lead you astray,
the Noble War will confuse him,
that he will not know truthfully
where he should go.

Der zwerchhaw

Zwerch benimpt
was von dem tage her kumpt
zwer mitt der störck
dein arbait da mitt mörck
zwer zu dem pflüg
zu dem ochsen hart gefüg
waß sich wol zwert
mitt springen den haupt gefert
veller wer füret
von vndenn nach wunsch rüret
verkerer zwinget
durch lauffer auch mitt ringet
den elnbogen gwyß nym springe
eine jn die wage
veller zwifach
trifft man den schnit mit mach
zwifach fürhaß
schreyt jn linck vnd byß nit las

The Zwerchhau (The Cross Strike)

The Zwerchhau takes
whatever comes from the roof.
Zwerch with the strong,
your work with this memorize.
Zwerch to the Plow;
to the Ox hard together.
He who Zwerchs well
with the jump protects the head.
Who leads the feint
hits from below as he wishes.
The Verkehrer forces,
a running through also brings wrestling.
The elbow take certainly,
jump into his balance.
Feint twice,
if you hit, also make the cut.
Twice further on,
step to the left and the cut not omit.

Der schilhaw

Schiller jn bricht
waß buffel schlöcht oder sticht
wer wechsel drawet
schiller in daruß beraubet
schill körtzt er dich an
durchwechsel gesigst jm an
schill zu dem ort
vnd nym den halß on forcht
schill zu dem obern
houpt hend wil du bedebern

The Schielhau (The Squinting Strike)

The Schielhau breaks,
what the Buffalo strikes or thrusts.
Who threatens to change through,
the Schielhau robs him out of it.
Schielhau when he strikes short to you,
change through, thrust to him.
Squint to the point,
and take the throat without fear.
Squint to the head above
if you want to damage the hands.

Der schaittelhaw

Der schaytler ist dem antlitz ge fere
mit seiner kere
der brust fast geuer
waß von im kumpt
die krone daß abnympt
schnyde der doch die krone
so brichst du sy hart schone
die strich druck
mitt schnitten sy ab zeüch

Die vier leger

Vier leger allain
da von halt vndd fleüch die gmain
ochß pflug alber
vom tag sy dir nitt vnmer

Die vier versetzen

Vier sind versetzten
die die leger ser letzen
vor versetzten hiet dich
geschicht es ser es müt dich
ob dir versetzt ist
vnd wie daß komen ist
hör waß ich dir rate
rayß ab haw schnell mitt drate
setz an vier enden
belyb daruff ler wilt du enden

Von nachraysen

Nachraysen lere
zwifach oder schnitt die were
zway ausser nym
der arbait darnach beginn
vnd brüff die geferte
ob sy sind waich oder herte
daß fulen lere
jn des daß wort schnidet sere
nachraisen zwifach
trifft man den alten snet mitt macht

The Scheitelhau

The Scheitelhau is a danger to the face.
With its turn,
very dangerous to the breast.
What comes from him,
the Crown will catch.
Cut through the Crown,
you will break it hard through.
Press the strikes,
with cuts take them off.

Vier Leger (The Four Guards)

Four guards alone hold;
and disdain the common.
Ochs, Pflug, Alber,
vom Tag should not be unknown to you.

Vier Versetzen (The Four Displacements)

Four are the displacements
which hurt four guards very much.
Beware of displacing.
If it happens to you, it troubles you greatly.
If you are displaced
and when that has happened,
hear what I advise to you:
Tear away and strike quickly with surprise.
Set upon the four ends.
Stay upon, if you want to learn to bring it to an end.

Nachreisen (The Traveling After)

The travelling after: learn
twice, or cut into the weapon.
Two outside takings.
The work after that begins.
And test the bind,
if it is soft or hard.
The feeling learn.
'Indes' – that word – cuts sharply.
Travel after twice,
if you hit, the old cut make along.

Von vberlauffen

Wer vnden rempt
überlaüff den der wirt beschempt
wenn er glitzt oben
so sterck das ger ich loben
dein arbeit mach
oder hört drück zwifach

Überlaufen (The Overrunning)

Who wants to strike below,
run him over, and he will be ashamed.
When he strikes from above,
then strengthen: this I truly do laud.
Do your work,
or press hard twice.

Von absetzen

Lere absetzen
haw stich kunstlichen
wer vff dich sticht
dein ort trifft vnnd sein an pricht
von baiden sytten
triff all mal wilt du schrytten

Absetzen (The Setting Aside)

Learn to set aside,
strike and thrust with skill.
Who thrusts at you,
your point hits and his is broken.
From both sides,
if you want to hit every time, you must step.

Von durchwechseln

Durchwechseln lere
von bayden syten stich mitt söre
wer vff dich bindet
durch wechsel jn schier findet

Durchwechseln (The Changing Through)

The changing through learn
from both sides, thrust with intent.
Whoever binds to you,
change through and find him exposed.

Von zucken

Tritt nahent in binden
das zucken gyt gut fünde
zeuch trift her
zeuch mer
arbait wind das tut jm we
zuck allen treffen
den maistern wilt du sy effen

Zucken (The Twitching)

Step close in binding.
The twitching provides good finds.
Twitch! If it hits,
twitch more.
Work and wind: that will hurt him.
Twitch in all meetings with
the Masters, if you want to imitate them.

Von durchlauffen

Durchlauff laß hangen
mitt dem knopf greyff wilt du rangen
wer gegen dir sterckt
durchlauff damitt mörck

Durchlaufen (The Running Through)

Run through, let hang
with the pommel. Grasp if you want to wrestle.
Who comes strongly at you,
the running through then remember.

Von abschnyden

Schnid ab die hertten
von vnden vnd baiden geferten
vier sind der schnitt
zwen vnden vnd zwen oben mitt

Abschneiden (The Cutting Off)

Cut off the hard ones,
from under and both bind.
Four are the cuts:
two from below and two from above.

Von hend trucken

Dein schnyde wende
zu flechenn drück dein hende

Hende Trucken (The Pressing of the Hands)

Your cutting edge turn,
to the wrists press your hands.

Von zwayen hengen

Zway hengen werden
vß ainer handt von der erden
in allen geförte
haw stich leger waich oder herte

Zwei Hengen (The Two Hangers)

There are two hangers
from one hand to the earth.
In all binds
strike, thrust, position - soft or hard.

Von sprechfenster

Sprechfenster mach
ste frölich besich sein sach
schlach nider das er erßnab
wer sich vor dir zücht ab
ich sag dir für war
sich schitzt kain man on far
hastu es vernommen
zu schlachen mag es clain kummen

The Sprechfenster

The Sprechfenster do.
Stand blithely and look at his matter.
Strike down so he snaps.
When he withdraws from you,
I say to you truthfully:
no one protects himself without danger.
If you have learned this,
to striking he barely comes.

Die beschliessung der zedel

Wer wol füret vnd recht bricht
vnd entlich garbericht
vnd bricht besunder
yegelicheß in dry wünder
wer recht wol hengett
vnd winden do mitt bringet
vnd winden achten
mitt rechten weg betrachten
vnd ir aine
der winde salb drette jch gemaine
so sein die zwenzüg
vnd fur zelt sie anzig
von bayden sytten
acht vnden lern mitt schrytten
vnd brüff die geört
nicht mer newe weich oder hert

The Conclusion of the Teachings

Who leads well and breaks properly
and finally makes it all right
And splits particularly
everything into three wounders
Who properly well hangs
and the windings brings along,
and the eight windings
views in a righteous way,
and one of
the winds with the same three I mean
so they are twenty and four.
And count them only,
from both sides.
Eight windings learn with stepping.
And test the bind
no more than soft or hard.

The author Christian Henry Tobler, in harness by Christian Fletcher.

Chapter 2
Basic Concepts

This is the start of Sigmund Ringeck's commentaries, his *glosa*, on Johannes Liechtenauer's teaching verse. The Master's words are usually presented a couplet at a time, though Ringeck sometimes offers several together. Commentary always follows, explaining the original mnemonic. What I call the "basic concepts" section of work deals with the fundamentals of Liechtenauer's fighting system; how to step as you strike, how to maintain control of the fight, and how the parts of the sword blade are important in engaging another's weapon. It also contains an introduction to the *"five secret strikes,"* as well as a sort of table of contents for the major longsword techniques.

Master Liechtenauer sets down the importance of footwork in his teachings and Ringeck emphasizes it. In striking a blow, the coordination of the footwork with movement of the hands is crucial. The foot must follow the hands, else the blow cannot be struck properly; when striking from the right, you must step with the right foot and when striking from the left, you must step with the left.

The concept of initiative is of paramount importance. When a combatant has the initiative he controls the fight and can stay on the offensive until his opponent finds himself overwhelmed. To fight maintaining the initiative is to fight in the *Vor*--the "Before"--which means striking *before* your opponent so he must react defensively. Combatants on the defensive are fighting in the *Nach*--the "After." An opponent who seizes the initiative forces you to react *after* he attacks. In the Liechtenauer School, the proper use of the *Nach*--as we shall see repeatedly--employs defensive techniques that also contain offensive capabilities; this allows one to win back the initiative while defending against an attack.

The next five chapters focus on Liechtenauer's five strikes; these epitomize his fighting philosophy: they can all be used as defenses that simultaneously counterattack. Put more philosophically, they are used in the *After* to win back the *Before*.

<u>**Ringeck Writes**</u>:

"*H)ere begins the interpretation of the teachings:*

This is the beginning of the interpretation of the Knightly Art of the Long Sword, written down in rhymes by a great master of these arts, Johannes Liechtenauer – God have mercy upon him. He recorded his teachings in secret words, so that the art may not be commonly spread. These secret phrasings were later interpreted and commented on in a book by Schirmaister Sigmund Ringeck, at the time Fechtmeister of Albrecht, Count Palatine of the Rhine and Duke of Bavaria, so that every fencer who already understands fencing can understand this art."

<u>**Liechtenauer writes**</u>:

"*Young knight learn, to love God and revere women, so that your honor grows. Practice knighthood and learn the Art that dignifies you, bringing you honor in wars.*

Wrestle well, and wield lance, spear, sword and dagger manfully, whose use in others' hands is wasted. Strike bravely and hard there! Rush to, strike or miss. Those with wisdom loath, the one forced to defend. This you should grasp: All arts have length and measure."

Illus. 2.1: *The only known image of Master Johannes Liechtenauer from the Rome copy of Peter von Danzig's fechtbüch. Photo courtesy the Library of the National Academy, Rome. Codex 44, A 8, f. 2v.*

"If you want to behold the art, left against him and right while striking. And left with right is how you strongly want to fight."

Ringeck Writes:

Note: This is the first tenet of the long sword: learn to strike blows equally well from both sides if you want to learn to fence well.

Note: If you want to strike from the your right side, make sure your left foot is forward [Illus. 2.3a & b] (at the beginning); if you want to strike from the left side, the right foot must be forward. [Illus. 2.5a & b]

"If you strike an Oberhau (a strike from above) from the right, follow the blow with your right foot. [Illus. 2.4a & b] If you do not the blow is wrong and ineffective, because your right side stays behind. Because of this the blow will fall short and cannot travel in its proper arc towards the left. If you strike from the left [Illustration 2.6a & b] and you do not follow the blow, it too is wrong. That is why no matter from which side you are striking follow the blow with the same foot so you will succeed in all techniques. This is how you shall strike all blows."

Christian Writes:

This is important advice. When you strike a blow, your body must move in such a fashion that it contributes to the power of the blow rather than hindering it. The motion of the body also extends the attack's range. A strike from the right should start with the right foot behind and finish with a step of that same foot. This way the energy of the footwork powers the strike both by adding momentum and the body's own mass to the blow's force.

Likewise, when you strike from the left, you step with the left foot. Mixing up your footwork inhibits the travel of your blade and weakens the blow.

Illus. 2.2a-c: *Christian stands in the basic ready stance; the left leg forward, most of his weight resting on the right. The stance is neither square to the opponent nor side-on; the body is carried at a 45 degree angle to the line of attack, compromising between chambering powerful attacks and minimizing visible targets.*

Illus. 2.3a & 2.3b: *This is how you begin a strike from the right side. The left foot is forward, with the weight of the body supported mostly on the right foot. The sword is held on the right side, in vom Tag, a position used primarily to chamber blows.*

Illus. 2.4a & 2.4b: *As Christian strikes an Oberhau from the right the right foot passes forward. This brings the weight of the body into the strike. The combatant generates power through the motion of the leg and the hips transmitted through the shoulders and arms. The whole body delivers a powerful strike and it must move in the direction of the blow – otherwise, it can impede it.*

Illus. 2.5a & 2.5b: *Here then is how you begin a strike from the left. The sword is held on the left side with the right foot forward and the weight resting on the left.*

Illus. 2.6a & 2.6b: *Christian attacks with an Oberhau from the left; as the strike is delivered the left foot moves simultaneously forward.*

Liechtenauer Writes:

"*He who goes after the strike can rejoice little in his art. To strike closing is what you wish, no change comes into your shield. To the head, to the body, the twitches do not shun. To fight with the entire body is what you powerfully want to do.*"

Ringeck Writes:

"*When you are closing to an opponent, do not watch his blows and do not wait for what he might use against you. Because all fencers who just wait for their opponent's blows and do not do anything else other than warding them off do not succeed very often. They are very often defeated.*

Note: Always fence using all of your strength! When you're close, strike at his head and at his body, [Illus. 2.7] so he may not be able to Durchwechseln--'change through'--in front of your point. After the blow, from the bind, strike light blows at his next opening, as is described in the section about different blows and other techniques."

Christian Writes:

This critical section reveals the mindset of the Liechtenauer tradition. A combatant should not focus on defending themselves, but on defeating their enemy. Put another way, a combatant should try to win rather than trying not to lose. Too much attention on defense and the opponent maintains the initiative, making him likely to triumph.

It is a caution against fighting tentatively, for doing so affords the opponent opportunities for deception. One way he can do this, if a combatant doesn't close as they attack, is to "change through"--*durchwecheln*. *Changing through*, explored in chapter 13, is a disengagement from a bind against a sword that frees the weapon to attack. Once the combatant has closed distance and bound the blade he can work on more subtle techniques. The phase of the fight wherein the combatant closes with an opponent is called the *zufechten* ("to the fight"), while the close-combat phase is called the *krieg* ("War").

Illus. 2.7:
Christian (left) closes the gap in the Zufechten to prevent Ben (right) from having an opportunity to change through, that is, to slide his sword out from the bind with Christian's sword and attack again.

Liechtenauer Writes:

"*Listen to what is wrong, do not fight above the left, if you are right; and if you are left, on the right you limp as well.*"

Ringeck Writes:

Note: This tenet is addressed to left-handers and to right-handers. If you are a right-handed fencer and you are closing to an opponent and thinking you can hit him, do not strike the first blow from (your) left side. Because you are weak there [Illus. 2.9a & b] and you cannot resist if he binds strongly against your blade. Because of this, strike from the right side [Illus. 2.8a & b], you can work strongly am Schwert--'on the sword'--and you can use all techniques you like. So, if you are left-handed, do not strike from the right side, since left-handers are usually not used to strike effectively from the right side and vice versa.

Christian Writes:

Right handers should strike first from their right, while left handers should strike first from their left. The reason for this is a matter of being able to hold strongly if a combatant binds against the opponent's sword. A right hander swinging from his left side strikes a weaker blow than if he struck from the right; he will also be weaker in the bind against the opponent's sword. This is because his wrists must cross in striking from the left. Crossing the wrists produces a tenuous grip and enables disarms.

It only follows then that a left hander striking from the right will cross the hands. There are certainly instances where the hands cross on purpose, but these are special applications for special circumstances. In general, powerful strikes should be delivered *without* crossing the hands.

Illus 2.8a & 2.8b: *The strong grip with the hands uncrossed. This can be done with the left hand on the grip or on the pommel. This is how the hands appear on the grip when a right-handed fighter strikes a blow from his right side.*

Illus. 2.9a & 2.9b: *This is the weaker, cross-handed grip. This can also be done with the left hand on the grip or on the pommel. This is how the hands appear on the grip when a right-handed fighter strikes a blow from his left side.*

Liechtenaeur Writes:

"Before and After, these two things, are to all skill a well-spring. Weak and Strong, Indes – that word – always remember. So should you learn with skill to work and defend. If you frighten easily, no fencing should you learn."

Ringeck Writes:

Note: Above all other things, you must understand the principles of Vor--'before'--and Nach--'after'--because the entire art of fencing is based upon it. Vor means pre-empting him with a blow or a thrust against an opening before he can hit you, so he must Versetzen--defend or displace. So, be flexible in your defense and aim your sword at one opening after the other so he cannot get through with his own techniques. But if he rushes in, start wrestling.

"Nach means: If you do not succeed with the Vor, wait for the Nach--the after. These are the defenses against all techniques he uses against you. So, if you have to displace him, make the displacement simultaneously (Indes) and from the bind strike immediately at his nearest opening. So you win the Vor and he remains in the Nach. Also, you should – during the 'before' and 'after' – notice simultaneously (Indes) how you can work against the strong or the weak of his sword.

Christian Writes:

The ownership of initiative in the fight is the most important tactical concept in Liechtenauer's tradition. When a combatant controls the fight, when he has the initiative, he fights in the *Vor.* This means he fights in such a fashion that he is on the offensive and the opponent is forced to defend. When he loses the initiative he fights in the *Nach,* which means he is now forced to defend under the attack. To succeed, he must win back the *Vor*--the "before"--that is, win back the initiative so that he can go on the offensive once more. In order to do this the combatant must decide what techniques to use *immediately* while in the bind against the opponent's sword or when he begins to strike. This split-second decision making is conceptually known as *Indes,* "while" or "during;" one of the decisions that must be made immediately is whether to work against the strong or weak of the enemy's sword.

Indes can also apply to the need for immediate response in countering a directed attack. The five strikes and the *Absetzen* techniques explored in this book (see chapter 12) are all examples of using *Indes* to recapture the initiative.

Ringeck Writes:

his means: The strong of the sword reaches from the cross to the middle of the blade, with it, you can hold opposed, if somebody binds against it. The weak reaches from the middle of the blade to the point. Here you cannot hold opposed. If you firmly understand this, you can work and defend yourself very well.

"Princes and Lords learn to survive with this art, in earnest and in play. But if you are fearful, then you should not learn to fence, because a despondent heart will always be defeated regardless of all skill."

Christian Writes:

There are two halves of a long sword's blade: the *strong*, which runs from the hilt to the middle of the blade, and the *weak*, extending from the middle of the blade to the point (See the photo on page 28). The strong of the blade offers leverage; using it the combatant has great strength in binding to his sword. The weak conversely offers little leverage and is not good for binding. But there are certainly reasons for using the weak. One of the tenets of the German sword tradition is that one should use strength against weakness, but weakness against strength. The weak part of the blade comes into play when the combatant needs to yield and let an opponent's blade slip by.

I've always found this to be a particularly satisfying passage. Courage is one of the chivalric virtues and it's significant that we find this passage referring to noblemen.

Without courage skill is useless. This is one of several instances where Ringeck connects the physical techniques with elements of a chivalric philosophy through the inclusion of specific virtues.

Liechtenauer Writes:

"*Five strikes learn from the right hand against the opposition.
Then we promise that your arts will be rewarded.*"

Ringeck Writes:

*Note, the teachings describe five secret strikes which sword
masters know to say nothing. You should learn to defend with
only these strikes when he comes against you from his right side.
And look for which of the five strikes that you should use to
meet his first attack. Whoever can counter you without injury
is praised by the master of these teachings and is more skilled
in this art than other fencers who cannot fence against the five
strikes. And you will find how you shall strike these five strikes
described in what follows.*"

Christian Writes:

These are Master Liechtenauer's five attacks, which came
to be known as *meisterhau* – master strikes. We are advised
to use these strikes to meet an opponent's incoming attack
from his right side. There is also a note here about the
difficulty of countering one of the strikes.

Liechtenauer Writes:

"*Zornhau, Krumphau, Zwerchhau, Schielhau,
with Scheitelhau, Alber;
Versetzen, Nachreisen, Überlaufen,
Absetzen, Durchwechseln, Zucken, Durchlaufen,
Abschneiden, Hände Drücken, Hangen, Winding to the openings;
Strike, cut, with thrusting.*"

Ringeck Writes:

Note: These are the names of the main techniques of the art of the long sword, whose names are chosen in such a way that you may understand them better. There are seventeen techniques and they start with the five strikes.

The first strike is the Strike of Wrath (Zornhau), the second one is the Crooked Strike (Krumphau), the third one is the Cross Strike (Zwerchhau), the fourth one is the Squinting Strike (Schielhau), and the fifth one is the Parting Strike (Scheitelhau). Sixth there are the Four Guards (Vier Leger), Seventh there are the four techniques of Displacement (Versetzen), Eighth there is the Traveling After (Nachreisen), Ninth there is the Overrunning (Überlaufen), Tenth there is the Setting Aside (Absetzen), Eleventh is the Changing Through (Durchwechseln), Twelfth is the Twitching (Zucken), Thirteenth is the Running Through (Durchlaufen), Fourteenth is the Cutting Off (Abschneiden), Fifteenth is the Pressing of the Hands (Hände Drücken), Sixteenth is the Hanging (Das Hangen), Seventeenth, finally there is the Winding (Das Winden)."

"*How you can use the Hanging and the Winding will be described, as well as how you can apply the other techniques, in the following.*"

Christian Writes:

An overview of the seventeen primary techniques, the *hauptstücke*. Each will be discussed in turn and as we will see, many of the techniques reference each other in the course of the commentaries.

Christian, having beat Ben's blade with a strong Zornhau, now prepares to strike to the other side.

Chapter 3
The Zornhau

The *Zornhau* or "Strike of Wrath" is the first and simplest of the five *meisterhau*--"Master strikes." Best characterized as an instinctive diagonal attack from the right shoulder, its name derives from the notion of an angry man naturally swinging his sword from this direction. The strike is accomplished by beginning with the left leg forward, and then striking from the shoulder while stepping forward and outward with the right leg – hearkening back to Master Ringeck's earlier admonition to always follow the blow with the foot.

When overwhelming with the counterattacking *Zornhau*, the combatant is free to thrust from the bind against his sword to his opponent's face. If his opponent instead holds strongly against the sword he is described as being "hard at the sword." The combatant must then find ways to work around the opponent's strength either by *Winden*--"winding"--the sword to recapture the leverage advantage or by striking around to the other side, letting his strength work against him.

While the *Zornhau* itself is simple, the chapter introduces many associated concepts that could be considered primary techniques. In learning *Zornhau* the student is exposed to *Zucken*--"twitching;" *Durchwechseln*--"changing through;" *Nachreisen*--"traveling after;" and last but certainly not least *Winden*. This is how the Liechtenauer tradition's teachings are structured – the primary techniques all reference one another and seem to have been introduced in context rather than as general principles, as modern students tend to expect.

Liechtenauer Writes:

"*Whoever strikes at you from above, Strike of Wrath and the thrust threatens him.*"

Christian Writes:

This technique is an almost single-time counterattack. I say almost, because the thrust along the blade is not quite the same motion as the swing into the strike. Both actions should happen as one continuous, smooth movement. How continuous the movement appears is largely dependent on range: if close to your opponent, draw your sword back to thrust; if you're farther apart, the strike and thrust can happen as if they are one motion. If the opponent doesn't bind too strongly (that is, he is soft at the sword) you can accomplish the thrust; otherwise he will have pushed you too far off line for the thrust to work. In either case, his attack is safely countered and this enables further techniques from the bind.

Ringeck Writes:

Note: When your adversary strikes at you from his right side with an Oberhau, [Illus. 3.2a] counter with a strike of wrath from your right shoulder against it. [Illus. 3.2b] Strike with your long edge and in your strong. When he is soft at the sword then, thrust into his face along his blade." [Illus. 3.2c & 3.2d]

Illus. 3.1: *Both combatants stand at the ready in vom Tag, swords chambered at their right shoulders.*

Illus. 3.2a & 3.2b *Ben opens with an Oberhau; Christian counters with a Zornhau, striking Ben's blade, disrupting his attack. As the strong of Christian's sword has been brought powerfully against Ben's attack Christian controls the leverage and hence holds the initiative.*

Illus. 3.2c & 3.2d *Ben is soft in the bind so Christian can complete the counterattack by thrusting to Ben's face along his blade.*

Liechtenauer Writes:

"*If he becomes aware of it, take it away above and drive on.*"

Ringeck Writes:

"*When you thrust against his face from the Zornhau and he notices this and displaces the thrust with strength,*[Illus. 3.3] *pull your sword upwards, away from his.* [Illus. 3.4] *And then strike to the head from the other side, also along his blade.*" [Illus. 3.5]

Christian Writes:

The opponent has strongly bound against you (that is, he is *hard* at the sword), making the thrust impossible. Rather than get into a pushing match, use his commitment to defense against him. This illustrates the German adage "use strength against weakness and weakness against strength." Yield to his strength and free your blade to strike the other side, keeping the sword between yourself and his sword. This "taking off" from the sword is known as an *Abnahmen*; this in turn is a form of *Zucken*, or "twitching" – another primary technique that will be explored later in detail.

Illus. 3.3: *Christian uses Abhahmen to disengage from Ben's sword and cut to the other side.*

Illus. 3.4: *Christian lifts his sword up and away to free himself from the bind.*

Illus. 3.5: *Stepping with the left foot Christian strikes Ben's head from behind Ben's sword. Christian strikes in such a way that he blocks Ben's line of attack.*

Liechtenaeur Writes:

"Be stronger against: turn, thrust. If he sees that, take it down."

Christian Writes:

This is the first instance in Ringeck's fechtbuch of *winden* or "winding." Winding is a turning of the sword about the axis of the blade. The result is superior leverage when in a bind and/or the angling of the point to find another vulnerability. In this particular case, you initially find yourself in a bind where the opponent presses strongly against your blade; that is, he is *hard at the sword*. In response you raise up your hilt so the strong of your blade is now in contact with the weak of his blade: this yields superior leverage. He who has the greater leverage in the bind is the one whose point will find its' mark. As you wind, keep your short edge in blade contact so your wrists are in a position of strength. Should he push your point away after the wind by raising his hilt, change your target from his face to his chest and drive your point home. [Illus. 3.10]

Ringeck Writes:

"When you strike a Zornhau and he displaces it, remaining hard at the sword, hold strongly against it. [Illus. 3.6] With the strong of your sword, slide up to the weak (schwech) of his blade, wind the hilt in front of your head while remaining on the sword (am schwert), thrusting into his face from above.[Illus. 3.7]

"When you thrust from the Winden as described [Illus. 3.8] *and he displaces the thrust by lifting up his arms and his hilt,*[Illus. 3.9] *stay in the Winden and take the point down*

You will see winding throughout this work – it is a cornerstone of the German *Kunst des Fechtens*. Further, the combatant's position while winding the hilt up and to the left side of the head corresponds with the left version of *Ochs*, a fundamental position. You will see variations of this position used many times in the techniques of the chapters that follow, especially in chapters 5, 6, 12, 16, 18 & 19.

Illus. 3.6: *Once again, Ben binds hard against Christian's counterattack.*

Illus. 3.7: – *Christian winds his sword upward so the strong of his sword is against the weak of Ben's. With this superior leverage, he then thrusts to Ben's face from above.*

Illus. 3.8: *Here Christian has wound his sword up to thrust to Ben's face.*

Illus. 3.9: *Before Christian can complete his thrust, Ben raises his hilt to set aside Christian's point.*

Illus. 3.10: *Undaunted by Ben's displacement of his point, Christian leans into the attack slightly and thrusts down into Ben's chest.*

Parts of a Sword

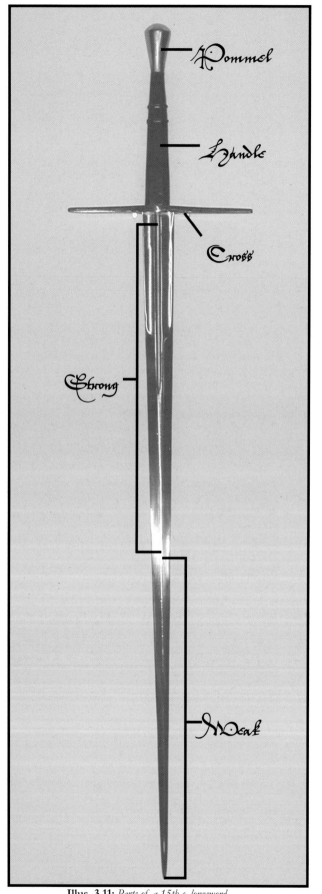

Illus. 3.11: *Parts of a 15th c. longsword*

Pommel

Handle

Cross

Strong

Weak

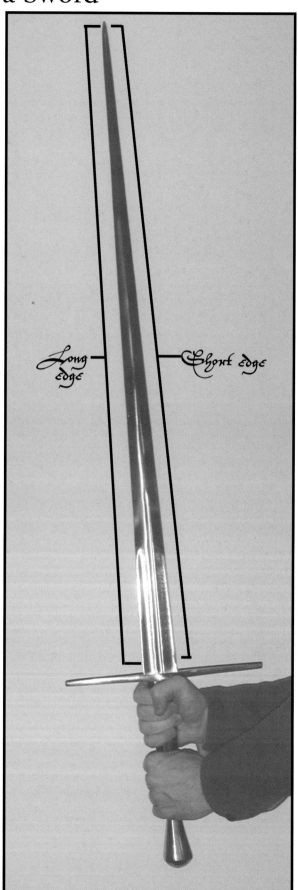

Illus. 3.12: *The "long" and "short" edges*

Long edge

Short edge

Christian Writes:

This is the counter technique for when the opponent "takes off" from your sword. To counter simply follow after him, aiming your long edge at his head. It's all about not being surprised by his attempt to leave the initial bind. This is one of the many cases where it's critical to sense changes in the pressure on your sword.

Ringeck Writes:

Note: When you bind at the sword with strength [Illus. 3.13] *and your adversary pulls his sword upwards* [Illus. 3.15] *and strikes at your head from the other side, bind strongly with the long edge and strike him on the head.*[Illus. 3.16]

Illus. 3.13: *The combatants are in a bind after Christian's Zornhau to Ben's attack.*

Illus. 3.14: *Since Christian is hard at the sword, Ben pulls his sword up and away. He will attempt to strike around to the other side of Christian's blade.*

Illus. 3.15: *Christian counters by turning his own long edge back upon him, preventing Ben's counterattack and striking his head in one motion. The counter succeeds because of its advantage in time and distance: Ben first has to free himself from the bind and then cut-over.*

Liechtenauer Writes:

"Memorize this: strike, thrust, position – soft or hard. Indes, Before and After heed. Your 'Krieg' [or 'War'] should not be in haste. Who tends to the War above, gets ashamed below."

Ringeck Writes:

"You must notice immediately if someone is soft or hard at the sword if he binds at your sword with a strike or a thrust. If you have noticed this you shall know simultaneously (Indes), if it is better to fight him in the Vor (Before) or the Nach (After). But don't engage rashly in close-combat (Krieg), this is nothing else than Winden at the sword.

"In close combat you should do the following: if you strike him with Zornhau and he displaces it, [Illus. 3.16] lift up your arms and, at the sword, wind the point to the upper opening. [Illus. 3.17] When he displaces (Versetzen) the thrust, [Illus. 3.18] stay in the winding and thrust to the lower opening. If he follows your sword in the displacement (Versatzung), [Illus. 3.19] lead your point through under his [Illus. 3.20] and thrust to the other opening on his right side.[Illus. 3.21] This is how you can defeat him above and below in close combat."

Christian Writes:

This is the most important admonishment in Liechtenauer's system. The combatant must be able to sense whether an opponent is hard or soft in a bind to understand his intent, letting it be the guide for how to proceed. If he is soft, fight him in the *Vor*; that is, fight him in something very close to single-time and simply follow through with the technique you started – never lose the initiative or control of the fight. If he's hard in the bind, he has thwarted the attempt to counter and attacked in one motion so he takes the initiative and leaves you in the *Nach*. You must then use another technique to retake the initiative, hoping to regain the *Vor*.

Master Ringeck further counsels us to be careful in resorting to fighting at close combat distance. One must be skilled at the *winden* to do this well, as this is what close combat is primarily about.

Should you find yourself in the close combat phase, or "war" (*Krieg*), here is a technique that forces your opponent to commit more and more to the defense of one side. When he has done this, you then perform a *Durchwechseln*--"changing through"--letting your blade slide out of the bind and thrust to another opening. Changing through is another one of Liechtenauer's primary techniques and it will appear throughout the techniques for the long sword.

Illus. 3.16: *Close combat, or "War" (Krieg). Both combatants in the bind.*

Illus. 3.17: *Christian winds by raising his hilt keeping his short edge in contact with Ben's sword. The point of Christian's sword is then ready to thrust.*

Illus. 3.18: *Ben displaces Christian's attempt to thrust.*

Illus. 3.19: *Christian seeks out the lower opening, but Ben continues to displace the point by binding strongly.*

Illus 3.20: *Ben is fully committed to the defense of his left side; Christian disengages by sliding his point from under Ben's sword.*

Illus. 3.21: *His sword free, Christian now finishes the 'krieg' engagement by thrusting to Ben's right side.*

Liechtenauer Writes:

"*In all meetings with the masters you want to imitate them. In all winding learn to find strikes, thrusts, and cuts. Also you should test along if you can strike, thrust, or cut.*"

Ringeck Writes:

"*Check when winding whether you should strike, cut or thrust; while winding you are to detect which of the three possibilities is best. You are not to strike if you should thrust; not to cut, if you should strike; and not to thrust if you should cut. Pay attention so that if he displaces one that you hit him with another. Thus: If your thrust is displaced, [Illus. 3.22] strike instead. [Illus. 3.23, 3.24] If he gets in under your sword, [Illus. 3.25, 3.26] lead a cut from below against his arm. [Illus. 3.27]*

"*Always consider these principles in each fight; if you want to achieve the art of the masters who face you.*"

Christian Writes:

Having introduced the *winden*--winding--earlier in this chapter, Ringeck now says that from a winding you can not only thrust to an opponent, but can also use a slicing cut or strike. In this example, he shows how you can strike from the *winden* if he displaces your sword or cut his arms if he tries to rush from the bind. The master then stresses the importance of this idea of using three types of attack from the wind.

Illus. 3.22: *Ben has displaced Christian's winding attack.*

Illus. 3.23: *Thrusts aren't the only techniques that may be used from winding; Christian attacks from the left by stepping with the left foot forward and to the left, striking high.*

Illus. 3.24: *Christian's strike connects.*

Illus. 3.25: *Christian has wound his hilt up trying a thrust to Ben's face.*

Illus. 3.26: *Defending himself from Christian's thrust, Ben raises his own hilt and begins to rush in by passing forward with his left foot.*

Illus. 3.27: *Christian slices Ben's arms under his sword, thus ending the assault.*

Liechtenauer Writes:

"*Four openings know, aim: so you hit certainly, upon all go without regard for how he acts.*"

Ringeck Writes:

These are the four openings you should aim at in combat. The first opening is the right side; the second is the left side above the belt. The other openings are the right and left side below the belt. Always pay attention to the openings when you are closing in; aim at the ones he (your adversary) exposes.

Thrust with the Langen Ort--'long point'--use the Nachreisen--'traveling after' and all other opportunities. Don't pay attention to what he's up to, fence securely and you'll hit so outstandingly that he'll not be able to get through with his own techniques."

Christian Writes:

Liechtenauer's system describes four "openings," or target areas on the opponent's body. He divided the body into four openings by imagining a line dividing the body into two zones vertically and another dividing into two halves horizontally at the bottom of the ribcage.[1] Thus there are two upper openings and two lower openings. Naturally, you should target those openings that his defense exposes.

Knowing the four openings you should attack them vigorously and not concern yourself with your opponent's actions. The man who tries too hard not to lose does not focus on winning. Among the techniques he advocates using to do this are the "long point" (*Langen Ort*) and the "traveling after" (*Nachreisen*). The long point is a position you end up in when you thrust with extended arms, while the traveling after is a way of following after his attack to catch him unprepared.

Illustr. 3.28:
The four target zones on the body according to the German system.

---

[1]*These same divisions of four quarters, first denoted by Liechtenauer, has been used in all successive traditions in European fencing; it is still used today in the Olympic sport.*

Liechtenauer Writes:

"**W**hen you want to consider how to break the four openings with skill: above Dupliere, below well Mutiere. I say to you truthfully: he can not defend himself without danger; if you have correctly learned, to striking he will barely come."

Ringeck Writes:

"**I**f you want to break one of the four openings by force, 'Dupliere' at the upper opening, against the strong (starke) of his sword, [Illus. 3.29, 3.30] and 'Mutiere' to another opening. [Illus. 3.31, 3.32] Against this he cannot defend himself and he will not be able to either strike or thrust."

Illus. 3.29: *In this sequence Duplieren and Mutieren are used together. Ben binds hard.*

Illus. 3.30: *Christian drives his pommel up, crossing his wrists, to Dupliere behind Ben's attack and strike to Ben's face behind his sword.*

Illus. 3.31: *Ben displaces Christian's Dupliere by raising his hilt high.*

Illus. 3.32: *In response to the displacement, Christian raises his own hilt and thrusts down the other side of Ben's blade to his lower opening on the right side.*

Ringeck writes:

Duplieren

"When you strike a strike of wrath (Zornhau) or any other Oberhau and he displaces it with strength, [Illus. 3.33] with the left hand immediately thrust the pommel of your sword under your right arm. [Illus. 3.34] With hands crossed behind his blade and in between the blade and his body, strike him diagonally through the face. Or strike him on the head." [Illus. 3.35]

Mutieren

"If you bind against his sword, with an Oberhau or otherwise, [Illus. 3.36] wind the short edge at his sword, [Illus. 3.37] raise your arms and thrust at the lower opening from the outside along his blade. [Illus. 3.38] You can use that from both sides."

Christian Writes:

Duplieren and *Mutieren* are two associated techniques used to "break" the four openings. They each involve winding to get behind your opponent's attack. A *dupliere* involves winding behind his blade by pushing your hilt up with your left hand; striking from the sword against his face. Done at speed, this technique has the very unnerving effect of making your sword appear to have passed through your opponent's! A *mutiere* is a winding technique where you raise your hilt and drop your point down the other side of his blade from which you initially engaged.

While a precise translation of these words is difficult, it's helpful to remember them with a couple of mnemonic tricks. *Dupliere* roughly means to double, and when one *duplieres*, one "doubles" the attack by striking a second time with a winding from an initial strike. *Mutiere* means to mutate or change, and when one *mutieres*, one "changes" from one side of the opponent's sword to another; from a strike into a thrust.

Illus. 3.33: *The combatants find themselves in a bind. Ben holds hard against Christian's Zornhau.*

Illus. 3.36: *The bind. Ben holds hard against Christian's sword.*

Illus. 3.34: *Christian begins to Dupliere by raising his left hand and winding his blade behind Ben's.*

Illus. 3.37: *Christian raises his hilt to his left side, winding the short edge of his blade against Ben's. It may appear to Ben that Christian is winding to menace his face, but instead Christian is moving to place his blade on the other side of Ben's sword, behind the bind.*

Illus. 3.35: *Christian strikes from Ben's sword to his face with his long edge. This attack could also be performed as a slicing cut across Ben's face.*

Illus. 3.38: *Christian drops his point down the other side of Ben's sword and thrusts to his lower opening along his opponent's blade.*

Chapter 7
The Krumphau

The *Krumphau* or "crooked strike" is a blow struck diagonally downward from the right towards the opponent's right side-- where the tip of the sword ideally strikes the hands. This trajectory forces your hands to cross at the wrists, that is to become krump or "twisted," as the blow is delivered. The *Krumphau* is the second of the five strikes, and one of the four displacements--*Vier Versetzen*--that are used to counter the four guards. In this case, the guard *Ochs*. Performed with crossed hands this peculiarity has caused considerable debate as to how to do the strike. Master Ringeck doesn't help to resolve the questions about the *Krumphau* – his commentary includes an oddity of phrasing and he doesn't specify whether the long or short edge should be used. My interpretation stays within the kinesthetic principles found elsewhere in the system[1], employing the simplest movements. Multiple interpretations are possible, and the debate will doubtless continue. Commentaries in the Peter von Danzig 1452 *fechtbüch* clearly indicate the use of the long edge[2] (which is how I have interpreted it), while Talhoffer's 1467 *fechtbüch* seems to indicate that the short edge is used.[3] Perhaps Master Ringeck is purposefully silent on this matter?

When a combatant strikes the *Krumphau* against an opponent's attack, there are three basic options. Ideally, he hits his opponent's hands to end the encounter in one motion. If especially quick, he may end up with his blade beneath his opponents', setting his opponent's attack aside. (a kind of *Absetzen*). If a little slow, he may end up striking his sword blade, binding against it. From the bind and can strike "from the sword" (*vom Schwert*) by attacking to his head with the short edge, or "on the sword" (*am Schwert*) by thrusting after a winding motion.

Master Ringeck also shows us how to work against a displacement with the *Krumphau*. Both techniques involve thrusting; while in a bind in the first case; in the second, by withdrawing from the bind and thrusting repeatedly until the point finds its mark. This is the "Noble War" (*Edel Krieg*), and is a fine example of Liechtenauer's--and hence Ringeck's-- fighting sensibilities: ideally, once the initiative has been seized, it is maintained until one's enemy has fallen.

---

[1] see Appendix 2
[2] Ibid
[3] Talhoffer, Hans, *Medieval Combat*, ed. Mark Rector, Greenhill Books, plate 19.

Liechtenauer writes:

"*Krump with nimbleness, throw the point to the hands.*"

Ringeck writes:

This is how you should strike the Krumphau at the hands. When he attacks you from his[4] right side with an Oberhau or Unterhau (a strike from below), jump out of the strike with your right foot towards his left side and with crossed hands strike against his hands using the point. [Illus. 4.3a & b] *Also use this when he stands against you in the guard Ochs.*" [Illus. 4.4]

Christian writes:

The *Krumphau* is performed with the hands crossed because it reaches across to the other side as it strikes. It is rather like striking a *Zornhau*, but instead the blow crosses the body to hit a target on your opponent's right side, in this case his hands. This strike is accomplished with a step outward, and only slightly forward, with the right foot, taking you out of the brunt of his attack owing to the diagonal line the *Krumphau* closes the line of attack from *Ochs*; hence, the *Krumphau* is one of the four displacements (*Vier Versetzen*) used to counter the four guards.

Illus. 4.1a & b: *Both men stand in vom Tag.*

---

[4] The manuscript actually says "deiner," rather than "seiner" here – that is, "your" rather than "his." Given that this is very strange phrasing for this manual ("strikes you from your right side"), and that none of the follow-on techniques for the Krumphau involve the opponent striking this way, I believe this is one of many scribe's errors. I have therefore interpreted it to be the usual attack from the opponent's right side. There's no practical way, in my view, to reconcile the two ideas of stepping toward his left side and stepping out of the strike if the opponent were indeed striking from his left.

Illus. 4.2a & b: *Ben begins with an Oberhau from his right. Christian begins to counter.*

Illus. 4.3a & b: *He counters by striking with crossed hands against Ben while stepping with his right foot. His footwork brings him more outward to his right than forward and he maintains a safe distance by throwing his point at Ben's hands.*

Illus. 4.3: *Placement of the attack to the hands.*

Illus. 4.4: *Ben, standing in Ochs, is the victim of a Krumphau delivered to his hands. Christian strikes as before — only now, slightly higher.*

Liechtenaeur writes:

"ho Krumps to displace with a step, he will strike last."

Ringeck writes:

This is how you can Absetzen--set aside--the cuts from above with the Krumphau: If he attacks your opening from his right side with an Oberhau, step towards his left side with your right foot and put your point against his sword into the Schranckhut. [Illus. 4.5-4.7] Practice this from both sides. From the Absetzeb [Illus. 4.8] you can strike him on the head." [Illus. 4.9]

Christian writes:

In this variation, pass forward with the right foot and moving the sword into position to set your opponent's strike aside from below. This position, with the point down and the hands crossed is the left side version of the *Schranckhut* – a secondary guard that Ringeck describes later in the manuscript.[5] From this position, you can deflect away your opponent's attack and immediately after cut strongly to his head.

Illus. 4.5: *Both fighters stand once more in vom Tag.*

[5] See chapter 20 on the "Nebenhut and Schranckhut."

Illus. 4.6: *As Ben strikes Oberhau, Christian steps forward and out with his right foot while striking his sword before Ben's attack.*

Illus. 4.7: *Christian has now struck his sword into the guard called the Schranckhut, from which he will deflect Ben's sword harmlessly away.*

Illus. 4.8: *Ben's sword is deflected.*

Illus. 4.9: *Striking from the Schranckhut, Christian hits Ben's head with a step forward with the left foot.*

Liechtenaeur writes:

"Strike Krump to the flats of the Masters when you want to weaken them."

Ringeck writes:

This means: If you want to weaken a master, then while he strikes an Oberhau from his right counter with a Krumphau using crossed hands against his sword." [Illus. 4.10 & 4.11]

Illus. 4.10: *Both combatants begin once again in vom Tag.*

Illus. 4.11: *Ben has struck an Oberhau, but Christian has countered by striking a Krumphau to the flat of Ben's sword.*

Liechtenaeur writes:

"*Wen he flashes from above, move away; this I will laud.*"

Ringeck writes:

This means: When you strike him with the Krumphau against his sword, from the sword (vom Schwert) immediately strike upwards against his head with the short edge. [Illus. 4.12] Or after the Krumphau wind the short edge at his sword and thrust him into the breast." [Illus. 4.13]

Christian writes:

Here the *Krumphau* is used to strike to the opponent's sword, preferably with the long edge to the flat of his blade. After this bind occurs, you have the option of either cutting from his blade to his head with the short edge or of staying in the bind and winding to thrust to him. One should stay on his sword if he's hard in the bind and depart from it to strike if he is soft.

Illus. 4.12: *From the bind Christian can either strike Ben's head with the short edge of his sword, or...*

Illus. 4.13: *...wind his short edge against Ben's sword so that he can thrust to his chest.*

<u>**Liechtenaeur writes**</u>:

"Strike the Krump short, changing through show with this."

<u>**Ringeck writes:**</u>

This means: When he strikes an Oberhau from his right shoulder, pretend as if you are going to bind against his sword with a Krumphau. But let your strike fall short, [Illus. 4.14 & 4.15] *lead your point through under his sword and wind your hilt over your head and to your right side.* [Illus. 4.16] *Then thrust him in the face."* [Illus. 4.17]

<u>**Christian writes:**</u>

The *Krumphau* may be used in conjunction with a *Durch-wechseln*--"changing through"--a sliding of the point through to another opening. The *Krumphau* is struck as if to bind against the opponent's sword, but is pulled so that the blade ends up beneath his. Then pull the hilt to the right side of your head, which drags your point out from under his sword, and thrust. It is important to remember to step far off line to your right as you strike *Krumphau* lest you be struck while performing the feint.

Illus. 4.14: *Christian and Ben in vom Tag.*

Illus. 4.15: *Ben strikes Oberhau while Christian throws a pulled Krumphau, ending up beneath Ben's attack.*

Illus. 4.16: *Christian pulls his sword hilt up to the right withdrawing his point from beneath Ben's sword.*

Illus. 4.17: *Christian thrusts to Ben's face.*

Liechtenaeur writes:

"*ho Krumps to lead you astray, the Edel Krieg ('Noble War') will confuse him, that he will not know truthfully where he should go.*"

Ringeck writes:

"*his is how you can break the Krumphau: If you attack from your right side with an Oberhau and he displaces with a Krumphau using crossed hands from his right side, strongly hold your sword against his.* [Illus. 4.18] *And thrust the point under his sword at his breast with your arms extended.*" [Illus. 4.19]

Illus. 4.18: *Here Ben has struck Krumphau against Christian's Oberhau attack, pinning his blade.*

Illus. 4.19: *Unfazed by the displacement of his initial attack, Christian thrusts to Ben with extended arms.*

Ringeck writes:

"*Another defense against the Krumphau: If you attack him from your right side with an Oberhau and he displaces (Versatzung) with a Krumphau using crossed hands from his right side and if he pushes your sword to the ground, [Illus. 4.20] wind towards your right side, raise your arms over your head [Illus. 4.21] and thrust at his breast from above. If he displaces, [Illus. 4.22] stand as you are with the hilt in front of your head and nimbly work with the point from one opening to the other. [Illus. 4.23] This is called the Edel Krieg--'Noble War'--and with this you'll confuse him so much that he will not know how to defend himself against your attacks.*"

Christian writes:

Here are two ways to defeat a *Krumphau* thrown against your sword. In the first, simply extend your arms to thrust from the bind. In the second, pull the point out from under his sword by winding the hilt to your head's and begin thrusting repeatedly until his displacement attempts fail. This is the "Noble War"--*Edel Krieg*[6]--and it probably derives its impressive sounding name epitomizing Liechtenauer's sensibilities: repeated attacks give the enemy no opportunity to seize the initiative.

Illus. 4.20
Ben has again displaced Christian's attack with the Krumphau, this time pushing his sword down.

Illus. 4.21
Christian frees himself from the bind by pulling his hilt up and back to the right side of his head.

Illus. 4.22
Christian begins thrusting to from this position. Ben displaces initially, but ultimately...

Illus. 4.23
he is hit by one of the thrusts. By attacking relentlessly, Christian has forced Ben into a purely defensive mode which is ultimately his undoing.

---

[6]The "Noble War" exemplifies the commentary in the *Zornhau* teachings that close combat is "no more than the winding." This techniques also typifies the concepts of Before and After - your opponent is forced to fight in the After while you repeatedly thrust to him, thereby staying in the Before.

Chapter 5
Zwerchhau

The third of the five strikes, the *Zwerchhau*, loosely defined as "Cross Strike," is a horizontal to diagonal cut that can be thrown high or low. When aimed at an opening on the opponent's left side, the short edge is employed; when the strike is to his right, use the long edge. In all cases the hilt is held high, affording considerable protection against counterattacks from above. Executing the *Zwerchhau* to either side brings you into a position corresponding roughly to the *Ochs*. When you strike his left you end up in the left *Ochs*; when you strike his right, you end up in *Ochs* on the right.

The *Zwerch* is also the 2nd of the four displacements (*Vier Versetzen*) – the four strikes – that counter the four guards (see chapters 8 & 9). It is used to counter *vom Tag* as it closes off the line of attack from above.

The first technique is the single-time case – the opponent's *Oberhau* is deflected while striking him with the short edge to the side of the head. If he's hard in the bind you can strike behind his blade (a *Duplieren*, see chapter 4 on the *Zornhau*), or use his strong pressure on your blade to tear his sword down to your right using your hilt as a hook. You can then tear down his sword and quickly strike around with the *Zwerch* to his right. If he is soft in the bind push his sword down with superior leverage, cutting his neck or throwing him to the ground by his neck.

The *Zwerchhau* is well-suited for throwing of rapid fire, successive blows. This is shown under the heading "How One Can Use the *Zwerch* to Strike the Four Openings," wherein the target is varied with each blow, forcing the opponent to scramble to defend himself. This ability to strike multiple targets is further brought to bear in the three feinting techniques described – again we see the Liechtenauer penchant for driving an opponent into defending one opening when he intends to strike somewhere else.

Liechtenaeur writes:

The Zwerchhau takes whatever comes from the roof."

Ringeck writes:

The Zwerchhau counters all downward strikes made from above. Do it like this: If he strikes an Oberhau at your head, jump to his left side with your right foot; while you jump, turn your sword so that your hilt is high in front of your head and your thumb is down [on the flat of the blade] striking at his left with your short edge. [Illus. 5.1a - 5.3b] You catch his strike with your hilt and hit him simultaneously on the head."

Christian writes:

This is a single-time counterattack to an *Oberhau*. As you raise your hilt, step out to your right and in a single action counter his attack with one of your own. The final position is very much the same as when you perform the "Winding to Regain Strength After a Displacement" technique from the *Zornhau* - this is the left side version of *Ochs* (see chapter 8, "Vier Leger"). The only difference here is that your blade is held horizontally.

This is a powerfully deceptive blow: the lift of the hilt, done in time with stepping causes the hips to twist strongly into the strike so that the *Zwerchhau* strikes with great force.

Illus. 5.1a & b: *Christian and Ben in vom Tag.*

Illus. 5.2a & b: *Ben attacks with an Oberhau; Christian responds by raising his hilt.*

Illus. 5.3a & b: *Christian catches Ben's strike on his guard while striking Ben's head with the short edge of his sword. Note how Christian's thumb is placed on the strong of his blade to help brace the sword.*

Liechtenauer writes:

"Zwerch with the strong, your work with this memorize."

Ringeck writes:

This is how you can work with the strong of the sword from the Zwerch: If you strike with the Zwerch, pay attention to strike strongly with your sword's strong against his blade. If he holds strongly against it [Illus. 5.4] *strike him at the sword on the head behind his blade with your hands crossed. Or, cut him through the face.*" [Illus. 5.5 & 5.6]

Christian writes:

If the counterstrike fails to reach the opponent's head you will find yourself in a bind. Ringeck counsels the use of *winden* and follow-on attacks rather than matching strength with strength. If he is hard at the sword let his strength work against him. One way to do this is simply wind *behind* his sword.

This is another application of *duplieren* – a "doubling" of the attack achieved by winding behind your opponent's displacement.

Illus. 5.5: *Christian winds his sword behind Ben's.*

Illus. 5.4: *Christian's Zwerchhau successfully stops Ben's attack, but without reaching his head. Ben decides to bind hard against Christian's sword.*

Illus. 5.6: *Christian completes the technique by striking Ben's head.*

Ringeck writes:

"*W*hen you bind using the strong of your sword with the Zwerch and he strongly holds against it, [Illus. 5.7] *push down his sword to your right side with your hilt.* [Illus. 5.8 & 5.9] *And immediately strike again with the Zwerch to the right side of his head.*" [Illus. 5.10]

Christian writes:

This is another option for when your opponent is hard against your sword: hook his sword's blade with your hilt and tear his sword down towards your right side. As you hook his sword with the hilt, the action of pulling his sword down also whips your blade to the other side and strikes him in the head with a second *Zwerchhau*; when done quickly, it is an impressive technique.

Illus. 5.7: *Ben again binds strongly against Christian's Zwerchhau.*

Illus. 5.8: *Using his hilt as a hook, Christian tears Ben's sword down to the right. Ben's strength in the bind has worked against him.*

Illus. 5.9: *The tear down helps Christian's sword whip around to the other side.*

Illus. 5.10: *Christian strikes the right side of Ben's head with the Zwerch. He steps to the left while striking the follow-up blow.*

More working with the strong of the sword with the Zwerchhau

Ringeck writes:

"If you bind against his sword with the Zwerch and he is soft at the sword, [Illus. 5.11] *place the short edge at the right side of his neck,* [Illus. 5.12] *jumping behind his left foot with your right and tearing him over with the sword."* [Illus. 5.13]

Christian writes:

Here, an opponent's softness in the bind allows you to throw him to the ground by hooking his neck with your sword. His lack of strong resistance allows you to place your sword at his throat for the throw.

Illus. 5.11: *Ben binds against Christian's Zwerchhau, but he is soft in the bind.*

Illus. 5.13: *Stepping right once more, Christian puts his right foot behind Ben's left and tears him to the ground.*

Illus. 5.12: *Christian pushes Ben's sword down, laying his short edge at Ben's neck. A step with the left foot enables this.*

Ringeck writes:

"*If you bind against his sword with the Zwerch and he is soft at the sword,* [Illus. 5.14] *push his sword down with the Zwerch and lay the short edge behind his arms at his throat.*" [Illus. 5.15]

Christian writes:

Another way to handle an opponent who is soft in the bind is to just place your edge on his throat, as in the previous technique. Rather than stepping in to throw him, however, the combatant simply slices with the sword's short edge.

Illus. 5.14: *Ben soft in his bind against Christian's Zwerch.*

Illus. 5.15: *Christian pushes Ben's sword down and slices his throat with the short edge.*

Ringeck writes:

" hen you bind at his sword with an Oberhau or another strike from your right [Illus. 5.16] *and he strikes around with the Zwerch to your other side,* [Illus. 5.17] *forestall this with a Zwerch to his neck under his sword."* [Illus. 5.18]

Christian writes:

The best defense against a *Zwerch* is...another *Zwerch*! Here the *Zwerchhau* is used to strike underneath an opponent's *Zwerch*, effectively defending against his strike and striking him at the neck. The attack must angle the counterattack so that the your hilt remains high enough to protect you against the opponent's attack as the blade passes beneath his.

Illus. 5.16:
Each combatant strikes an Oberhau with an ensuing bind.

Illus. 5.17: *From the bind, Ben strikes a Zwerch to Christian's right side.*

Illus. 5.18: *Stepping to his right, Christian counters Ben's Zwerch with one of his own, directed under Ben's attack to his neck.*

Liechtenaeur writes:

"*Zwerch to the Plow; to the Ox hard together.*"

Ringeck writes:

This is how you can strike to the four openings with the Zwerch: When you close in with your adversary with Zufechten, at the right moment, jump towards him and strike with the Zwerch to the lower opening of his left side.[Illus. 5.19] *This is called 'striking towards the plow' ('zum Pflug schlagen').*

"*When you have attacked the lower opening with the Zwerch, immediately strike another Zwerch to the other side, at his head. [Illus. 5.20 & 5.21] This is called 'striking towards the ox' ('zum Ochsen schlagen'). And then strike swiftly alternating the Zwerch towards the plow and the ox, crosswise from one side to the other. You can then disengage from him with an Oberhau to the head.*"

Christian writes:

The *Zwerch* can be used in rapid succession to attack both high and low. Liechtenauer describes the four openings here in terms of the guards that would be held in those positions: *Ochs* and *Pflug* on both sides. By varying the attacks among the four openings, you can force your opponent to commit fully to defending himself, leaving no time for him to counterattack. This is one of the few times in Ringeck's *fechtbüch* that we see an attack described, rather than a counterattack. It's also another example of fighting in the *Vor* and thereby forcing your opponent to remain in the *Nach*.

Illus. 5.19: *Christian steps right and attacks Ben with a low targeted Zwerch "to the Plow." Ben displaces the strike.*

Illus. 5.20: *Christian swings his sword around to the other side. He accomplishes the blow by stepping left.*

Illus. 5.21: *Christian strikes "to the Ochs," that is, to one of the upper openings, once again forcing Ben to displace. Christian will keep striking until he either hits Ben or has confused him enough to strike with a simple Oberhau.*

Liechtenaeur writes:

"*He who Zwerchs well, with the jump protects the head.*"

Ringeck writes:

"*When you strike the Zwerch you shall always jump to his flank, namely towards the side on which you want to hit him so you can hit his head. And pay attention that you cover the front of your head with the hilt while jumping.*"

Christian writes:

This is an admonition to always hold your hilt high while striking the *Zwerch* so that your head is protected as you attack.

Liechtenaeur writes:

"*Who leads the feint, hits from below as he wishes.*"

Ringeck writes:

"*All fencers who rely on* displacing *are deceived and defeated with the feint. When you close with him, feint any Oberhau to his left side.* [Illus. 5.22] *From there (when he wants to displace it)* [Illus. 5.23] *you can easily hit a lower opening.*" [Illus. 5.24]

Christian writes:

This feint is another example of driving the opponent into defending one opening, when the intended target is really somewhere else. Strike high, forcing him to displace your attack, then strike *Zwerchhau* to the lower opening on the same side.

Illus. 5.22: *Christian strikes with an Oberhau from his right, which Ben displaces.*

Illus. 5.23: *Christian lifts his hilt high, bringing his sword away from the displacement.*

Illus. 5.24: *Christian strikes a Zwerch to Ben's lower left opening.*

Liechtenaeur writes:

"*The Verkehrer forces a running through and also brings wrestling. The elbow take certainly, jump into his balance.*"

Ringeck writes:

"*If you bind at your adversary's sword with an Oberhau* [Illus. 5.25] *or an Unterhau, invert your sword so that your thumb is down and thrust to his face from above* [Illus. 5.26] *so you force him to displace the thrust.* [Illus. 5.27] *While he displaces, grab his right elbow with your left hand, place your left leg in front of his right and toss him over.* [Illus. 5.28] *Or, run under his weapon and close to wrestle, as will be explained in detail later.*"

Christian writes:

The *Verkehrer*--"Inverter"--is similar to winding the hilt high from the *Zornhau* ("Winding to Regain Strength After a Displacement"). As the sword inverts, it assumes the same position a *Zwerchhau* does when struck towards the head. The point stands against the opponent's face. This forces him to displace it by pushing your blade to his left, thereby exposing his right side. As he displaces, rush in with the left foot and throw him by his elbow over your leg.

Illus. 5.25: *Christian strikes an Oberhau from his right. Ben displaces it.*

Illus. 5.26: *Christian inverts his sword to menace Ben with the point.*

Illus. 5.27: *Feeling menaced by Christian's point, Ben displaces it.*

Ilus. 5.28: *Christian steps aggressively forward with the left foot, and rushes into the opening created by Ben's displacement. He then throws Ben by the elbow over his knee.*

Liechtenaeur writes:

"*Feint twice, if you hit also make the cut.*"

Ringeck writes:

"*Here, you must deceive him twice while closing in. When you come close to him with the Zufechten, jump towards him with the foot and feint a Zwerch to the left side of the head.* [Illus. 5.29] *But then turn the blow around* [Illus. 5.30] *and strike to the right side of his head.*" [Illus. 5.31]

Illus. 5.29: *Christian steps right and strikes the Zwerch with little commitment to Ben's left side. Ben displaces this blow.*

Illus. 5.30: *From this feint, Christian swings the sword around to the other side, stepping left.*

Illus. 5.31: *Christian's blow reaches Ben's right side, where Ben displaces it (sequence continued on p. 62).*

More on the double feint

"*Twice further on, step to the left and the cut not omit.*"

Christian writes:

The "double feint" seeks to deceive the opponent twice about the real target of your attack in order to make him completely over-commit his weapon. The first strike goes to the left side of his head; when he then predictably displaces, the sword is quickly pulled around so as to strike the right side of his head. This is the first deception. If he displaces again, instead of striking back around to the left side once more, strike again to his right side, against his blade. This is the second deception. To finish the encounter, wind the sword behind his to cut his face with a step to the left.

Ringeck writes:

"*If you have attacked him on the right side of the head as described, strike immediately at the same spot.* [Illus. 5.32 & 5.33] *Then go over his sword with the short edge and your hands not crossed, jump to your left side and cut through his face with the long edge.*" [Illus. 5.34 & 5.35]

Illus. 5.32: *Christian withdraws his sword from the bind, as if to strike back to the other side.*

Illus. 5.33: *Instead of striking to the other side, Christian strikes again at Ben's sword. Ben is fooled a second time.*

Illus. 5.34: *Christian winds his short edge behind Ben's sword.*

Illus. 5.35: *Stepping further to his left side, Christian cuts Ben through the face behind Ben's sword.*

 Chapter 6
The Schielhau

The *Schielhau* or "Squinter" is the fourth of the five strikes, and, like the *Zwerchhau,* is accomplished by striking with the short edge. The *Schielhau* should be thrown with almost the same motion as the *Zwerchhau* – the only difference is that its trajectory is vertically down, rather than horizontal, and this requires that it be "hooked" into the target area, which is the opponent's right shoulder. Another similarity that the *Schielhau* shares with the *Zwerch* is the appearance of the final position, corresponding to the left guard *Ochs*.

The "Squinter" is also one of the four displacements--*Vier Versetzen*--that are used to counter the four guards. It is used against the guard of the Plow (*Pflug*) as it closes off the line of attack that this guard enables and it is also effective against thrusts from *Pflug* as well.

The *Schielhau* derives its colorful name from how the striker looks when he delivers the blow – attacking from the right side all the way over to the opponent's right puts the combatant in a position such that only one eye is on the opponent, i.e. "squinting" at him.

"*The Schielhau breaks what a Buffalo strikes or thrusts. Who threatens to change through, the Schielhau will rob him out of it.*"

Christian writes:

"Buffalo" is a slang term for a combatant who relies on raw strength instead of skill. The "squinting strike" is well-suited to countering such an opponent. When someone pulls back far to take a powerful swinging blow from their right shoulder, the *Schielhau* can be used to close off their line of attack by driving a wedge between the opponent's attack and his own head and neck.

Should you strike the adversary's blade, he may *change through*, by sliding his point past your attack in order to thrust to you. Because your point is already facing him, you need only push the thrust to him as he does this.

Master Ringeck also tells us here to use the *schielhau* against the *Pflug*. As the *Pflug* is the source of thrusts from below, the strike also works as a counter to those because it puts your sword into a position similar to the left side *Ochs*, thus closing off your opponent's line of attack.

Ringeck writes:

The Schielhau is a blow which primarily 'breaks' the strikes and thrusts of those fencers who rely only on their strength. Do it like this: If he attacks you from his right side, strike from your right side with the short edge and extended arms against the weak of his sword and hit him on the right shoulder. [Illus. 6.1a & b - 6.4a & b] If he changes through, [Illus. 6.5 & 6.6] thrust him into his breast with your arms extended. [Illus. 6.7] You should strike like this, too, if he faces you in the guard of the plough (Pflug) or if he wants to thrust you from below." [Illus. 6.8]

Illus. 6.1a & b: *Christian stands in the guard vom Tag, while Ben pulls his sword far back to begin a powerful swinging blow.*

Illus. 6.2a & b: *As Ben attacks from his right Christian moves to counter.*

Illus. 6.3a & b: *Christian steps forward and out with his right foot striking by raising his hilt and bringing the point forward, closing off Ben's line of attack.*

Illus. 6.4a & b: *The short edge of Christian's blade impacts simultaneously against Ben's sword and his right shoulder, creating a "single-time" parry and counterstrike. Here you can see why this blow is called the "squinter" – Christian's angle of counterattack puts him in a position wherein he is "squinting" at his opponent with one eye.*

Illus. 6.5: *In this variation, Christian succeeds in thwarting Ben's attack but fails to reach the right shoulder target.*

Illus. 6.6: *Escaping the bind, Ben changes through--durchwechseln- -to his other side, intending a thrust.*

Illus. 6.7: *Before Ben can begin his attack, Christian pushes his point forward, thrusting to Ben's chest.*

Illus. 6.8: *In a separate maneuver, Christian demonstrates how the Schielhau can be used to break the Plow (Pflug): Christian strikes the Schielhau against Ben's guard and thrusts to his chest in single time.*

Liechtenauer writes:

Schielhau when he strikes short to you, change through; thrust to him.

Ringeck writes:

Note: *You should always deceive him with your line of vision. Pay attention, if he fights short (feints). You will know this when he does not extend his arms when striking. You should strike then too; move your point through under his sword and thrust him into the face."* [Illus. 6.9]

Christian writes:

If you use *Schielhau* against his strike and he pulls the blow, you are still in position and stand safely with your blade between your body and his sword. From here thrust to his face or any high target.

Illus. 6.9: *Ben feints by pulling his strike so Christian extends his arms to thrust.*

Schielhau--The Squinter

How to break the long point with the Schielhau (Langenort)

<u>**Liechtenauer writes**</u>:

"Squint to the point, and take the throat without fear."

<u>**Christian writes**</u>:

<u>**Ringeck writes**</u>:

Note: The Schielhau (squinter) breaks the Longenort (long point) and is done as follows: When he faces you and points his tip against your breast or face with extended arms, [Illus. 6.10] *place your left foot forward and look at his tip. Feint a strike against his point,* [Illus. 6.11] *striking strongly against his sword with the short edge and thrusting with a forward step with the right foot, your point against his throat, with your arms extended."* [Illus. 6.12 & 6.13]

The *Langenort* or "Long Point," while not a primary guard, is a position that keeps an opponent at a safe distance by extending the point against them. In this technique the combatant uses line of sight to convey a false intent of striking for the opponent's head, but instead strikes his sword with a *Schielhau*, so that the short edge against his blade. The feint requires no footwork. The *Schielhau* to the blade and the thrust to the throat are done with an accompanying step with the right foot.

Illus. 6.10:
Christian stands in vom Tag. Ben stands against him in Langenort.

Illus. 6.11:
Without stepping Christian feints a strike to Ben's point.

Illus. 6.12:
Christian steps right to strike Schielhau against Ben's sword.

Illus. 6.13:
Leaning into the strike Christian thrusts to the throat along Ben's blade.

---

[1] The Four Primary Guards are the *Vier Leger* (see chapter 8). While Liechtenauer only advised using these four guards, most later masters included others, even while including Liecthenauer's verse that includes only the four guards. Ringeck himself includes the *Langenort*, *Schranckhut*, and *Nebenhut*.

Liechtenauer writes:

"*Squint to the head above, if you want to damage the hands.*"

Ringeck writes:

"*When he strikes an Oberhau look at his head, as if you intend to strike him there. But then strike against his blow with the short edge* [Illus. 6.14 & 6.15] *and strike at the hands with your point, along his blade.*" [Illus. 6.16]

Christian writes:

In this technique, the combatant uses line of sight to convey a false intent of a strike at the opponent's head but instead strikes his sword with *Schielhau* so that the short edge is brought to bear against his blade. The point is then slid down against the opponent's hands.

Illus. 6.14: *Both men stand in vom Tag.*

Illus. 6.15: *While his line of sight leads Ben to believe he will attack the head, Christian instead attacks Ben's sword with the Schielhau.*

Illus. 6.16: *Christian now slices his point down on to Ben's hands.*

Chapter 7
The Scheitelhau

The last of the five strikes, the *Scheitelhau*--"Parting Strike"-- works a little differently than the other four. Rather than attacking the opponent's blade while counterattacking it works through the principles of geometry: a high, extended strike will always *outreach* a low strike or guard. Unless the opponent raises his sword, there is no need to contact his blade while striking *Scheitelhau*. We'll see this principle described explicitly later in Ringeck's chapter on *Überlaufen* (Overrunning- -chapter 11) and the concept appears similarly in Fiore Dei Liberi's early 15th century Italian manual, "Fior di Battaglia."[1]

We will also find the *Scheitelhau* listed as one of the four displacements --*Vier Versetzen* - that counters *Alber,* the "fool's guard." It is the only one of the four strikes used to counter the four guards that uses the concept of outreaching an opponent without making blade contact.

The blow is accomplished by striking vertically down with the arms extended. The target of the strike should be the face or top of the chest - the closest available targets. The footwork involves a step outward and forward with the right foot. One must be careful to not step too far forward as maintaining a safe range from the sword is key.

Before leaving the *Scheitelhau*, I'm compelled to remind the practitioner about the importance of reach when using this attack. Practice so that it becomes instinctive to extend the arms fully, but without locking, while doing the strike; if you lock the elbows you'll find yourself within range of a strike to your legs.

---

[1] Fiore dei Liberi, *Fiore di Battaglia*, 1409, 26r.

Liechtenauer writes:

he Scheitelhau is a danger to the face."

Ringeck writes:

Note: The parting strike is aimed at the face or breast. Do it like this: If he is in the guard Alber,[Illus. 7.1a & b] *strike vertically downward with the long edge. And while striking, keep your arms up high and move your point to his face.*" [Illus. 7.2]

Illus. 7.1a & b: *Christian starts in vom Tag; Ben in Alber.*

Illus. 7.2: *Christian steps outward and slightly forward with his right leg while striking vertically towards Ben's face. The extension of Christian's arms while striking the Scheitelhau is very important, as this attack works by outreaching an opponent who either lies in a low guard or is striking to a low target.*

Liechtenauer writes:

"*With its turn, very dangerous to the breast.*"

Christian writes:

The first technique is the single time version; in one movement the opponent's sword is evaded and the strike hits its' mark. If the opponent raises his hilt and successfully thwarts the attempt to hit him, raise your hilt to get around his displacement and thrust down to his chest. Once again, in doing this wind and thrust we find ourselves in a variation of the familiar position of the left side version of *Ochs*.

Ringeck writes:

"*If you move the point at his face from above with the parting strike and he displaces the point with his hilt up,*[Illus. 7.3] *turn your sword, lift your hilt high above your head and thrust him down into the breast.*" [Illus. 7.4]

Illus. 7.3: *Christian strikes with Scheitelhau, but Ben raises his hilt to displace.*

Illus. 7.4: *Christian regains the initiative by inverting his sword so that his hilt is high and his short edge is against Ben's blade. From here, he thrusts down to Ben's chest. This Verkehrer, an "inversion," is a form of winding and must be done without breaking blade contact.*

How the Crown breaks the Schietelhau

Liechtenauer writes:

"*What comes from him, the Crown will catch.*"

Ringeck writes:

"*When you strike a schietelhau--'parting strike'--and he displaces with the hilt high above his head, this displacement is called the Crown (Kron).*[Illus. 7.5] *From there one can rush in.*" [Illus. 7.6]

Christian writes:

This is another way your opponent can displace your *Scheitelhau*. If he raises his sword vertically then he is using the displacement called the "Crown" (*Kron*). With the Kron, the swordsman steps directly into the attack, lifting his hilt and catching the cut at the juncture of the blade and cross guard. *Kron* allows him to run in under your sword and grapple or disarm you.

Illus. 7.5: *Ben counters Christian's Scheitelhau by raising his sword up high from Alber into the "Crown" displacement.*

Illus. 7.6: *From the Crown, Ben could rush in to grapple with his opponent, in this case using a common but very effective elbow push.*

Liechtenauer writes:

"*Cut through the Crown, you will break it hard through. Press the strikes, with cuts take them off.*"

Ringeck writes:

"*If he breaks the parting strike or any other Oberhau with the crown and tries to rush in, cut him in the arm under his hands and push upward, so that the crown is broken.* [Illus. 7.7] *Then turn your sword from the cut from below into one from above and in this way free yourself.*" [Illus. 7.8]

Christian writes:

Use a slicing cut from below to his arms to force him out of the displacement, saving yourself from being disarmed or thrown. You then finish him with a particularly gruesome type of winding technique, one where the winding is done against his arms, rather than at his sword. This leaves you in a position to now cut down onto his arms and force him away from you. This "winding while slicing" action will appear again as one of Liechtenauer's primary techniques, the *Hende Trucken* "Pressing of the Hands."

Illus. 7.7: *As Ben begins to rush in, Christian steps with his left foot and cuts upward to the underside of his arm. This forces Ben's attack up and away from him, thwarting any possible grappling.*

Illus. 7.8: *Christian completes the counter to the Crown by winding the long edge of his sword at Ben's arms, and then cutting down onto the arms from above. This forces Ben away from him.*

Chapter 8
Vier Leger

Liechtenauer writes:

"*Four guards alone hold; and disdain the common. Ochs, Pflug, Alber, vom Tag should not be unknown to you.*"

Ringeck writes:

"*There are only four basic positions that are useful in combat; these are Ochs, Alber, Pflug, and vom Tag.*"

In his verse, Master Liechtenauer advises to use only four guards: *Ochs* ("the Ox"), *Pflug* ("the Plow"), *Alber* ("the Fool"), and *vom Tag* ("from the roof"). Later students of Liechtenauer's system, including Sigmund Ringeck, added others. In the chapter on the *Krumphau* we were introduced to the *Schranckhut* while the commentaries on the Schielhau described how to counter a guard called *Langenort*, the "Long Point." These two are presented formally later in the book. There is another position that we have yet to encounter, the *Nebenhut*, which Master Ringeck describes outside of his commentaries in a separate chapter.

The guards *Ochs* and *Pflug* are a matched set - it seems no accident that both are allusions to the same agrarian activity: using oxen to plow fields. Each are thrusting guards protecting the inside; a solid understanding of them is necessary to comprehend a number of other concepts in the system. *Ochs* thrusts from above while *Pflug* thrusts from below. They can also set aside blows--*Absetzen*--so corresponding to the positions wherein you bind an opponent's sword.

Because they are used in so many ways, one must understand that they are symmetrical. There are mirror positions on the left side of the body for both guards. *Ochs* on the left involves standing with the right leg leading and holding the sword at the left side of the hand with uncrossed hands. *Pflug* on the left has a right leg lead and the sword held at the left side with the hands uncrossed. This is very important; many of the binds described require the left *Ochs*.

If *Ochs* and *Pflug* are inside thrusting guards, *Alber* and *vom Tag* are outside guards that threaten to strike or rush in. *Vom Tag* is an easy position to understand - it's an obvious starting place for delivering powerful hewing blows from above (that is, "from the roof"). Master Sigmund provides two different interpretations. It is possible that the more conservative version (at the shoulder) is intended for use when one is wearing more restrictive clothing (or even a light armour?) or they could be intended to create different kinds of invitation to attack.

Alber--the "fool's guard"--requires a bit more speculation. Perhaps part of its function invites an opponent to attack by appearing unguarded, luring a fool to attack. While this is interpretation, I find *Alber* especially useful as a place to start the Crown displacement (*Kron*) that appears in the chapter on the *Scheitelhau*, and a good starting position for some of the "rushing in" techniques discussed later. It has a right leg lead so you can also raise your sword from *Alber*, and with a step of the left foot attacking from the left. The combatant should remember Master Liechtenauer's advice to not throw an initial strike from the left - it is inherently weaker (for a right-hander). But if your first strike from the right missed the opponent you could end up in *Alber* and could strike as described.

The four guards are the framework on which the rest of the Liechtenauer's system is built; every technique can be described in terms of transitions from one guard to another. For instance, when you strike a *Zornhau* against an opponent's blade, you begin the strike in *vom Tag* and strike into the left *Pflug*. In like fashion when you strike a *Zwerch* or *Schielhau* you start in *vom Tag, Ochs* or *Pflug* on the right and end in the left *Ochs*. Master the transitions between all four primary guards and you will be able to work a great many of the techniques.

Ringeck writes:

"*Stand with your left foot forward, holding your sword at the right side of your head, your point directed at his face.*" [Illus. 8.1a & b]

Christian writes:

The *Ochs* creates menace by directing the point towards the opponent from above. It should be no surprise that this guard is used to thrust downward to the face or chest. It derives its name from the way the point hangs like the horns of an ox.

Illustr. 8.1a: *The guard of 'the Ox', Ochs. Note how the point is directed at the opponent's face.*

Illustr. 8.1b: *The guard Ochs from the front.*

Ringeck writes:

"*Stand with the left foot forward and hold your sword at your right side above your knee, with your hands crossed, your point directed at his face.*" [Illus. 8.2a & b]

Christian writes:

Where *Ochs* threatens from above *Pflug* threatens from below and from this position you should thrust upward. It derives its name from the position one assumes while pushing a plow.

Illustr. 8.2a: *The guard Pflug, "The Plow."*

Illustr. 8.2b: *The guard of "The Plow," Pflug, from the front.*

Ringeck writes:

"*Stand with your right foot forward and hold your sword in front of you with your arms extended, your point directed at the ground.*" [Illustr. 8.3a & b]

Alber is an invitational guard. Carried low it seems to invite an attack. One can, however, raise the sword from *Alber* to counter or begin a strike. Some have speculated that *Alber* derives its name from the idea that a only a fool relies on a purely defensive posture.[1] I find it unlikely that Liecthenauer would include a guard that shouldn't be used. I'm inclined to believe that its intended to lure fools into attacking what seems to be a vulnerable posture.

Illustr. 8.3a: *The guard of "the Fool," Alber.*

Illustr. 8.3b: *Alber from the front.*

---

[1]S. Matthew Galas, 'Kindred Spirits', *Journal of the Asian Martial Arts*, Vol. 6, No. 3, 1997, p. 32.

Christian writes:

Vom Tag is a guard from which powerful blows may be struck. It threatens to attack strongly against any who approach. *Vom Tag* may be done in two ways: one variation holds the sword at the shoulder, the other carries it high overhead. It derives its name from its high position: blows struck from it come down "from the roof."

Ringeck writes:

"*Stand with your left foot forward and hold your sword at the side of your right shoulder* [Illus. 8.4a & b] *or above your head with your arms extended.* [Illus. 8.5a & b]

"*And in this book, you'll find written down how to fence from these guards.*"

Illustr. 8.4a: *The guard "from the roof," vom Tag. See the next page for the alternate position, with the hands held above the combatant's head.*

Illustr. 8.4b: *The guard vom Tag from the front.*

Illustr. 8.5a: *The alternate Vom Tag.*

Illustr. 8.5b: *The alternate vom Tag seen from the front.*

Vier Versetzen

The four displacement--*Vier Versetzen*--are four of Master Liechtenauer's five strikes used to counter the four guards. Every technique has its counter and in turn every guard its displacement. In this context a displacement is a parry or block impeding a blow or thrust. Liechtenauer scorned any displacement that only provided defense - if one merely blocks an attack it means the opponent can easily attack again and thereby maintain the initiative.

Liechtenauer's four displacements are thus active defenses; they attack while protecting. A *Zwerchhau* used to attack an opponent in *vom Tag* enjoys considerable protection during the attack - the worst an opponent can do is to engage your blade. It is possible to "displace" his guard without hitting his sword. These displacements can be used against a man lying in guard or they can displace, in the more conventional sense, an attack coming from that guard.

We are also advised to eschew displacements used by "bad fencers." I interpret this to mean "empty displacements" - one devoid of any counterattacking capability. Overuse of this kind of passive defense causes you to remain on the defensive (or, as Liechtenauer would have it, in the *Nach*--the "After") and it is probably only a matter of time before you are hit by your opponent, who remains on the offensive (in the *Vor*, the "Before"). The better approach is to displace in a way that allowing a counterattack with a simultaneous defense, to "strike when he strikes, and thrust when he thrusts," the core idea behind the Master's five strikes.

In the latter part of the verse on displacing Liechtenauer includes two options for how to handle an opponent's counter to your attack. One option is to "snap out" from under the bind created by the displacement; the other is to strike around in search of another opening. Ringeck includes two techniques for each option; the last two introduce the concept of *Halbschwert*, the "half-sword" where the sword is shortened, "halved," by releasing the left hand from the grip and grasping the blade and turning the sword into a short, powerful spear.

Liechtenauer writes:

"*Four are the displacements which hurt four guards very much. Beware of displacing. If it happens to you, it troubles you greatly.*"

Ringeck writes:

"*You have heard previously, that you shall fight only from four guards. Now, you shall get to know the four displacements, which are four strikes.*

The first strike is the 'crooked strike' (Krumphau). It counters Ochs. [Illus. 9.1]

The second strike is the 'cross strike' (Zwerchhau). It counters vom Tag. [Illus. 9.2]

The third strike is the 'squinter' (Schielhau). It counters Pflug. [Illus. 9.3]

The fourth strike is the 'parting strike' (Scheitelhau). It counters Alber." [Illus. 9.4]

Christian writes:

Master Ringeck tells us that four of the five strikes may be used to counter the four primary guards. His remarks are brief at best, but then, he has really already told us how these four strikes do this in previous chapters.

Illustr. 9.1: *The Krumphau breaking Ochs. Ben's line of attack from above is closed off by the strike.*

Illustr. 9.2: *The Zwerchhau breaking vom Tag. Ben cannot bring his sword down to strike as he is hit.*

Liechtenauer writes:

"*If you are displaced and when that has happened, hear what I advise to you. Tear away and strike quickly with surprise.*"

Ringeck writes:

"*And beware of all displacements used by bad fencers. Note: Strike, when he strikes; thrust, when he thrusts. And in this chapter and in the chapter on the five strikes you shall find written down how you shall strike and thrust.*"

Christian writes:

Ringeck advises never use "bad" displacements; one that has no offensive potential; a parry or block that only deflects your adversary's strike. One should displace attacks in such a way that they also counterattack your opponent. In order to regain or maintain the initiative every defense must comprise an offense.

Illustr. 9.3: *The Schielhau breaking Pflug. The line of attack from below is closed.*

Illustr. 9.4: *The Scheitelhau breaking Alber. Ben is at an angular disadvantage as he tries to raise from Alber to counter Scheitelhau, delivered with the arms extended.*

A technique against displacement

Ringeck writes:

"*If a strike of yours has been displaced, note: if an Oberhau of yours is displaced* [Illus. 9.5] *stay in the bind, move your pommel* [Illus. 9.6] *over his forward hand, tearing it down and striking him on the head simultaneously.*" [Illus. 9.7]

Illustr. 9.5: *Ben displaces Christian's Oberhau.*

Illustr. 9.6: *Christian drives his pommel forward.*

Illustr. 9.7: *Hooking Ben's hands with his own pommel, Christian strikes Ben's head.*

Liechtenauer writes:

"*Set upon the four ends. Stay upon, if you want to learn to bring it to an end.*"

Ringeck writes:

"*If you strike Unterhau from the right side and he falls on your sword (i.e., he pushes it downwards), so that you cannot lift it up,* [Illus. 9.6] *move the pommel over his sword* [Illus. 9.9] *and, with a snapping motion, strike him on the head with the long edge.* [Illus. 9.10] *Or, if he falls on your sword from your left,* [Illus. 9.11] *strike him with the short edge.*" [Illus. 9.12]

Christian writes:

These two techniques both address the same portion of Liechtenauer's verse, concerned with what should be done when *you* are displaced. Both advocate "tearing away" by snapping your sword out of the bind. This is done by pushing the pommel forward, which frees your blade from beneath.

Illustr. 9.8: *Ben displaces Christian's Unterhau, which has struck from his right.*

Illustr. 9.9: *Christian pushes his pommel forward over Ben's hands in time with a step of the left foot.*

Illustr. 9.10: *Freeing himself from the bind Christian strikes Ben's head.*

Illustr. 9.11: *In this variant Christian strikes an Unterhau from his left; Ben binds strongly.*

Illustr. 9.12: *Freeing himself from the bind, Christian steps forward with his right foot and strikes Ben with the short edge.*

Christian writes:

Here are another pair of techniques useful for countering a displacement. In these two cases, escape from the bind by striking around to another opening. In the first, grab your blade with the left hand and strike, setting up a thrust with what the German masters call the *halbschwert* (half-sword).

If the thrust from the half sword is then displaced the second of the two counters is used. *Change through* with the pommel, striking with it to his head or using it as a hook to throw him over your right leg.

Ringeck writes:

"*If you strike an Oberhau from the right and if you want to end the fight, note: when he displaces,* [Illus. 9.13] *immediately strike around (i.e., to the other side)* [Illus. 9.14] *with the Zwerchhau. Grab the blade of your sword with the left hand and thrust into his face.* [Illus. 9.15 & 9.16] *Or attack one of the other openings you can reach best.*"

Illustr. 9.13: *Both men stand in the bind.*

Illustr. 9.14: *Christian steps with the left foot and strikes*

Illustr. 9.15: *Christian releases his left hand from his hilt and moves it to grasp the middle of his own blade.*

Illustr. 9.16: *Christian thrusts to Ben's face at the half-sword.*

Ringeck writes:

"*If you thrust at his face at the halbschwert (half-sword) and he displaces this, [Illus. 9.17] immediately strike him on the other side of the head with the pommel. [Illus. 9.18] Or jump with the right foot behind his left, move your pommel around his neck from the right shoulder (i.e., his right side) and tear him down over your right leg.*" [Illus. 9.19]

Illustr. 9.17: *In this technique, Ben displaces Christian's half sword attack to the face.*

Illustr. 9.18: *Christian counters by stepping with his right foot and changes through with his pommel, smashing Ben in the face.*

Illustr. 9.19: *Another option: a deeper step with the right foot puts Christian's foot behind Ben's left. Using the pommel as a hook about Ben's neck, Christian can now throw him.*

Chapter 10
Nachreisen

Nachreisen, "Traveling After," is a technique used to take back the initiative from an opponent who has made the first move. It relies primarily on out-timing the opponent and striking him as he prepares to attack or after a strike of his has missed and he is attempting to recover. The same two things can be done if he is thrusting.

A special case of *Nachreisen*, the two *Ausser Abnahmen*--"Outer Takings"--are a kind of traveling after done "at the sword" (*am Schwert*). Once you are on his sword, follow his movement and push his sword aside while pursuing your own thrusting attack. The first technique does this from above, the second from below; both are done from the outside of his blade.

Before showing a final *Nachreisen* that uses a slicing cut to finish the encounter, Liechtenauer and Ringeck both remind us of the importance of sensing an opponent's intention while in a bind. This sense is called *Fühlen*--"feeling"--and is all about knowing what an opponent will do based on his pressure on your blade. *Fühlen* is used to determine *immediately* what you should do. This on-the-fly decision-making, the notion of "while" or "during," is known as *Indes*, first introduced in the chapter on the basics. *Indes*, says Ringeck, is the key to the art: knowing what to do during a bind is what allows the swordsman to make the right choice of technique in each situation. "*Indes* - that word - cuts sharply."

Liechtenauer writes:

"The traveling after: learn twice, or cut into the weapon."

Ringeck writes:

"There are two kinds of Nachreisen, and you should learn both. Use the first against an Oberhau. If he raises the sword to strike, travel after him with a strike or a thrust and hit him in the upper opening before he can complete the strike. [Illus. 10.1 & Illus. 10.2] Or fall on his raised arms with the long edge and push him away from you." [Illus. 10.3]

Illus. 10.1: *Both men stand in vom Tag.*

Illus. 10.2: *Christian strikes as Ben raises his sword to attack.*

Illus. 10.3: *Christian falls upon Ben's arms with a slicing cut as Ben raises his sword to attack.*

Christian writes:

Liechtenauer tells us there are two kinds of *Nachreisen*-- "Traveling After." Ringeck explains that there is one kind in which you follow him as he pulls back to strike. You can either strike to one of his upper openings or you can forcefully cut into his arms if he begins striking to you. The other kind of *Nachreisen* involves striking him after he has attacked--and missed. Catch him as he tries to recover and begin anew. This same method works when your opponent pulls back to prepare a thrusting attack - simply follow after him with your point and thrust before he is able to execute his attack.

Ringeck Writes:

"*W*hen he strikes an Oberhau and brings the blade down with the attack, [Illus. 10.4] *travel after him with a strike on the head before he can get his sword up again.* [Illus. 10.5] *But if he wants to thrust at you and pulls the sword back to prepare for the thrust, travel after him and thrust before he can do it himself.*" [Illus. 10.6]

Illus. 10.4: *Ben strikes short, missing Christian.*

Illus. 10.5: *Christian strikes Ben's head before the latter can finish raising his sword.*

Illus. 10.6: *Ben has cocked back to thrust, but Christian has traveled after and thus thrusts first.*

Nachreisen from the outside ("Ausser abnahmen")

Liechtenauer writes:

"Two outside takings. The work after that begins. And test the bind, if it is soft or hard."

Ringeck writes:

Note, there are two Ausser Abnahmen from the outside, which are two Nachreisen at the sword (am Schwert). Do them like this: If his strike falls short, [Illus. 10.7] travel after him. If he displaces that, [Illus. 10.8] stay at the sword (that is, maintain blade contact) and check whether he's hard or soft in the bind. When he pushes up your sword with strength, place your blade on the outside of his blade and thrust at his lower opening." [Illus. 10.9]

Illus. 10.7: *Ben again strikes short as Christian moves his midsection away from the attack.*

Illus. 10.8: *Christian travels after, but Ben raises his hilt in time to displace.*

Illus. 10.9: *Christian stays on Ben's blade and, from the outside, thrusts to his lower opening by raising his own hilt.*

Ringeck writes:

"*Also, if you fence against him with low strikes or other techniques and he forestalls this, winding against your sword from above so that you cannot move up, [Illus. 10.10] maintain strong contact with his sword from below. If he then attacks your high opening [Illus. 10.11] follow with your sword, taking the weak of his blade with your long edge and pushing it down and thrusting into his face.*" [Illus. 10.12]

Christian writes:

These two techniques are called *Ausser Abnahmen*, or "Takings from the Outside;" a special type of *Nachreisen* that involves traveling after your opponent without leaving his blade. In the first technique, an attempt to hit his head after he pulls a strike is thwarted by his displacement. If he's soft in the bind, press on with your initial attempt to travel after. If he is hard in the bind stay on his sword and, with a winding motion, thrust down to one of his lower openings. In the second *Ausser Abnahmen*, your opponent attempts to thrust after pinning your low strike. Bring the strong of your sword to bear against the weak of his and force his blade aside while thrusting to his face. Both techniques work by taking his sword off-line from the outside, hence the name.

Illus. 10.10: *Ben pins Christian's attempted Unterhau.*

Illus. 10.12: *Using the strong of his sword against the weak of Ben's, Christian forces Ben's attack away and delivers his own thrust.*

Illus. 10.11: *Ben moves to thrust upward; Christian remains on his sword.*

Liechtenauer writes:

The feeling learn. 'Indes' – that word – cuts sharply."

Ringeck writes:

"You shall learn and understand both the word 'Fühlen' and the word 'Indes', because these two belong together and together account for the greatest art and skill in fencing. Therefore remember: if one binds against the others sword, you shall notice - right in the moment when the blades make contact - whether he has bound hard or soft. And as soon as you have noticed this, remember the word 'Indes': this means that you should attack the next opening immediately and nimbly, hard or soft. So he will be defeated before he knows it himself.

"Likewise, you shall remember the word 'Indes' during all binds at the sword, because 'Indes' duplieres and 'Indes' mutieres, 'Indes' rushes through and 'Indes' slices, 'Indes' wrestles and 'Indes' disarms, 'Indes' – in the art of fencing – does what your heart desires.

"'Indes' is a sharp word that cuts all fencers who don't know anything about it. And 'Indes' is the key that unlocks the art of fencing."

Christian writes:

As the last two techniques have depended on knowing whether the opponent is hard or soft in the bind, this is a fitting place to address the concept *Indes*, "simultaneity." When in a bind, determine immediately how the opponent has bound to you: is he holding hard against the sword, or is he soft in the bind? What you do next depends on this determination.

Recall the ability to determine an opponent's intent by his blade pressure--*Fühlen*--loosely "the feeling of the steel;" this may be the single most important skill to master in Liechtenauer's fighting system. *Fühlen* lets you determine--*Indes*--what to do. If he is hard at the sword, don't get into a pushing match with the blades. Wind to regain strength or find another opening. If he is soft at the sword, you don't want to let up pressure as this would free him to act against you - instead make use of your superiority in the bind to complete your initial action.

Indes allows us to decide whether to fight in the *Vor* ("Before") or the *Nach* ("After"). *Fühlen* applies there as well; it is the skill used to make that determination instantly. *Fühlen* and *Indes* go hand in hand and Master Ringeck does not exaggerate their importance - they are the key to the art. By developing a sense for blade pressure you learn how to direct your reactions so that they always give you the initiative.

Liechtenauer writes:

"Travel after twice, if you hit, the old cut make along."

Ringeck writes:

"*When* he attacks short in front of you, [Illus. 10.13] *travel after him with a strike to the high opening. If he moves up and winds against your sword from below,* [Illus. 10.14] *note: as soon as the swords clash together* [Illus. 10.15] *fall on his arms with the long edge and push him away from you.* [Illus. 10.16] *Or cut through his face.* [Illus. 10.17] *Practice this from both sides.*"

Christian writes:

Liechtenauer says to "travel after twice." In this technique, this seems to mean that you travel after his first feinting strike, and then again travel after him when he displaces that from below. After he hits your blade, you make the cut, either into his arms with an aggressive push or through his face.

Illus. 10.13: *Ben strikes short, having misjudged his range.*

Illus. 10.14: *Christian travels after the strike, but Ben raises to displace.*

Illus. 10.15:
Ben displaces the blow.

Illus. 10.16:
Ben's displacement is soft, so Christian forces his way through it and cuts Ben's arms.

Illus. 10.17:
Ben's displacement is hard and it may be preferable to not try forcing his blade down: never oppose strength with strength. Instead, Christian merely exploits a gap and slices Ben through the face.

Chapter 11
Überlaufen

Überlaufen is simply the concept of outreaching your opponent. The case that Ringeck comments on uses a high line of attack to outreach, or "overrun," an attack along the low line. This concept illuminates the application of the *Scheitelhau* against *Alber*, and reveals why we don't find any leg strikes being taught with longswords in this or other German manuals. A strike to the legs is easy to avoid, and likely to yield a simultaneous counterstrike to one's head.

Ringeck only provides commentary for one of the two types of *Überlaufen* described by Liechtenauer's verse. The other is a technique for overrunning your opponent's high line attack by doing something to go over it, such as hooking one's pommel over his blade and grabbing his grip or pommel to disarm him. A number of other *fechtbücher* ("fight books") describe this variant. The idea there is that if he attacks high, you "take him down a peg" by going even higher and pulling him down. *Kron*--the crown displacement--described in the chapter on the *Scheitelhau* is probably a good place to start this kind of a "pulling down" action.

Liechtenauer writes:

"Who wants to strike below, run him over, and he will be ashamed. When he strikes from above, then strengthen: this I truly do laud. Do your work, or press hard twice."

Ringeck writes:

"When your adversary aims at the lower openings with either a strike or a thrust while closing in, do not displace this, [Illus. 11.1 & 11.2] *but wait until you can overrun him with a strike to the head or a high thrust.* [Illus. 11.3] *So you'll defeat him because the high strikes and thrusts all have a longer reach than the low ones.*"

Christian writes:

In this technique--the only one in the chapter--your opponent strikes a low targeted blow to you. Rather than displacing the blow, avoid it and outreach his attack with a high targeted strike of your own. The technique works because of a geometric advantage: high strikes outreach low ones. The same is true for thrusts. This is the same principle that allows the *Scheitelhau*--"Parting Strike"--to outreach and ultimately counter *Alber*.

Illus. 11.1: *Both combatants stand in their guards.*

Illus. 11.2: *As Ben strikes to Christian's lower openings, Christian slips the blow with a step back with his left foot. As he steps, he begins to attack.*

Illus. 11.3: *Christian extends his arms to complete his strike, outreaching Ben's attack and hitting him on the head with a Scheitelhau (Parting Strike).*

Chapter 12
Absetzen

An *absetzen*--"setting aside"--is a deflection of an opponent's attack. There are four "primary" *absetzen*[1], whose positions correspond to the guards *Ochs* and *Pflug* on the left and right sides. We've seen these *absetzen* indirectly throughout the techniques previously covered. When you strike a *Zornhau* against an *Oberhau*, bind in a position akin to *Pflug* on the left, and this is the lower left *absetzen*. In a similar vein, when you strike a *Zwerchhau* or *Schielhau*, you counter his attack by arriving in the left *Ochs*, which is the upper left *absetzen*. It follow then that the opposite side guards/*absetzen* would be used if your opponent attacked from his left side.

The particular techniques described in this chapter are done as single-time counterattacks. If the five strikes are *meisterhau* that defend and attack in one motion, then we could almost consider these techniques to be "master thrusts:" in one motion; essentially a change of guards that encompass a simultaneous attack and defense. The opponent's attack is deflected and his face is attacked with your point. It should therefore be no surprise to find that the conclusion of each of the two techniques looks remarkably like the conclusion of some of the techniques from the chapters on the five *meisterhau*.

---

[1] Ringeck adds at least one more: the deflection done using the Schranckhut.

<u>**Liechtenauer writes**</u>:

"*Learn to set aside strike and thrust with skill. Who thrusts at you, your point hits and his is broken. From both sides, if you want to hit every time you must step.*"

<u>**Ringeck writes**</u>:

This means: You shall learn how to set aside strikes and thrusts skillfully so that his thrust is countered and yours hits.

"*Do it like this: If he stands before you as if he is about to thrust at your lower opening, assume the guard of the plow (Pflug) on your right side [Illus. 12.1] and open up your left. If he then thrusts at your left opening, wind your sword against his to your left side and take a step forward with your right foot, thus your point will hit and his will miss.*" [Illus. 12.2]

Illus. 12.1:
Both combatants begin in right-sided Pflug.

Illus. 12.2:
Ben attempts to attack Christian's left side, but Christian steps forward with his right leg into Pflug on his left which deflects Ben's attack and puts the point into his face.

Ringeck writes:

"*If you face him in Pflug on your left* [Illus. 12.3] *and he strikes at your left high opening, move up with your sword on your left, the hilt in front of your head. Take a step forward with the right foot and thrust to his face.*" [Illus. 12.4]

Christian writes:

These two techniques both use the same kind of setup: standing in a particular guard leads the opponent to attack an opening that appears to be unprotected. In the first *absetzen*, stand in the guard of the plow (*Pflug*) on the right, opening your left side to attack. When he attacks the left, step forward with you right foot and change to *Pflug* on the left, simultaneuously deflecting his attack and putting your point into his face.

The second technique works in a similarly. Here you protect a lower opening and he attacks a high one. Begin in the left *Pflug* and when he attacks transition into the left *Ochs* by raising your hilt. Already in a right leg leading stance, you take only a small step forward with the right foot to propel your thrust to his face at the same time try to set his attack aside.

Illus. 12.3: *Ben stands in the guard vom Tag, Christian in the guard Pflug on his left side.*

Illus. 12.4: *Ben attacks Christian's upper opening on his left side, but Christian winds his hilt high, and with a forward step of the right leg, sets aside the attack and lands his own thrust to Ben's face.*

Chapter 13
Durchwechseln

Durchwechseln--"changing through"--describes a disengagement from the opponent's blade accomplished by sliding the sword out of the bind. It is best done when your opponent has committed strongly the displacement. His strong commitment to defending one opening has two consequences that facilitate a *durchwechseln*: it makes another opening all the more available and it pushes your blade far enough away from him that you have room to drag your point free.

The third technique against displacement (see chapter 9 on the *Vier Versetzen*) features a variation on changing through. The *durchwechseln* is accomplished by driving the pommel to free the sword. The result is the same - the sword slides out of the engagement and is now free to work once more.

Durchwechseln - Changing Through
Intro to the Durchwechseln

Liechtenauer writes:

The changing through learn from both sides, thrust with intent. Whoever binds to you, change through and find him exposed."

Ringeck writes:

"*Do it like this: If he wants to bind with you in the Zufechten against a strike or a thrust,* [Illus. 13.1] *allow your point to slide through under his sword* [Illus. 13.2 & 13.3] *and thrust at him on the other side.* [Illus. 13.4] *There you find him exposed.*"

Christian writes:

Durchwechseln is simple to do - just slide your sword out of the bind and thrust somewhere else where the opponent is vulnerable. The trick is knowing *when* to use the technique. Here a *durchwechseln* is used in response to a strong displacement of a thrust or strike. The *durchwechseln* should only be used when the opponent is committed to a defensive bind; if he is soft in the bind, he'll be able to respond easily to your attempt and press his attack aggressively.

Ilus. 13.1: *Christian thrusts to Ben's left side. Ben displaces the thrust and binds with strength.*

Ilus. 13.2: *Christian begins to slide his point out of the bind.*

Ilus. 13.3: *Christian's point is freed.*

Ilus. 13.4: *Christian drives his point into Ben's right side*

Chapter 17
Zucken

Twitching (*Zucken*) is a colorful term for suddenly breaking free from a bind with an opponent's sword and striking around to the other side for a follow-on attack. *Zucken* is a close cousin to the previous chapter's *Durchwechseln*: a "twitch" is a freeing from the bind followed by an attack to an opening on the other side, while a "changing through" is a sliding out from the bind followed by a thrust to the other side. The rule that applies to changing through also applies to twitching: you don't do it unless your opponent is strongly committed to a displacement.

We have seen twitching used elsewhere: the *abnahmen* ("taking off") that appears in the chapter on the *Zornhau* is really a twitching, and the *Zwerchhau* to the "Four Openings" might also be considered an example.

Liechtenauer writes:

"Step close in binding. The twitching provides good finds. Twitch! If it hits, twitch more. Work and wind: that will hurt him. Twitch with all meetings with the masters, if you want to imitate them."

Ringeck writes:

"If you come at him in the Zufechten, strike him from the right with an Oberhau to the head. If he binds against your sword, [Illus. 14.1] step into the bind near to him, 'twitch' (that is, rapidly move away) your sword above and away of his [Illus. 14.2] and strike at the other side to his head. [Illus. 14.3] If he displaces you again, [Illus. 14.4] strike again to the other side, [Illus. 14.5] and work skillfully to the upper openings with duplieren [Illus. 14.6] and other techniques."

Christian writes:

Zucken is used as a response to a strong displacement from the opponent. In this solitary example of the technique, the Zucken is used twice, followed by a dupliere or other technique once you've gotten the opponent expecting you to keep twitching. In practice, either of the two "twitches" could yield a successful attack. The initiative is kept through continued striking and working of other techniques until the opponent is overcome.

Illustr. 14.1: *Ben strongly displaces Christian's strike.*

Illustr. 14.2: *Christian begins to step to move in towards Ben while raising his sword.*

Illustr. 14.3: *Christian steps in with his left foot and strikes to Ben's other side. Ben catches this in time, again displacing Christian's blow.*

Illustr. 14.4: *Christian again begins to raise up his sword away from Ben's displacement.*

Illustr. 14.5: *Christian "twitches" again, this time back to Ben's left. Again Ben displaces the blow.*

Illustr. 14.6: *Having led Ben to expect another Zucken to the opposite side, Christian instead duplieres behind Ben's displacement.*

Chapter 15
Durchlaufen

This chapter derives quite a bit of technique from relatively little of Liechtenauer's verse. *Durchlaufen*--"running through"-- doesn't involve putting your point through someone's body - it is a method for circumventing a rushing attack by going under and through the attack to throw the opponent. This concept, covered by the first two techniques, seems to be all the verse implies. Ringeck includes some variations on this theme which he calls "wrestling at the sword." He seemingly goes even farther afield in grouping some "sword takings" in this chapter. All of the techniques involve grappling on some level, so it's unsurprising that they should be learned together. However, it is interesting how much Ringeck adds to Liechtenauer's teachings on the concept.

All of these techniques can be used as yet another set of options for when one must deal with a strong opponent or one who is simply very strong in a particular bind. Rather than oppose his strength with your own, yield to it and slip through his attack. This illustrates the German swordfighting adage "Use strength against weakness, and weakness against strength."

Liechtenauer writes:

"*Run through, let hang with the pommel. Grasp if you want to wrestle. When one comes strongly against you the running through then remember.*"

Ringeck writes:

Note: If he runs at you with his arms raised and wants to overwhelm you from above with strength [Illustr. 15.1] *lift your arms and hold the sword with the left hand at the pommel over your head so that the blade hangs behind your back.* [Illustr. 15.2] *Duck through under his right arm and jump with your right foot behind his. While jumping seize him with the right arm around the body, take him on the right hip and throw him before you to the ground.*" [Illustr. 15.3]

Christian writes:

These first two techniques are really a pair. In each of them, the sword is held only by the left hand with the blade hanging protectively over the back. The right leg is then used as a point to throw the opponent over. In the first technique, the right leg is placed behind the opponent's right leg and he is thrown backwards. In the second technique, the right is put before the opponent's right and he is thrown onto his face. In both cases, the rushing attack is not opposed with an attempt to simply displace it; rather, one "runs through" the attack and unbalances the attacker.

Illus. 15.1: *Both men stand in vom Tag.*

Illus. 15.2: *As Ben approaches with a strike from above, Christian lets go of the sword with his right hand. His sword hang protectively from his left hand as he begins to close with Ben.*

Illus. 15.3: *Christian "runs through" the attack by stepping to place his right foot behind Ben's right. With his right arm about Ben's chest, Christian throws him over his right leg.*

Ringeck writes on a second technique:

"*If he runs in and wants to overwhelm you with strength from above, hold your sword with your left hand at the pommel and let the blade hang over your back. Duck through under his right arm, however leave your right leg in front of his. Seize him then with the right arm around his back and throw him over the hip behind you.*" [Illustr. 15.4]

Illus. 15.4: *An alternate conclusion to the last encounter. Instead of stepping behind Ben's right foot, Christian steps to place it in front of the foot, and with his right arm about Ben's back, throws Ben behind him.*

Ringeck writes:

"*If he runs at you, let go of your sword with your left hand and hold it in the right. Strike his sword with your hilt to your right side. [Illustr. 15.5 & 15.6] Jump with the left foot in front of his right, seize him with the left arm around the body, taking him on your left hip and throwing him before you to the ground. [Illustr. 15.7] Pay attention so that you do not fail to throw him.*"

Illus. 15.5: *Ben has rushed in on Christian, who engages his blade.*

Illus. 15.6: *Releasing his left hand from his sword, Christian hooks Ben's blade with his hilt.*

Illus. 15.7: *Christian steps forward with his left foot to place it before Ben's right. With his left hand he grasps Ben about the back and throws him.*

Ringeck writes:

"*If he runs at you, let go of your sword with your left hand and hold it in your right. Strike his sword with your hilt to your right side. Jump with the left foot behind his right, seize him with the left arm around the chest and throw him over your leg to the rear.*" [Illustr. 15.8]

Christian writes:

Here is another pair of techniques. This time, the left hand is released from the sword, while the right is used to move the opponent's sword aside with the hilt. The left leg is used in each technique. Depending on whether you step in front of his right leg or behind it, you throw him forward or backward to the ground. You maintain pressure against his weapon with your hilt as the throw is accomplished, making this a "wrestling at the sword" *ringen am schwert.*

Illus. 15.8: *An alternate conclusion to the previous technique. Rather than placing his foot before Ben's foot, Christian places it behind the foot. He also puts his left arm about Ben's chest to throw him backwards.*

Durchlaufen -- Running Through
Third wrestling at the sword

Ringeck writes:

"*If you run in at him let go of your sword with the left hand and hold it in the right.* [Illustr. 15.9] *Move your pommel over his right arm from the outside* [Illustr. 15.10] *and tear it downward. With the left hand seize his right elbow, jump with the left foot in front of his right, pulling him in such a way over your leg to your right side.*" [Illustr. 15.11]

Christian writes:

This is another way to wrestle at the sword. Here the right hand, which alone holds the sword, drives the pommel to hook your opponent's right arm and push it down. Step in with the left foot and with your left hand grab his elbow, throwing him over your left leg.

Illus. 15.9: *Ben has rushed in - Christian moves to intercept.*

Illus. 15.10: *Releasing his left hand from the grip, Christian moves to grab Ben's elbow while his right hand drives his pommel forward over Ben's right arm.*

Illus. 15.11: *Christian steps in, placing his left foot in front of Ben's right while pushing his right arm downward with his pommel and shoving him by the right elbow with his left hand, all of which conspires to make Ben fall.*

Durchlaufen -- Running Through
A fourth wrestling at the sword

Ringeck writes:

"*If he runs at you, pass your left inverted hand over his right arm* [Illus. 15.12-14] *and grab your own right arm.* [Illus. 15.15] *Press with your right arm over your left to his right, and jump with your right foot behind his, turning to your left side: thus you throw him over the right hip.*" [Illus. 15.16]

Christian writes:

This time, your left arm - freed from gripping the sword - is used to grab around the opponent's right arm and throw him backwards over your left leg, which you have conveniently placed behind his right.

Illus. 15.12: *Christian again binds against Ben's attempt to rush in.*

Illus. 15.13: *Christian releases his left hand from his sword and begins to drive it over Ben's right arm.*

Illus. 15.14: *Christian steps in, placing his left foot behind Ben's right in order to drive his left hand over and through Ben's right arm.*

Illus. 15.15: *Having encircled Ben's arm with his left, Christian grabs his other arm with his left hand.*

Illus. 15.16: *Using his tight hold on Ben's right arm, Christian throws Ben backwards over his left leg.*

Durchlaufen -- Running Through

A fifth wrestling at the sword

Ringeck writes:

"*If he runs at you work with your left hand, moving over his right arm,* [Illustr. 15.17 - 15.18] *seizing his sword at the grip between his two hands,* [Illustr. 15.19] *and tearing it to your left side.* [Illustr. 15.20] *Thus you take his sword and it will go badly for him.*"

Christian writes:

This sequence is a "sword taking"--*Schwert nehmen*--although Ringeck doesn't call it such. With your free left hand, you grab his hilt while pressing with your own hilt against his blade. A strong jerk to your right side frees him from the burdens of sword wielding.

Illus. 15.17: *Again, the bind as Ben attempts to rush in.*

Illus. 15.18: *Christian releases his left hand from the sword and drives it over Ben's right arm.*

Illus. 15.19: *Christian steps in with his left foot and grabs Ben's grip betwen the hands. His hilt remains in contact with Ben's sword.*

Illus. 15.20: *Christian pulls up with his left hand, while maintaining pressure with his hilt against Ben's blade. Ben is dismayed to find himself disarmed.*

Durchlaufen -- Running Through
A sword taking (Schwert nehmen)

Ringeck writes:

"*If he binds with a displacement or otherwise to your sword, seize both swords at the center of the blades with your left hand.* [Illustr. 15.21 & 15.22] *Hold them together firmly, and force your pommel under and through with your right hand over both of his hands.* [Illustr. 15.23] *And then pull upward toward your right side: thus you take both swords.*" [Illustr. 15.24 & 15.25]

Christian writes:

This is another technique for helping relieve an opponent of his sword. Grab the swords where they cross in the bind with your left hand, and drive your pommel with your right over his hands and pull up hard.

Illus. 15.21:
The bind from the rushing in.

Illus. 15.22:
Christian grabs both swords in the middle where they have bound together.

Illus. 15.23:
Holding both blades together, Christian drives his pommel under the bind and over Ben's hands.

Illus. 15.24:
Christian pulls upward towards his own right side with his pommel, breaking Ben's grip.

Illus. 15.25: *The sword capture is completed.*

Chapter 16
Abschneiden

The teachings on Abschneiden, or "Cutting Off," comprise techniques for delivering slicing cuts with the longsword. While we have seen slicing cuts used earlier in Ringeck's *fechtbüch*, this chapter focuses on them and explains them in a more systemized fashion. Cutting, along with thrusting and striking, is one of the "Three Wounders"--*Drey Wünder*--the three different ways of injuring with the long sword. Like many other techniques in Liechtenauer's system, these slicing cuts--*schnitts*--are done from positions that correspond to *Ochs* and *Pflug* on both sides. Hence, there are four basic cuts: two from above (*Obere Schnitten*), using the left and right *Pflug*, and two from below (*Untere Schnitten*), using the left and right *Ochs*. These are not light slashing cuts; considerable force is use to push up with from below or down with the cut from above. The idea is to injure the opponent while pushing his attack safely off-line.

In two of the three techniques described, Ringeck is silent about what footwork should be done with the cuts. Perhaps this is not always important. He is explicit about which edge to use, at least for the *Untere Schnitten*: against an attack from the left, you should use the long edge with your hands crossed, while on the right side you should use the short edge and uncrossed hands. In any case, you can draw your sword's edge on your enemy by either pulling the cut or pushing it.

Liechtenauer writes:

"Cut off the hard ones from under and both bind. Four are the cuts: two from below and two from above."

Ringeck writes:

Note, there are four schnitte (slicing cuts), two from below and two from above. Do it like this: If he runs at you, raising his arms up and wanting to overwhelm you on your left side, wind your sword and fall on his arm under his hilt with your long edge with crossed hands and press upward with the cut. [Illus. 16.1 - 16.2] If he runs at you however to your right side, fall on his arm with the short edge and press it upward like before." [Illus. 16.3 & 16.4]

Christian writes:

The four slicing cuts--*schnitts*--are done from positions approximating *Ochs* and *Pflug* on both sides. Cuts from below generally correspond to *Ochs*, while those from above generally correspond to the *Pflug*. In this first technique we learn how to use the cuts from below against an attacker who is bearing down from above. On the left side, the short edge is used; on the right, the long. These draw cuts can be done with either a pulling or pushing motion along the edge, but should always be done accompanied by a strong push upward with the sword so that your opponent is forced away.

Illustr. 16.1: *Christian begins in Pflug, Ben in vom Tag.*

Illustr. 16.2: *Ben moves to strike to Christian's left side, but is stopped by Christian's slicing cut under his arms.*

Illustr. 16.3: *This time, Ben moves to attack Christian's right side.*

Illustr. 16.4: *Christian falls onto Ben's arms from below with the short edge of his sword.*

Ringeck writes:

"*If you bind strongly against his sword,* [Illus. 16.5] *and he then snaps his sword over yours to strike at your head,* [Illus. 16.6] *wind your sword with the hilt in front of your head and slice under to his arm. As you cut set the point down into his chest.*" [Illus. 16.7]

Christian writes:

Here is a variant using the a position corresponding to *Ochs* to slice an opponent's arm as he makes a follow-on attack following a bind. The slicing cut in this case is used in tandem with a thrust to the chest. This is a particularly satisfying technique: the high position of the hilt puts the blade into a protective position, the slice negates the attack, and the thrust finishes the opponent, all in one motion.

Illus. 16.5: *A bind.*

Illus. 16.6: *Ben moves to strike around from the bind to the right side of Christian's head. Christian raises his hilt.*

Illus. 16.7:
Christian slices the underside of Ben's right arm, plunging the point into his chest as he does.

Ringeck writes:

"*If he binds at your sword on your left side* [Illus. 16.8] *and changes from the sword to your right side with the Zwerchhau* [Illus. 16.9] *or another technique, jump with the left foot out of the blow to his right side and fall onto both of his arms with the long edge from above.* [Illus. 16.10] *Practice this from both sides.*"

Christian writes:

This technique shows the cut from above in action. As the opponent strikes around from a bind to strike the *Zwerchhau* to your right side, you step and cut down onto his arms from a position akin to the right side version of *Pflug*. If this happened on the other side, you'd be in a position approximating the left *Pflug*.

Illus. 16.8: *The combatants bound against each other.*

Illus. 16.9: *Ben strikes around with the Zwerchhau to the right side of Christian's head.*

Illus. 16.10:
Christian cuts from above to Ben's arms, stymieing Ben's attack.

Chapter 17
Hende Trucken

Hende Trucken--the "pressing of the hands"--is a really an extrapolation of *Abschneiden*, "slicing cuts." In order to press the hands, the combatant changes from a cut from below to one from above. This is accomplished by winding the long edge at your opponent's wrists, while stepping. The beauty of the technique lies in its defensive quality: with the wind to the cut from above, the opponent is pushed safely to the side.

Liechtenauer writes:

"*Your cutting edge turn, to the wrists press your hands.*"

Ringeck writes:

"*From the change of the cuts: If you can hit him with the lower cut into his arm, so that your point faces his right side, press with the cut strongly upward.* [Illus. 17.1 & 17.2] *At the same time jump with the left foot to his right side, and wind your sword with the long edge above his arms, so that your point faces to his left side.* [Illus. 17.3] *Then press his arms away from you.*" [Illus. 17.4]

Christian writes:

This rather grisly application of a slicing cut involves not a winding at the sword, but a winding at the opponent – in this case, his wrists. With a winding at his wrists and a step to the left, change from a cut from below to one from above, thereby forcing his attack away from you.

Illus. 17.1: *Christian stand in Pflug, while Ben moves to attacks with an Oberhau.*

Illus. 17.2: *Stepping in with his right foot, Christian pushes strongly upward as he cuts the underside of Ben's arms.*

Illus. 17.3: *Christian steps to the left and winds his long edge against Ben's wrists.*

Illus. 17.4: *While cutting from above, Christian forces Ben's attack to the ground.*

Chapter 18
Zwei Hengen

The positions of the *Zwei Hengen*--"Two Hangers"--should be familiar to the reader by now. In the lower hanger position, which is equivalent to *Pflug*, the pommel hangs down, while the point is aimed at the opponent's face. For the upper hanger, the hilt is held high with the point hanging down to the opponent's face – this is the *Ochs*.

The hangers are close kin to the *absetzen*. The technical difference is that an *absetzen* is a movement that sets aside the enemy's blade while the hangers are used once you are already in the bind with him. It's interesting that the technique is called *Zwei Hengen* as you could say there are really *four* hangers, not two: the upper and lower hangers can be done on both sides, like most of the techniques in Liechtenauer's system.

The admonition about being competent with various techniques from the hangers is an important one – the hangers are intimately associated with winding. In fact, the windings are all performed *from* the hangers.

Liechtenauer writes:

"There are two hangers - from one hand to the earth. In all binds strike, thrust, position - soft or hard."

Ringeck writes:

Note, there are two hangings on each side. Do it like this. If you bind at his sword on your left side with the lower Absetzen, [Illus. 18.1] let your sword's pommel hang to the ground and thrust to his face from below. [Illus. 18.2] If he displaces your point high, [Illus. 18.3] stay at the sword and move up high, too. And let your point hang towards his face from above. [Illus. 18.4] And from both hangings you shall nimbly practice all techniques: strikes, thrusts and slices, depending on whether you feel he is hard or soft when you engage."

Christian writes:

The "two hangers" are intimately connected with two of the *vier leger* - Ochs and Pflug, and are thus also connected to the *absetzen*. In this technique, the two hangers, upper and lower, are used together. If you are in a bind in the lower *absetzen*, a position corresponding to *Pflug*, you should let the pommel drop a bit and thrust to your opponent's face. If he moves that aside, you then wind your hilt high such that your *point* hangs from the upper hanger – this position is akin to *Ochs*. From there you can thrust again.

Illus. 18.1: *Both men stand in the bind. As their positions correspond roughly to Pflug, the bind they are in is also a lower Absetzen.*

Illus. 18.2: *Christian lets his pommel "hang" to the ground in order to thrust to Ben's face. This is the lower hanger.*

Illus. 18.3: *Ben raises his hilt to try to displace Christian's point high.*

Illus. 18.4: *Winding his own hilt high, Christian changes to the upper hanger to counter the displacement and thrust anew to Ben's face.*

Liechtenauer Writes:

"The Sprechfenster do. Stand blithely and look at his matter. Strike down so he snaps. When he withdraws from you, I say to you truthfully: no one protects himself without danger; if you have learned this, to striking he barely comes."

Ringeck Writes

Note: If he binds with your sword with a strike or displacement, then remain hard at the sword with the long edge with outstretched arms and with your point at his face, [Illus. 18.5] calmly paying attention to what he tries to use against you. If he strikes from the sword with an Oberhau over to your other side, [Illus. 18.6] follow his blow strongly in the bind with the long edge, to his head. [Illus. 18.7] Or, if he strikes over with the Zwerch, [Illus. 18.8 & 18.9] fall with the upper cut onto his arms. [Illus. 18.10] Or, if he actually tears your sword down [Illus. 18.11 & 18.12] and wants to thrust to your lower opening, [Illus. 18.13] travel after him at the sword and thrust at him from above. [Illus. 18.14] If however he wants to neither take off nor change, work at the sword with duplieren [Illus. 18.15 & 18.16] and other techniques, depending on whether he is hard or soft at the sword."

Christian Writes:

This technique explores some of the possible actions an opponent may be taken when you bind with an opponent. The *Sprechfenster* is a probe, and in this technique remain in the bind to sense the opponent's intent through blade pressure. It is critical to be able to determine immediately whether he is hard or soft, as this indicates his intent and thus your response. You should be able to feel through your blade if he moves to strike around to another opening; if he goes to drive your weapon down, or if he simply remains too long in the bind.

Illus. 18.5: *Christian stands in the bind with his point directed towards Ben's face. He awaits Ben's next move.*

Illus. 18.6: *Ben moves to strike around to Christian's right side. Christian is already moving to counter, having sensed the departure of Ben's sword from the bind.*

Illus. 18.7: *Christian steps left and strikes Ben's head while preventing Ben's strike from finding its mark.*

Illus. 18.8: *Christian stands again in the bind against Ben's sword.*

Illus. 18.9: *Ben strikes from the bind with Zwerchhau.*

Illus. 18.10: *Stepping left, Christian counters Ben's Zwerchhau with a cut from above to Ben's arms.*

Illus. 18.11:
The bind with the Sprechfenster.

Illus. 18.12:
Ben tears down Christian's sword with his hilt. Christian senses this because pressure ceases to be applied on one side and is transferred to the other.

Illus. 18.13:
Ben moves his sword to thrust to Christian's lower body, but Christian travels after him, maintaining blade contact.

Illus. 18.14:
Still in contact with Ben's sword, Christian thrusts from above.

Illus. 18.15: *Once again, both men stand in the bind.*

Illus. 18.16:
As Ben has made no move, Christian duplieres to attack behind Ben's blade.

Ringeck Writes:

Note: if you come close to him in the Zufechten, put your left foot forward and direct your point with outstretched arms against his breast or his face. [Illus. 18.17] If he then strikes from above to your head, wind your sword against his blow and thrust to the face. [Illus. 18.18 & 18.19] Or, if he strikes from above or below against your sword and wants to strike your blade to the side, [Illus. 18.20 & 21] change through [Illus. 18.22] and thrust to his opening on the other side. [Illus. 18.23] If however he hits your sword with strength, [Illus. 18.24] let it snap around [Illus. 18.25] and hit him with it on the head. [Illus. 18.26] If he rushes in, [Illus. 18.27 & 28] then wrestle [Illus. 18.29] or cut. [Illus. 18.30] Always pay attention so that he does not fool you!"

Christian Writes:

This is an alternate application of the *Sprechfenster*. Lure the opponent into showing his hand by standing in the guard *Langenort*, which puts a lot of distance between you and him, thereby forcing him to try to take your blade off line before he can attack you. Part of knowing his intent is through visual observation, but the key element of *fülen,* which this technique is based upon, is sensing the degree of strength he uses to displace your sword.

Illus. 18.17: *Christian now stands in the guard of the Long Point (Langen Ort) with his point menacing Ben from a safe distance. He awaits his opponent's next move.*

Illus. 18.18: *Ben goes to strike to Christian's head. Christian moves to intercept.*

Illus. 18.19: *Using the upper left Absetzen, Christian sets aside Ben's attack and thrusts to his face.*

Zwei Hengen -- Two Hangers
How to use the Long Point against an attempt to move the sword aside

Illus. 18.20: *Christian begins in the Langenorte, Ben in Pflug.*

Illus. 18.21: *Ben tries to knock Christian's blade aside.*

Illus. 18.22: *Christian steps in with his right foot while changing through. His point is now on the other side of Ben's attack.*

Illus. 18.23: *Christian thrusts to Ben's exposed right side.*

Illus. 18.24: *Here Ben strikes hard at Christian's blade as the latter stands in Langenort.*

Illus. 18.25: *Gathering momentum from this forceful blow, Christian begins to snap his sword around.*

Illus. 18.26: *With a step of his right foot, Christian strikes Ben's head.*

Illus. 18.27: *Christian stands against Ben in the guard of the Long Point.*

Illus. 18.28: *Ben tries to rush in.*

Illus. 18.29: *Christian leans in to begin grappling.*

Illus. 18.30: *Alternately, Christian steps in with his right foot to cut Ben's arm.*

Chapter 19
Conclusion of the Teachings

We now reach the end of the commentaries on Master Liechtenauer's secret verses. A good story should always have a satisfying finish, and like an orchestral work whose finale draws off of its previous motifs, the conclusion of the master's teachings ends by tying together a number of important concepts previously taught.

The conclusion is really all about the techniques of winding the sword. We have already been exposed to winding throughout the previous chapters. The winding, and hanging, is the focus of the teaching. The two hangers (*Zwei Hengen*) on each side are the positions from which the windings at the sword are done. As we have seen before, these hangers correspond to the ever-important guards *Ochs* and *Pflug*, which in turn are the upper and lower *Absetzen*. The system is a closed circle, with the guards informing all movement: the guards are the absetzen, the hangers, and the windings all at once.

There are eight windings at the sword, and these are used in pairs. These pairs exist above and below (that is, in *Ochs* and *Pflug*) and the pairings are on *one side of his blade*. So, there are four windings above and four below, or looked at from a different angle, four windings done with the *Ochs* positions and four done with the *Pflug* positions.

When you bind at the sword, thrust from *Pflug* provided that your opponent is relatively soft in the bind. If he is strong, you need to wind your hilt high into *Ochs* to gain the precious advantage of leverage. Once you are using one or the other, you can thrust. Should he displace, wind to the other side of your body (for the *Pflug*) or head (for the *Ochs*) in order to regain the leverage advantage. When you change windings from one side to the other, you are changing what side version of the guard you are using, but you never leave the side of your opponent's blade that you started on.

Liechtenauer characterizes the three modes of attack--the strike, the thrust, and the cut--as the "Three Wounders." These three may be used from any of the windings at the sword. As there eight windings, it follows that there are twenty-four techniques of attack that may be done while winding. One must use the skill of sensing blade pressure to know which to use: if you try to thrust while winding to an opponent who displaces you slightly off target, you might still be able to slice him somewhere. In like fashion, if he is especially soft at the sword, you might achieve a strike. Sensing blade pressure is also important in knowing whether or not you need to change the side that you are winding to. If your opponent is soft in the bind, you should be able to accomplish your attack from the winding you are using, but if he is hard at the sword and begins to displace you, you must wind to the other side. You must use the skill of testing blade pressure to know which to use: if you try to thrust while winding to an opponent who displaces you, you may still be able to strike somewhere else with a cut.

The conclusion therefore ties together a number of concepts: winding, hanging, binding, striking, thrusting, cutting, sensing of blade pressure, and of course, the guards *Ochs* and *Pflug*. We began our study of Liechtenauer's long sword method with the *Zornhau* and its winding technique, and we end here with the winding, explained in depth. If the notion of initiative, with its concepts of Before, After, and *Indes*, is the philosophical heart of this art, then the *Winden am Schwert* ("winding at the sword") is the heart of its distinctive method of movement. To fight in accordance with Liechtenauer's teachings, you must master the eight windings and be capable of using all three "wounders" from them.

While we have now finished with the commentaries on Master Liechtenauer's teachings, we have some more long sword work ahead. Master Ringeck hereafter extrapolates from the teachings, adding his own[1] techniques to the corpus of German long sword arts.

---

[1] *Perhaps* they are his own. More work needs to be done to determine if Ringeck's *fechtbüch* contains the first occurrence of these additional techniques.

Liechtenauer writes:

"*Whoever leads and properly breaks and finally makes it all right – And splits particularly everything into three wounders – who properly well hangs and the winding brings along, and the eight windings views in a righteous way – and one of the winds with the same three I mean – so they are twenty and four, and count them only, from both sides. Eight windings learn with stepping. And test the bind no more than soft or hard.*"

Ringeck writes:

"*In the following the teachings are briefly summarized. Note: you are to be in the art of fencing always ready and experienced, so that you can apply counters against any techniques that your opponent uses. From each counter you are to be able to work with the three wounders. You are to know the hanging on the sword and from the hanging how to use the eight windings. And from windings you are to strike, cut likewise and be able to thrust.*"

Christian writes:

Master Ringeck begins his comments on the final section of Liechtenauer's verse by telling us that we will be using the "three wounders" in all of these techniques. These "wounders" are thrusts, cuts, and blows. We are also reminded here of the inextricable connection between the *hengen* and the *winden,* and that there are eight windings.

Ringeck writes:

ꟼote: there are four binds with the sword, two upper and two lower. From each bind you are to master two winds. So: if he binds above to your left side, [Illus. 19.1] wind the short edge at his sword and raise your arms high. Let the point hang and thrust to his face. [Illus. 19.2] If he displaces the thrust, [Illus. 19.3] leave the point at the sword hanging from above and wind to your right side. [Illus. 19.4] Those are two winds at one side of the sword."

Christian writes:

There are four binds at the sword. These correspond to the left and right versions of *Ochs* and *Pflug*, the upper and lower *Absetzen*, and the *Zwei hengen* on each side. This paragraph also reaquaints us with winding the hilt high (into *Ochs* on the left side) to regain the advantage of leverage in the bind. Next, if the opponent displaces the winding thrust to the side, wind to your other side while staying at his sword. It is usually best to do this with a step of the left foot so that your body does not become twisted as you wind; this gains back your leverage from the right *Ochs*.

Illus. 19.1: *Both combatants bind on their left sides after striking from their right. Ben holds hard against Christian's sword.*

Illus. 19.2: *Christian raises his hilt high and, with the strong of his short edge against the weak of his opponent, moves to thrust to Ben's face. This is the 1st Winding.*

Illus. 19.3: *Ben displaces Christian's thrust to the side.*

Illus. 19.4: *In order to gain back the leverage he has lost to Ben's displacement, Christian steps in with his left foot and winds his hilt to the right side of his head, thrusting once again. This is the 2nd Winding.*

Conclusion
The third and fourth windings

Ringeck writes:

"*ℒikewise, if he binds above to your right side,* [Illus. 19.5] *wind also above your long edge at his sword. Raise up your arms, let the point hang and thrust to his face.* [Illus. 19.6] *If he displaces the thrust with strength,* [Illus. 19.7] *leave the point at the sword hanging from above, winding to your left side and thrust.* [Illus. 19.8] *Those are four winds from both upper binds of the left and right sides.*"

Christian writes:

What can be done on one side with winding can also be done on the both sides. The opponent has struck from his left to your right and you have bound to him there. Wind your *long* edge so that you are in *Ochs* on the right. If he displaces, remain at the sword and with a step of the right foot wind you hilt to the left side of your head. This brings you to the left *Ochs* and renewed strength in the bind. These are four of the eight winds. These four all use the *Ochs* and are used in pairs on one side of his blade.

Illus. 19.5: *The same bind, only this time the combatants have struck from their left sides.*

Illus. 19.6: *Christian now winds his long edge into the guard of the Ochs on the right side. This is the 3ʳᵈ Winding.*

Illus. 19.7: *Ben prevents Christian's thrust by displacing the blade.*

Illus. 19.8: *Christian steps in with his right foot and into the Ochs on the left side. This is the 4ᵗʰ Winding.*

Ringeck writes:

"*Likewise you are to master the two lower binds with four winds* [Illus. 19.9 - 19.16] *with all techniques, like those from the upper: together these are eight. And it follows that you can apply strike, thrust and cut* [Illus. 19.17 - 19.19] *from each winding, so that one can execute all together twenty-four techniques from winding. And you are to learn the eight winds in such a way from both sides so that you check with each strike, whether he is soft or hard at the sword. And if you have felt that, then do all techniques that pertain to winding. If you don't, you will be struck while you are winding.*"

Christian writes:

Master Ringeck indulges in bit of shorthand and refrains from describing in detail how the remaining four windings are done. Yet he gives us all the necessary clues. These windings are done from the two lower binds, which we know correspond to the two lower *absetzen* and in thereby to the left and right versions of the *Pflug*. Once again, the windings are used as pairs. If one wind at a side of his blade is displaced, you should step and wind to the other side of your body, i.e., change from the left to the right *Pflug* or vice-versa.

The commentary concludes with the admonition to use the three wounders with all winding techniques. From any of the eight windings, you can strike, cut, or thrust. As there are eight windings, and three attacks from each, there are twenty-four attacks that may be done. Knowing which of these to use and when you must wind to the other side is, like so much else in Liechtenauer's system, a matter of sensing whether your opponent is hard or soft in the bind.

Illus. 19.9: *The bind on the left side. Both combatants have struck from their right.*

Illus. 19.10: *Christian pushes Ben's sword down and using the lower hanger, which is really also the guard Pflug, moves to thrust to Ben's face. This is the 5th Winding.*

Illus. 19.11: *Ben displaces the thrust with strength.*

Illus. 19.12: *Christian steps with his left foot and winds from the left Pflug into the right Pflug to thrust to Ben's face. This is the 6th Winding.*

Illus. 19.13: *This is the bind on the right side. Both fighters have struck from their left.*

Illus. 19.14: *Christian pushes down into the lower right hanger, which is the guard Pflug on the right side. He goes to thrust to Ben's face. This is the 7th Winding.*

Illus. 19.15: *Ben displaces the thrust.*

Illus. 19.16: *Christian steps with his right foot to wind into Pflug on the left and again menace Ben's face. This is the 8ᵗʰ and last winding.*

Illus. 19.17: *You can strike from any winding: here Christian strikes from the 1ˢᵗ Winding, a technique that is effectively an application of the Zwerch-hau.*

Illus. 19.18: *You can thrust from any winding: here Christian thrusts from the 1ˢᵗ Winding into Ben's chest.*

Illus. 19.19: *You can cut from any winding: here Christian slices Ben's hands from the 1ˢᵗ Winding.*

Chapter 20
Nebenhut & Schranckhut

While the commentary on Master Liechtenauer's long sword verse ended in the last chapter, Ringeck continues his instruction with some additional techniques not described by the old master. Of the *Nebenhut* in particular, he says that although they are not described in the teachings, they are nonetheless derived from them; which is to say that they are built around the same basic principles.

The *Nebenhut* and *Schranckhut* are two additional guards. *Nebenhut*--"near guard"--is held close to the body on either side with the point directed to the ground. Ringeck advises using the left *Nebenhut* in particular as it is "more effective." *Nebenhut* on the left is also useful as it is a position one can easily end up in after striking strongly from the right side. Most of the techniques involve deflecting your opponent's strike by 'catching' it from the outside. This application of the left *Nebenhut* is interesting as it goes against the grain of a number of other German manuals, which primarily teach the right side version. There is an additional technique whose placement in the manuscript would seem to suggest that it be done from *Nebenhut*. This is an *absetzen* ("setting aside") technique, and without the context of its placement, its execution would be rather difficult to divine.

Another guard described by Ringeck is *Schranckhut*--"barrier guard"--also done on both sides. The *Schranckhut* is held in a similar fashion as the *Nebenhut* but where the latter is held near the body at the side, the former is held more in front of the body with the point hanging down diagonally. Unlike *Nebenhut*, we have seen *Schranckhut* before – it is used by Ringeck to clarify how one can set aside a blow with the *Krumphau*. It should be no surprise then that the *Schranckhut* is also a good place from which to start a *Krumphau*, which is what the techniques here are concerned with.

The last technique of this chapter is an exotic strike called *das Redel*--"the Wheel"--done by extending the arms and swinging the sword around in a horizontal arc. This powerful blow is best done from a low, backward pointing guard, so it makes sense that it is grouped with the above guards and techniques.

21.1a

21.1b

21.1c

21.1d

Ringeck writes:

"*Here note, from the Nebenhut – that is, from the strikes – to fence well.*

"*Although they are not described in the teachings, nevertheless all the techniques that you fence with are derived from them. And you should start the strikes from the left side* [Illus. 20.1a & b]*, because from the right* [Illus. 20.1c & d]*they are not as effective.*"

> **Illus. 20.1a-d:** *Nebenhut poses on the right and left, page opposite.*

Christian writes:

The *Nebenhut*--"near guard"--is an additional guard Master Ringeck adds. The guard's stance is not described but rather must be inferred from other actions and from expositions in other Liechtenauer-tradition fighting manuals.[1] While most *fechtbücher* favor the right-sided *Nebenhut*, but Ringeck declares that it is best used on the left; *from the strikes*. By "from the strikes," he seems to mean a position that you can arrive at by having struck from your right.

The *Nebenhut* therefore, is a good place to launch a follow-on attack. To hold the sword in the *Nebenhut*, one stands with the right foot forward, with the sword beside the left leg, the tip pointing to the ground. For those familiar with Italian medieval swordsmanship, think of Ringeck's *Nebenhut* as a more conservatively held tail guard.

Illus. 20.2: *Ben begins in the guard vom Tag, Christian in the Nebenhut on the left.*

[1]Joachim Meyer's fechtbuch (1570) describes it in Folio VIII.

Ringeck writes:

"*If you are on your left side in the Nebenhut* [Illus. 20.2] *and he strikes an Oberhau, strike (angled against the opposing blade in such a way that the strike forces it to the side) from below with the short edge strongly against his sword.* [Illus. 20.3] *If he holds strongly against it and his hands are not too high, dupliere between the man and his sword with the short edge to the left side of his neck.*" [Illus. 20.4 & 20.5]

Christian writes:

From the left *Nebenhut* on the left, strike with the short edge to "snatch" his attack from the outside. Should you encounter resistance in the bind, you can *dupliere* – that is, attack behind his blade, in this case with the short edge.

Illus. 20.3: *Christian steps with his left foot and catches Ben's strike from the outside.*

Illus. 20.4: *As Ben has held hard in the bind, Christian moves to dupliere – wind behind Ben's attack.*

Illus. 20.5: *Christian completes his dupliere, striking to Ben's head with his short edge.*

Ringeck writes:

"*If you strike like before against his sword* [Illus. 20.6 & 2.0.7] *and he is soft at the sword with his hands down low, strike at him immediately with the long edge to the upper opening.* [Illus. 20.8] *Or if he falls strongly upon your sword,* [Illus. 20.9] *move with the pommel over his sword, remain thereupon with your hands and direct your point to the rear of your left side.* [Illus. 20.10] *And snap to his head with the short edge.*" [Illus. 20.11 & 20.12]

Christian writes:

In the first of these two variations, your opponent is soft in the bind and his hands are low. After setting aside his attack, you can simply strike with your long edge. In the second variation, he is hard at the sword, you snap out of the bind to strike with your short edge to his head. This should be familiar, as it is an application of the "Techniques Against Displacement" that figure in the chapter on *Vier Versetzen*.

Illus. 20.6: *Christian stands in the Nebenhut.*

Illus. 20.7: *As Ben strikes, Christian again catches the attack from the outside.*

Illus. 20.8: *Deflecting the attack, Christian notes Ben's softness in the bind and strikes to the head with his long edge.*

Illus. 20.9: *In this variation, Ben holds hard in the bind.*

Illus. 20.10: *Rather than directly fighting Ben's strength, Christian drives his pommel forward over Ben's sword.*

Illus. 20.11: *Snapping out from the bind, Christian strikes around with his short edge with a step of the right foot.*

Illus. 20.12: *Christian's strike, which is really a Zwerchhau, reaches Ben's head.*

Ringeck writes:

"*If you strike like before against his sword* [Illus. 20.13] *and he moves up and winds,* [Illus. 20.14] *strike him with a step backwards with outstretched arms to his right side.*" [Illus. 20.15]

Christian writes:

Here, the opponent tries to wind from the bind. To counter this, you simply step away from him while out-reaching his attack. This is an application of *Überlaufen,*, "overrunning."

Illus. 20.13: *Here again is the bind with the short edge.*

Illus. 20.14: *Ben winds his hilt high to menace Christian's face with his point.*

Illus. 20.15: *With a backwards step of the right foot, Christian strikes Ben's right with outstretched arms.*

Ringeck writes:

"*If you strike like before against his sword* [Illus. 20.16 & 20.17] *and he moves up and winds,* [Illus. 20.18] *strengthen your bind by winding the long edge.* [Illus. 20.19] *If he then strikes around with the Zwerch,* [Illus. 20.20] *strike him while withdrawing to the left side.*" [Illus. 20.21]

Christian writes:

This is another counter for when you opponent winds after binding against your strike from the *Nebenhut*. You in turn should wind, into *Pflug* on the right, using your long edge to maintain strength. If he strikes around, you again withdraw while striking.

Illus. 20.16: *Again, the combatants stand on guard.*

Illus. 20.17: *Christian binds to the outside of Ben's sword.*

Illus. 20.18: *Ben winds his hilt high.*

Illus. 20.19: *Christian strengthens his bind against Ben's sword by bringing the long edge to bear.*

Illus. 20.20: *Ben moves to strike around with the Zwerchhau.*

Illus. 20.21: *Christian backs away from the Zwerch with a step of his left foot and strikes Ben with outstretched arms, out-reaching his attack.*

Ringeck writes:

"*If you strike against him first,* [Illus. 20.22] *and he holds his sword diagonally in front of him with raised arms and wants to fall on your sword, strike him from below against his sword* [Illus. 20.23] *and hit him on the arm or thrust to the chest.*" [Illus. 20.24]

Christian writes:

This technique involves striking into his sword hard to overwhelm a weak defense. The opponent drops his point to cover his body, so you simply fall upon the weaker part of his blade and strike his arm, or thrust to his body.

Illus. 20.22: *Ben stands in Pflug on the right . Christian stands in the left Nebenhut.*

Illus. 20.23: *Christian moves to strike, while Ben covers.*

Illus. 20.24: *Christian's blow still reaches Ben's arm.*

Ringeck writes:

"*If his hands are low and he wants to fall on your sword,* [Illus. 20.25] *strike through to the other side* [Illus. 20.26 & 27] *and thrust to his chest.* [Illus. 20.28] *This is a changing through.*"

Christian writes:

In this technique, you draw off of familiar knowledge and simply "change through" (*Durchwechseln*) from his bind against your sword to thrust to his other side.

Illus. 20.25: *Both men in their guard.*

Illus. 20.26: *Ben's attack provides mighty resistance as Christian binds against it.*

Illus. 20.27: *Christian changes through from the bind to free himself for a new attack.*

Illus. 20.28: *The final thrust follows.*

Ringeck writes:

"*If your strike passes by his,* [Illus. 20.29 & 20.30] *fall on his sword with the long edge* [Illus. 20.31] *and wind to your left side, so that your thumb is situated down.* [Illus. 20.32] *Lay the strong of your long edge on the right of his neck, jump with the right foot behind his left, and with a step tear him over.* [Illus. 20.33]"

"*If you change through from striking and end up above his sword on the other side, you can do all the techniques like before with light blows and all others.*"

Christian writes:

This technique works rather much like a classic *Durchwechseln*. However, in this case you change through in front of the opponent's strike, rather than after binding to it. Your sword ends up in front of his attack, where you must intercept him with your long edge. This evolves into a "tear down," similar to what we learned from the techniques in the chapter on the *Zwerchhau*: the sword is used to hook the opponent about the neck in order to throw him over one of your legs.

Illus. 20.29: *The fighters begin in vom Tag and Nebenhut.*

Illus. 20.30: *Christian's strike from the Nebenhut "out-times" Ben's attack.*

Illus. 20.31: *Christian turns his sword to intercept Ben's with his long edge.*

Illus. 20.33: *Christian turns his sword to bring the long edge against Ben's neck.*

Illus. 20.34: *Stepping deeply behind Ben's left foot with his right foot, Christian pulls Ben over his leg with his sword.*

Ringeck writes:

"*When you come close to him in the fight, go into Pflug. Do this quickly by winding from one side to the other and aim your point where you want.* [Illus. 20.35 & 20.36] *And from that you can displace anything that comes near. And you can strengthen the bind with the long edge and execute from this all of the techniques specified before. Also, you can use blows and thrusts and counter him with the winding,* [Illus. 20.37] *and find his opening with the point.*"

Christian writes:

This enigmatic paragraph bears some scrutiny. If it appeared anywhere else in the *fechtbüch*, I'd be quick to assume that this is an alternate description of how one can set aside blows by winding from *Pflug* on one side of the body to the one on the other. As it follows hard upon the techniques of the *Nebenhut*, I've chosen to interpret the technique as starting from the *Nebenhut* on the left (although this would clearly work on both sides). From the *Nebenhut*, wind to your right to set aside his attack with the lower right *absetzen*,. ending in the right *Pflug*. This is a powerful *absetzen* with a counter-thrust. This technique could also be done with the *Schranckhut*.

Illus. 20.35: *Ben begins in the guard vom Tag, Christian in the left Nebenhut.*

Illus. 20.36: *Christian sets aside Ben's attack by stepping with his left foot into the right Pflug. This also thrusts his point forcefully to Ben's face.*

Illus. 20.37: *Alternately, Christian could have stepped into Ochs on the right and thrust from there.*

Ringeck writes:

"**W**hen you come close to him in the fight, put the left foot forward and place your point at your right side to the ground, so that the long edge is up. [Illus. 20.38a & b] *And on the left side the short edge is down and the right foot is forward.*" [Illus. 20.39a & b]

Christian writes:

We have seen the *Schranckhut* before, in one of the techniques for the *Krumphau*. *Schranckhut*--"barrier guard"--is another position not explicitly called out in Liechtenauer's teachings. It is a low position wherein the point hangs diagonally to the ground. Like the *Nebenhut* it can be done on both sides.

Illus. 20.38a & b: *The Schranckhut on the right.*

Illus. 20.39a & b: *The Schranckhut on the left side.*

Ringeck writes:

"*If he strikes with an Oberhau or an Unterhau at you, step out of his strike and strike with a Krumphau to his opening.* [Illus. 20.40 - 43] *Or strike a Krumphau to his blade,* [Illus. 20.44 & 45] *and as soon as the swords meet one another, strike immediately to the next opening with the short edge.* [Illus. 20.46] *Or wind your sword in the bind (Verkehrer) and thrust to his face.* [Illus. 20.47] *If he binds against you then, hold strongly with the long edge against him. Otherwise you can try the techniques which were described with the strikes before.*"

Christian writes:

When striking *Krumphau*, you can easily end in the left *Schranckhut*, as we saw some chapters ago. The *Krumphau* can also *start* in the right *Schrankhut* and attack towards its mirror on the left side. You can strike to one of his openings while keeping clear of his attack (the main strength of the *Krumphau*). You can also bind against him and work the familiar follow-on *Krumphau* technique.

While Ringeck doesn't describe it,[1] the *Krumphau* may also be struck from the left *Schranckhut* – the hands begin crossed, uncrossing as the blow lands with the short edge.

Illus. 20.40: *Christian begins in the right Schranckhut, Ben in vom Tag.*

---

[1]Peter von Danzig's *fechtbüch* (c. 1452) describes how to do this

Illus. 20.41: *Ben moves to strike – Christian moves to intercept.*

Illus. 20.42: *Stepping outward with the right foot, Christian strikes a Krumphau to Ben with his long edge.*

Illus. 20.43: *Maintaining a safe distance from Ben's attack, Christian hits Ben with the counter.*

Illus. 20.44: *Both men stand in their previous guards.*

Illus. 20.45: *As Ben strikes from his right, Christian strikes a Krumphau against his blade.*

Illus. 20.46: *From the bind with the Krumphau, Christian strikes Ben's head with his short edge.*

Illus. 20.47: *An alternative from the bind: Christian winds and thrusts to Ben's chest.*

Ringeck writes:

"𝔚hen you close with him, then stretch the arms and hold the thumb above on the sword [Illus. 20.48] and move the point like a wheel before you from below to your left side. And go in such a way toward him. [Illus. 20.49] From this you can change through [Illus. 20.50 - 52] or bind on either side, and if you bind up, you can do whatever techniques seem best to you, as before."

Christian writes:

Evocatively named, *das Redel*--"the wheel"--is a technique done by swinging the sword wide from one side to the other, like the turning of a wheel. It appears in this portion of the manual as it is best done from a position like the *Nebenhut*. This technique is a very powerful attack with a lot of reach.

Illus. 20.48: *Ben stands in vom Tag, while Christian takes the right Nebenhut, his thumbs atop the sword.*

Illus. 20.49: *Christian whips his sword horizontally, powering through Ben's strike to hit him in the head.*

Illus. 20.50: *To counter, Ben has held against Christian's strike with das Redel.*

Illus. 20.51: *Christian changes through from the bind...*

Illus. 20.52: *...and finishes Ben with a thrust to the chest.*

Chapter 21
Additional Counter Techniques

This handful of counter-techniques are Ringeck's final teachings on the long sword. Like the chapter on the *Nebenhut* and *Schranckhut*, this material does not come directly from Liechtenauer's verse; it is derived from the fundamental tactical and bio-mechanical principles expressed in the *merkverse*.

All of these techniques work on the same principle: you can break an attack or counterattack by falling down onto it to cut and/or thrust. While we leave the long sword after this chapter,[1] we will see the principles that we have learned put to good use later when in the realms of armoured fighting on foot and on horseback.

---

[1] There is actually one more section of long sword work: a section that features an incomplete re-exposition of Liechtenauer's verse followed by some alternate commentaries for the *Zornhau* and *Krumphau*. As this section doesn't seem to include any unique or new information, and is difficult to follow, I have assigned it to Appendix 2.

Ringeck writes:

"*If you are in vom Tag* [Illus. 21.1] *and he strikes a Zwerchhau against you,* [Illus. 21.2] *immediately strike a Zornhau with strength against his sword,* [Illus. 21.3] *and find an opening to strike with the point.* [Illus. 21.4] *And if he wants to then change and strike with the Zwerch to the other side,* [Illus. 21.5 & Illus. 21.6] *attack him first with the Zwerch under his sword to his neck.* [Illus. 21.7] *Or cut with the long edge into his arm, when he changes.*" [Illus. 21.8 & Illus. 21.9]

Illus. 21.1: *Christian stands in the guard vom Tag, Ben in the right Pflug.*

Illus. 21.2: *Ben starts to strike with the Zwerchhau.*

Illus. 21.3: *As Ben's Zwerchhau strikes, Christian falls upon it with a Zornhau.*

Illus. 21.4: *Christian presses down Ben's sword to make an opening for his point.*

Illus. 21.5: *In a different engagement Christian has struck Zornhau against Ben's Zwerchhau.*

Illus. 21.6: *Ben strikes out from the bind and around with a Zwerch to the other side.*

Illus. 21.7: *Christian stops this attack by striking a Zwerchhau beneath Ben's Zwerchhau, striking Ben's neck in the process.*

Illus. 21.8: *In another variation Christian has bound against Ben's Zwerchhau.*

Illus. 21.9: *As Ben frees himself from the bind to strike around with the Zwerch, Christian falls upon his arms with a cut from above.*

Ringeck writes:

"*If you strike a Zwerchhau and he wants to forestall you with a Zwerch under your sword to the neck,* [Illus. 21.10 & 21.11] *fall down strongly with the long edge onto his sword,* [Illus. 21.12] *thus the technique is broken. And find the next opening which becomes available.*" [Illus. 21.13]

Christian writes:

This is the first counter-technique with the long sword that is not directly described by Liechtenauer's verse. When your opponent strikes *Zwerchhau* as you stand in *vom Tag*, strike down with a Strike of Wrath (*Zornhau*) and attempt to thrust. Should he strike around to the other side, use the familiar techniques for breaking the *Zwerchhau*: cut to the arm or "counter-*Zwerch*" beneath his own *Zwerchhau* that lands on his neck.

A counter to this "counter-*Zwerch*" technique is described wherein you fall upon his *Zwerchhau* to your neck to prevent it from finding its mark. This is really the same idea repeated – that a *Zwerchhau* can be broken by falling down onto it with the long edge.

Illus. 21.10: *Christian moves to strike a Zwerchhau.*

Illus. 21.11: *Ben counters with a Zwerch of his own.*

Illus. 21.12: *Christian falls upon Ben's Zwerchhau.*

Illus. 21.13: *Christian presses Ben's sword down and finds an opening with his point.*

Ringeck writes:

"*If you strike an Oberhau and he binds* [Illus. 21.14] *and lifts up his hilt, and you do the same and rush in,* [Illus. 21.15] *try the cut from below.* [Illus. 21.16] *If, however, he wants to slice you with a cut under your hands into the arm,* [Illus. 21.17 - 21.19] *follow his sword downward and press strongly down with the long edge so that the cut is broken.* [Illus. 21.20] *Find an opening immediately.*" [Illus. 21.21]

Christian writes:

This technique details how to cut under the arms and how to counter such an attack. From the bind raise your hilt and if he does the same slicing his arms from below. But is he does the same to you, use the same trick as above against the *Zwerchhau* by falling upon his sword with your long edge. It isn't surprising that the same technique would work in both cases: a cut from below looks very much like a *Zwerchhau* – they both finish as permutations of *Ochs*.

Illus. 20.14: *A bind.*

Illus. 20.15: *Both combatants raise their hilts.*

Illus. 21.16:
Christian cuts Ben's arm with a cut from below.

Illus. 21.17:
In this variation, the combatants find themselves in a bind.

Illus. 21.18:
Both combatants raise their hilts.

Illus. 21.19:
Ben moves to slice under Christian's arms.

Illus. 21.20:
Christian reacts by falling upon Ben's sword from above.

Illus. 21.21:
While pressing Ben's sword down, Christian thrusts to Ben's face.

Ringeck writes:

"*If you strike an Oberhau and he binds* [Illus. 21.22] *and raises up his hilt, and you do the same,* [Illus. 21.23] *and he tries to push his pommel under your hands and into your face or against your chest,* [Illus. 21.24] *move strongly down with your pommel and the strike is broken.*" [Illus. 21.25]

Christian writes:

Once again the idea of falling down upon the opponent's sword comes to the rescue in this counter to a pommel strike.

Illus. 21.22: *Another bind.*

Illus. 21.23: *Both men raise their hilts.*

Illus. 21.24: *Ben rushes in to strike with his pommel.*

Illus. 21.25: *Christian falls upon Ben's sword by pressing down his pommel, repelling the assault.*

A counter to a thrust with Half Sword

Ringeck writes:

"*If you bind with him,* [Illus. 21.26] *and he changes through with the pommel and switches to half sword,* [Illus. 21.27] *counter it with a cut from above.* [Illus. 21.28] *And as you slice you can switch to half sword and thrust.*" [Illus. 21.29]

Christian writes:

In this last counter-technique, the long edge is used to cut from above against an attempt to thrust with the half sword (*halbschwert*). From this cut, you can grab your blade and finish him with your own half sword thrust.

Illus. 21.26: *Once again, the bind.*

Illus. 21.27: *Ben changes to the half sword.*

Illus. 21.28: *Christian cuts down onto Ben's arm.*

Illus. 21.28: *Changing to the half sword, Christian converts the slicing cut into a thrust to Ben's chest.*

Chapter 22
Techniques with the Buckler

This short section comprises six extended sequences, "plays," with the single-handed sword and buckler providing the foundations for a complete fighting system. They appear to have been influential, as they are copied verbatim in several fighting treatises throughout the 15th century, also translated into French in the 16th.[1]

While there is no *merkeverse* in this part of the manuscript, the method for fighting with sword and buckler is clearly similar to Liechtenauer's long sword system in terms of tactics and terminology. A number of previously examined terms appear--*Zwerchhau*, *Scheitelhau*, *Oberhau*, and *Unterhau* --while some "new" words make their first appearance--*Wechselhau*, *Mittelhau*, and *Sturzhau*. Ringeck doesn't explain these other terms, so we must depend on knowledge from other *fechtbücher* to fill in the gaps.[2]

Plays one to five explain how to begin from a particular angle of attack. The first starts with a strike from above, the second with one from below. The third begins with a *Wechselhau*, or "Changing Strike," which is a cut that "changes" (*wechsel*, as in *Durchwechsel*, or "changing through") in mid-blow from one target to another, in this case from a high target to a low one. The fourth starts with a *Mittelhau*, or "Middle Strike," a horizontal blow to the opponent's mid-section. The fifth begins with a *Sturzhau*, or "plunging strike," which is a downward blow wherein the sword is turned with the strike to "plunge" down with the short edge over the opponent's defense. The last play essentially involves using the sword and buckler together in a half sword technique that finishes with a disarm of the shield. The techniques are presented in the manuscript without any indication of their origin. However, the 1452 fechtbuch of Peter von Danzig[3] ascribes them to a Master Andres Lignitzer.[4]

---

[1] Andre Pauernfeindt, *La Noble Science es joueurs d'espee*, Antwerp, 1538

[2] Notably, Joachim Meyer's work from 1570, *Grundtliche Bechreibung der Freyen Ritterlichen unnd Adelichen kunst des Fechtens*.

[3] von Danzig, Peter, *fechtbüch* (1452), pp. 80r - 80v.

[4] Perhaps this is the same Master Lignitzer mentioned by Paulus Kal in his 15th century *fechtbüch* as being one of Liechtenauer's teachers.

The same tactical sensibilities are discussed in the long sword chapters. Liechtenauer's methods tend to gravitate towards driving an opponent to commit himself more and more to the defense of one opening to the detriment of others. This is even more pronounced with the buckler, because the separation of defense from offense that arises from having a sword *and* a shield allows for a wider range of targets - the leg now becomes a viable target. The leg isn't generally considered a good target with the long sword because of the *Überlaufen* principle: high line attacks outreach low line attacks. Here, that principle is suspended because you can still protect your head while you strike to your opponent's legs. Four of the six plays capitalize on this by luring your opponent into defending his upper openings, exposing his legs or groin.

Those familiar with the earliest surviving medieval fighting manuscript, the I.33--the "Tower Manuscript,"[5] will see some similarities in approach. Both I.33 and Ringeck's buckler work make use of the shield to protect the sword hand. This means that the sword and buckler at times function as a single unit. The trick in interpreting Ringeck's buckler techniques is deciding at what points the sword and buckler stay together, and when they separate. Given the brevity of Ringeck's descriptions, this has required some interpolation.

When reading the translation for these six plays, be aware that they are written in a very condensed way. In the long sword chapters, Ringeck more thoroughly spells out the sequence of events. For example, he'll say *"if* he displaces your strike, *then* wind to his opening." In these techniques, we have to assume the "if," because he runs all the follow-on moves together. It is possible that, at each step of the way, a "sub-technique" could succeed that ends the fight.

---

[5] Ms. I.33, in the Royal Armouries at Leeds collection, is a c.1300 south German work that exclusively depicts sword and buckler combat. At the time of this writing, a full translation and analysis of this manuscript is being prepared for publication by Dr. Jeffrey Forgeng has prepared a translation facsimile of the volume released as "The Medieval Art of Swordsmanship: A Facsimile & Translation of Europe's Oldest Personal Combat Treatise, RA MS I.33," Chivalry Bookshelf, 2003.

Ringeck writes:

"*F*rom the Oberhau: [Illus. 22.1 & 22.2] *When you strike an Oberhau, place the pommel of your sword on the inside of your buckler close to your thumb. And thrust from below high into his face,* [Illus. 22.3] *winding against his sword,* [Illus. 22.4 & Illus. 22.5] *and letting yours snap over it.* [Illus. 22.6, Illus. 22.7] *This works from both sides.*"

Illus. 22.1: *Christian stands on the left in a guard akin to vom Tag, one of the four primary long sword guards. Ben stands in a guard closely resembling Pflug.*

Christian writes:

In this sequence the opponent is driven to defend his left side through multiple and varied assaults on that side, finally surprised by an attack to his right.

One of the key dangers when fighting with the shorter, single-handed sword are counterattacks to the sword-hand or wrist. When striking the *Oberhau*, the buckler shields the sword hand so that you can attack with relative safety. If the opponent binds your sword, thrust to him. If he displaces the thrust, wind your sword by raising the hilt, which should result in a leverage advantage. Should this too be displaced, snap around and attack him with a cut to the other side.

There are several analogues for long sword primary techniques here: a thrust from a bind (*Zwei Hengen* and/or *Absetzen*), a winding at the sword (*Winden*), and a "twitching" out from under his displacement (*Zucken*). This play looks like an amalgamation of the sub-techniques of the *Zornhau*, applied to the sword and buckler.

Illus. 22.2: *Christian passes forward with his right foot to strike an Oberhau, his buckler shielding his sword hand. Ben binds to Christian's sword, displacing his strike. Note that Ben is actually displacing with his sword, while his buckler protects his hand.*

Illus. 22.3: *Christian bears down in the bind with Ben's sword to thrust to his face. This is similar to thrusting from the lower hanger in the chapter on Zwei Hengen from the long sword techniques.*

Illus. 22.4: *Ben displaces Christian's thrust by moving his sword and buckler to his left side.*

Illus. 22.5: *Christian winds his sword and buckler high on his left side, into a position corresponding to the left Ochs. This increases his leverage in the bind and creates the opportunity for a thrust.*

Illus. 22.6: *Ben displaces Christian's thrust from above by driving even harder with his sword and buckler to his left side.*

Illus. 22.7: *Now that Ben has over-committed himself to defending on his left side, Christian snaps his sword out from the bind to strike around to Ben's right side, hitting him in the head. This is done with a pass forward of the left foot.*

Second technique of the buckler

Ringeck writes:

"*From the Unterhau:* [Illus. 22.8 & 22.9] *When he strikes an Oberhau from his right shoulder, wind against him towards your left side against your shield so you have a double shield.* [Illus. 22.10] *Then wind towards your right and aim for his face.* [Illus. 22.11] *If he defends by lifting his shield,* [Illus. 22.12] *strike at his left leg.* [Illus. 22.13] *This works from both sides.*"

Christian writes:

This technique uses binds and deceptions, showing the advantage of fighting "double" (with two weapons). It begins with an *Unterhau*. When the opponent displaces, wind with both sword and buckler together (the "double shield") to regain leverage. Then, separate the sword from the buckler; the buckler remains in place to tie up his weapon while the sword winds to the right side menacing his face. If he deflects the thrust, surprise him by switching targets and strike the left leg.

Illus. 22.8: *Both Christian and Ben stand with a left leg lead in vom Tag.*

Illus. 22.9: *With a kind of "scooping" motion that directs the sword up from below, Christian strikes Unterhau. Ben counters by keeping his buckler between himself and harm.*

Illus. 22.10: *Christian winds both sword and buckler to his left. Keeping the sword and buckler together creates the "double shield" so that he can move Ben's sword aside with relative safety.*

Illus. 22.11: *Christian winds his sword to his right but leaves his buckler in place so that it can continue to pin Ben's sword. From here he can thrust to Ben's face.*

Illus. 22.12: *Ben prevents Christian's thrust by countering with the buckler.*

Illus. 22.13: *Christian passes backward with his right leg, freeing his sword from Ben's buckler and allowing him to attack the Ben's left leg.*

Third technique of the buckler

"**F**rom the buckler. From the Wechselhau: [Illus. 22.14 & 22.15] *strike from the left from the buckler over him to his sword,* [Illus. 22.16] *and strike him then from the left side to the head,* [Illus. 22.17] *winding to the opening and thrusting to his face.* [Illus. 22.18] *If he defends with sword and buckler,* [Illus. 22.19] *strike at his right leg with the long edge.* [Illus. 22.20] *This also works from both sides.*"

The third play teaches the *Wechselhau*, or "changing strike" - a deceptive blow that changes trajectory to strike another target. The attack changes from a high line to a low one; the sword ultimately striking towards the forward leg. If unsuccessful, the sword leaves the buckler and slaps aside the opponent's weapon. Strike then to his head by whipping the sword around in a complete circle. If he thwarts this attack, deceptively change targets and again attack the leg.

Illus. 22.14: *Christian stands in vom Tag, while Ben stands in the right-side Pflug.*

Illus. 22.15: *Christian passes forward with his right leg and strikes a Wechselhau, or changing strike. With it he deceives Ben into thinking he will be hit high, but then changes targets to strike low. Note how Ben has raised his weapons to defend his head and Christian falls short of hitting the leg ending up in a low position similar to Alber.*

Illus. 22.16: *Separating his sword and buckler, Christian strikes his sword to Ben's sword, knocking it aside.*

Illus. 22.17: *With a forward pass of his left leg Christian strikes to the right side of Ben's head while shielding his own with his buckler. Ben displaces the blow with his sword and buckler together ("double shield").*

Illus. 22.18: *Remaining in contact with Ben's sword, Christian winds his hilt high so that he can find an opening to thrust down at.*

Illus. 22.19: *Ben shifts his weight forward to drive Christian's sword up, displacing his thrust.*

Illus. 22.20: *Christian keeps his buckler forward to protect himself as he passes back with his left leg and frees his sword to strike to Ben's right leg.*

Ringeck writes:

"**F**rom the Mittelhau: [Illus. 22.21 & 22.22] *Strike the Zwerch to both sides* [Illus. 22.23 & 22.24] *and the Scheitelhau with the long edge,* [Illus. 22.25] *thrusting to his groin."* [Illus. 22.26 & 22.27]

Christian writes:

In this play, attack the opponent's mid-section with a horizontal blow, the *Mittelhau*. If displaced, strike *Zwerchhau* to both sides. As with the long sword, the short edge is used to strike the left side of your adversary's head, while the long edge is used to strike the right. If both *Zwerchs* are displaced, strike with *Scheitelhau*, also familiar from the chapters on the long sword, to his head. Should that too be displaced, leave the buckler defending high while dropping the point of your sword low, thrusting at the groin.

Illus. 22.21: *Christian stands in vom Tag, while Ben stands ready in Pflug.*

Illus. 22.22: *Christian passes forward with his right leg to strike a Mittelhau, or horizontal strike. Ben meets Christian's sword with both sword and buckler--"double weapon"--displacing the blow.*

Illus. 22.23: *Christian inverts his sword so that his right thumb is situated down on the strong of his blade. He strikes the Zwerchhau to the left side of Ben's head, but Ben's raised buckler displaces it.*

Illus. 22.24: *From Ben's displacement, Christian now passes forward with his left foot and strikes a Zwerchhau to the right side of Ben's head. Again, Ben displaces with sword and buckler, the "double-shield."*

Illus. 22.25: *Passing back with his left foot, Christian strikes a Scheitelhau to Ben's head. Ben displaces by raising both buckler and sword.*

Illus. 22.26: *Christian frees his sword from Ben's displacement by drawing the sword back. This puts him in a good position to thrust.*

Illus. 22.27: *Christian thrusts to Ben's groin.*

Fifth technique of the buckler

Ringeck writes:

"*From the Sturzhau:* [Illus. 22.28 - 22.29] *Pretend as if you're about to thrust to his left side over his shield, moving down and through with your point to thrust at his body on the inside of his shield.* [Illus. 22.30] *And wind – immediately (Indes) – towards your left side.* [Illus. 22.31] *If he defends this,* [Illus. 22.32] *strike at his right leg with the long edge."* [Illus. 22.33]

Christian writes:

The *Sturzhau* is a downward blow that strikes with the short edge, not unlike the *Schielhau*, or "squinter." It's called the "plunging cut" because the blade is turned to bring the short edge into play as the blow is struck, which enables the sword to "plunge" over the opponent's defense. You deceive the opponent by making him believe that you intend to thrust to his face. Instead, plunge the point down between his buckler and his body. Once behind his defenses, wind to your left side with your sword to thrust. Note that all of these attacks are targeted at the adversary's upper openings. If he fends off the last thrust, switch to a lower opening by striking at his right leg.

Illus. 22.28: *Christian stands in vom Tag, while Ben stands ready in Pflug.*

Illus. 22.29: *Christian passes forward with his right leg to strike a Sturzhau, or plunging cut, at Ben. The Sturzhau is performed with a turn of the sword in mid-strike so that it reaches over your opponent's defense and strikes downward with the short edge. Even if Christian's edge does not find its mark, the strike puts his point in a position to thrust.*

Illus. 22.30:
Instead of thrusting at Ben's face, Christian thrusts down between Ben's buckler and his body. Christian's sword is now behind Ben's defenses.

Illus. 22.31: *Having penetrated Ben's defenses, Christian immediately winds his sword and buckler to his left, thrusting at Ben's face.*

Illus. 22.32: *Ben moves his sword and buckler to displace Christian's sword by forcing it up.*

Illus. 22.33:
Christian passes back with his right leg to free his sword to strike at Ben's right leg. His buckler remains in place before Ben's sword.

Combat with the Buckler
Sixth technique of the buckler

Ringeck writes:

ake the blade into your left hand together with the buckler [Illus. 22.34] and wind against him as with the half sword. If he strikes or thrusts high at your face or low at your leg, [Illus. 22.25] let go your right hand and displace this with sword and shield. [Illus. 22.26] Grasp his shield on his right side from below with your right hand [Illus. 22.27] and turn it to your right side; you have then taken his shield." [Illus. 22.28]

Christian writes:

This is a fascinating play that hybridizes the techniques of half-swording and buckler work. The left hand is used to hold both the buckler and the middle of your sword. After deflecting the opponent's attack with both sword and buckler, let go with your right hand, freeing it to grab his buckler and wrench it painfully out of his grip.

Illus. 22.34: *Christian stands on guard with his left leg forward, the sword and buckler held together so that his left hand holds both his buckler and the middle of his sword's blade. Ben stands in vom Tag.*

Illus. 22.35: *Ben strikes an Oberhau, which Christian displaces with the face of his buckler by passing forward with his right leg.*

Illus. 22.36: *Christian releases his right hand from his sword's grip. He continues to bind Ben's sword with his left hand holding both his buckler and his sword's blade.*

Illus. 22.37: *Christian grabs the edge of Ben's buckler on Ben's right side from below.*

Illus. 22.38: *With a strong clockwise rotation, Christian removes the buckler from Ben's hand.*

Chapter 23
Wrestling Techniques

Ringeck writes:

"*Here begins good wrestling techniques with counters.*"

Ringeck's wrestling appears to be haphazard in its organization. We may be seeing techniques drawn from a variety of earlier sources; the mansucript certainly feels different here; as if we are looking at what appear to be at least three separate wrestling subsystems compiled together.

The nine techniques in this chapter are culled from the earliest parts of Ringeck's wrestling material. The first six are grouped together, while the remaining three are scattered amongst some of the other early techniques, which themselves are grouped together by type - there are groups of holds, ground fighting methods, strikes, etc. This seemingly disorderly presentation is difficult to scrutinize; but perhaps this section of the manuscript is a compendium of techniques garnered from various sources by the scribe who set it to paper.

In a way, this first section provides a bit of a "sampler" of the groups of techniques that in later chapters. An interesting feature about the wrestling techniques preserved is the use of striking blows to "soften up" an enemy before grappling with him. The strike to the neck in the eighth technique is a good example of this concept in action. We'll see more of these in a later chapter on *Mortstöße* – "Murder Strikes."

Ringeck writes:

"*Let him take hold of you, even if you can prevent it. If he seizes you then under the arms around the chest and actually presses you, wanting to raise you.* [Illus. 23.1] *Allow yourself to drop down and grab him under the knee. Resist his pressure and bend him with both hands, the head to the rear over the back.* [Illus. 23.2] *Thus you can throw a strong man as well as a weaker one to the ground.*"

Christian writes:

In this simple technique, an opponent's attempt to bind you around the chest is countered by pulling out the support from one of his legs while pushing him backwards at the neck. The technique will appear repeatedly throughout the wrestling chapters. Note that it doesn't rely on superior strength: it simply throws the opponent off balance and uses a knee lift to break his connection to the ground.

Illus. 23.1: *Ben binds Christian about the chest.*

Illus. 23.2: *Christian drops down to grab beneath one of Ben's knees. At the same time he uses his other hand to push at the neck, which forces Ben to fall backwards.*

Ringeck writes:

"*If you want to seize him and he tries to use arm leverage,* [Illus. 23.3] *release his arm immediately and reach for his hair.* [Illus. 23.4] *Pull his hair to your shoulder, then run with his head against the wall. Thus he is defeated.*" [Illus. 23.5]

Christian writes:

Here, an attempt to grab the opponent's arm has failed. The opponent has grabbed your arm, so you seek a new target: his hair. This gives you a handhold from which to use his own momentum against him.

Illus. 23.3: *Christian seizes one of Ben's arms, but Ben has begun to apply leverage with his other hand.*

Illus. 23.4: *Christian grabs Ben by the hair.*

Illus. 23.5: *Having released his hand from Ben's arm, Christian uses it to help run Ben into an obstacle, in this case an obliging tree, by the hair.*

Ringeck writes:

*"**Note**: if you approach him and he pulls both arms in, then step with the left side forward. Allow the left arm to quickly slide around his neck, the right between his legs. Thus throw him over the head: he is then dazed."* [Illus. 23.6]

Christian writes:

This is essentially a variant of the first technique, with the opponent's neck and lower extremities providing a big lever with which to through him off balance. In this case, it is done as an attack, and the right hand is placed between the legs, rather than grabbing at one of the knees. Ringeck's dry comment that "then he is dazed," is something of an understatement.

Illus. 23.6: *An attack. Christian puts one hand to Ben's neck and the other between his legs to aggressively throw him backwards.*

Ringeck writes:

"*If you approach an equally strong opponent, you must not hesitate. If you seize him in full run, he cannot prevent it. Seize him from below and throw him this way.* [Illus. 23.7] *However, pay attention and make sure that he does not do this to you!*"

Christian writes:

This is a simple tackling move. Your momentum is used to throw your opponent off balance.

Illus. 23.7: *Christian tackles Ben by grabbing his legs while running into his body, forcing him off his feet.*

Ringeck writes:

"*From a full run seize his right hand with your left and hold it. Pass under his right arm, lead through your left hand and seize his thigh. Take him then on the shoulder and throw him on his head.*" [Illus. 23.8]

Christian writes:

This is a shoulder throw done by restraining the opponent's arm and running under it. A side benefit of this technique is that the opponent may break his arm over your neck depending on how he falls. This is very similar to *Durchlaufen* in the long sword section – you "run through" your enemy's attack.

Illus. 23.8: *Christian has grabbed Ben's right arm and run underneath it. He picks up Ben's right leg while jamming his shoulder into him to throw him.*

Ringeck writes:

"*If you close with him, seize his left arm with your left, his left leg with your right hand. Grab him quickly, he must then turn his back to you.* [Illus. 23.9] *You can then strike him on the head* [Illus. 23.10] *or push him to the ground. However, if he bends down rapidly and slips through under your arm,* [Illus. 23.11 & 23.12] *then he has repelled the technique.*"

Christian writes:

Here you use leverage to turn the opponent about so that he can pose no threat to you as you continue your offensive. You must be careful, however, not to let your opponent escape by slipping underneath the grab.

Illus. 23.9: *Christian grabs Ben's left arm and leg to turn him around.*

Illus. 23.10: *With Ben now facing away from him, Christian strikes to his head.*

Illus. 23.11: *Once again, Christian seizes Ben's arm and leg.*

Illus. 23.12: *Ben thwarts Christian's attack by passing under his arm.*

Ringeck writes:

"*If you close with him, bring in both arms before your chest and push against his neck.* [Illus. 23.13] *Then bend down, seize his leg underneath the calf with both hands and throw him.*" [Illus. 23.14]

Christian writes:

In this technique, a hard shove to the opponent's neck knocks him off balance. This is followed by a leg lift, toppling him over backwards.

Illus. 23.13: *Christian slams full force into Ben's neck with his arms folded before him.*

Illus. 23.14: *Christian grabs one of Ben's legs with both hands to finish toppling him over.*

Ringeck writes:

"*Seize one of his hands with both hands, grab two fingers that are next to each other, and tear them apart.* [Illus. 23.15 & 23.16]

Christian writes:

In this gruesome technique you simply rip apart two of your opponent's fingers, leaving him in agony (and still maintaining your grip on that hand, for further actions).

Illus. 23.15 & 16: *As Ben reaches to grab, Christian tears two of his fingers apart.*

Ringeck writes:

"*As you approach: strike him with the second hand against his neck; then wrestle.*" [Illus. 23.17]

Christian writes:

This is the first example of a concept we'll see repeated in Ringeck's wrestling techniques. A strike is used to soften up an opponent, before actually throwing him.

Illus. 23.17: *Christian takes some of the fight out of Ben, before grappling by striking his neck.*

Chapter 27
Drei Ringen

The "Three Wrestlings" are really three entering techniques – that is, they are good opening moves in a wrestling encounter. Each utilizes a simple "push-pull" mechanic that drives the upper body backwards, at the same time the "base" of the legs is uprooted, forcing the opponent to fall. The second technique particularly evinces the sensibilities of the Liechtenauer tradition: if your first attack is thwarted, keep attacking. All three techniques enjoy left/right symmetry – indicated by the characteristic phrase "this works from both sides" – a familiar line from Ringeck's longsword commentary.

Of all of the grappling techniques taught in Ringeck's treatise the greatest attention should be spent understanding these three techniques. Much as the *Vier Leger* encapsulate the techniques of the longsword, these three techniques--particularly when combined with the *Drei Ringen*--form the basis for much of Ringeck's Art of Wrestling.

Ringeck writes:

he first wrestling: lead your lower arm across his upper arm in front of his neck and the other arm into the hollow of the knee. [Illus. 24.1] This can be done on both sides."

Christian writes:

The first technique is a throw that unbalances the opponent through simple "push-pull" leverage. It is performed by pressing one arm at the opponent's neck, while the other pulls one of his legs out from under him. The end result is that his upper body's mass is unbalanced backwards as his legs are pulled forward, affecting the throw. This simple form appears again and again throughout the system both in wrestling and in grappling with weapons.

Illus. 24.1: *Christian throws Ben by putting one arm before his neck and the other under his knee. By lifting the knee and pushing at the neck, he can pull Ben's leg out from under him and throw him to the ground.*

Ringeck writes:

"*A counter: exchange the hand, which is above and grabbing for the front of his neck, with the other hand at the leg. If you cannot do the first wrestling,* [Illus. 24.2 & 24.3] *then exchange both hands, so that one is at the neck and the other one at the leg.* [Illus. 24.4] *This can be done from both sides. This counter is called the 'leg break at the arm.'*"

Christian writes:

This is a variant on the first technique, that teaches what to do if the adversary resists or retreats. A simple switch of which arm presses high, while the other pulls low, uses the opponent's resistance against him, causing the throw to succeed.

This technique also marks the first appearance of the term *Beinbruch* ("leg break") – which does not refer to literal leg breaking, but rather a counter technique that break the legs' connection to the ground.

Illus. 24.2: *Here Christian tries to seize Ben at the neck and knee once again. However,…*

Illus. 24.3: *Ben escapes the technique by backpedaling.*

Illus. 24.4: *In response to Ben's escape, Christian follows after him with a step of the right foot and switches the hand that grasped for the neck with the one that seized the knee.*

Ringeck writes:

"*Strike your lower arm over his,* [Illus. 24.5] *grabbing also with the second hand and placing the foot of the same side to the rear. And throw him in front of you on his face.* [Illus. 24.6] *That can be done on both sides. Or use both hands together, pull him down by the neck and step behind him with both feet.* [Illus. 24.7]

"*Those are three wrestling techniques. You can use them when approaching from either side, and also use the defense techniques from them.*"

Christian writes:

The third technique is another variation of the same, using both of your arms against one of his. Stepping backwards with one of your feet, throw him. An alternate outcome is also presented here: as you step back, grab his neck and force him to ground. I have interpreted this throw as essentially a pull; my strong, two-handed grip, combined with the pivoting step of my back foot, pulls him off-balance and locks his arm as he falls.

Illus. 24.5: *Christian has stepped in to seize Ben's left arm using both of his.*

Illus. 24.6: *Stepping backwards with his left leg, Christian pushes Ben to the ground. Note how the action of both arms locks Ben's arm.*

Illus. 24.7: *In this alternate conclusion to the third technique, Christian's hands leave Ben's arm and seize the back of his neck. He's easily put down from this advantageous position.*

Chapter 25
Countering Grabs

Simple and practical, these are some of my favorites among the many wrestling techniques in Ringeck's book. Each describes what to do when an opponent has seized in a hold. Four of the techniques deal with a grab from the front, the remaining three with a grab from behind. In general, they show the bias in earlier sections of Ringeck's wrestling towards using strikes, "pain-compliance," and leg lifts as counters and setups for throws and holds.

Counters to Grabs
Countering the under-arm grab

Ringeck writes:

"*If he wants to grab you under the arms and hold you strongly or throw you,* [Illus. 25.1] *move both arms to his throat and push.* [Illus. 25.2]

"*Or, turn him over with both hands to his head, one at the chin, the other at the back of the head.* [Illus. 25.3]

"*Or, put both thumbs to the throat and the other fingers into the eyes.* [Illus. 25.4]

"*Or, press with both thumbs against his temples.*" [Illus. 25.5]

Christian writes:

These techniques describe four ways to respond to the classic wrestling "hug." All involve pushing or striking to sensitive parts of the head and neck. At first, these techniques may seem obvious, until you realize that most people's impulse in such a scenario is to simply try to *force* themselves free.

The first technique uses simple leverage - where the head goes, the body must follow. Pressing back the throat, move his entire upper body back, breaking his hold.

The second technique is a more sophisticated version of the first. The head turn not only moves his center of balance backwards, but, if he tries to free his head by turning it to either side, he actually further unbalances himself by helping you to "corkscrew" him into the ground.

The third and fourth technique use direct pain-compliance to break his hold.

Illus. 25.1: *Ben has seized Christian under the arms and holds him fast.*

Illus. 25.2: *In this response to Ben's grab, Christian puts both of his hands to Ben's throat with vigor.*

Illus. 25.3: *Another option for countering a grab: Christian uses both hands to wrench Ben's head backwards.*

Illus. 25.4: *A third option for countering a grab: Christian pushes his thumbs into Ben's throat and his fingers into his eyes.*

Illus. 25.5: *A fourth unpleasant comeuppance: Christian uses his thumbs to strike to his temples.*

Ringeck writes:

"*If he grabs you from behind around the hip,* [Illus. 25.6] *grasp the index finger of his upper hand.* [Illus. 25.7] *Turn and step behind him.* [Illus. 25.8] *From here you can wrestle as you please. And also bend his finger.*

"*Or, turn a little so that your feet move near to either one of his.* [Illus. 25.9] *Seize that leg with both hands above the knee.* [Illus. 25.10] *If he doesn't release you, throw him on his head.*

"*Or, grab him behind you between the hands, and press him thus.*" [Illus. 25.11]

Christian writes:

These three techniques deal with a grab from *behind*. As this kind of grab doesn't allow you to bring your hands to bear as easily against your opponent, they are by necessity a bit more creative.

The first technique uses pain compliance to break his hold (a finger lock), combined with leverage gained from turning and stepping. From here, proceed with any of other throws or holds previously learned.

The second technique again uses a knee lift to break his balance, as we've seen before.

The last technique required considerable creativity on the part of my students. I think this must be the single most cryptically worded passage in the entire manuscript, and hence required more interpretation than the others.

Illus. 25.6: *Having not learned his lesson from the unpleasantness of the last encounter, Ben this time grabs Christian from behind.*

Illus. 25.7: *Christian pries one of Ben's hands away from his person by grabbing the index finger and bending away.*

Illus. 25.8: *Distracting Ben with pain, Christian steps out of the grab and behind him.*

Illus. 25.9: *Here is another way to free oneself from a grab from behind. Christian moves slightly to get near one of Ben's legs.*

Illus. 25.10: *Bending down, Christian seizes the nearest leg and lifts it to either throw Ben backwards or force him to release his hold.*

Illus. 25.11: *Another counter to the grab from behind: Christian reaches behind with both of his hands to grab Ben by the head, in this case by the hair.*

Chapter 26
Unterhalten

These techniques provide Ringeck's answer to the question "What do I do after I throw someone to the ground?" The answer is to pin him before proceeding further. These holds are used for this purpose. While only three are described, they well convey an important strategy: use both hands to gain control of the opponent, and then transfer that control to just one of your hands. Once accomplished, the adversary is restrained and you have a hand free to continue the offensive. This is best done on the ground, as the ground itself helps to provide that restraint. This is shown in the first technique where the opponent is initially held while standing and then thrown on his face, where the same hold can be done even more effectively while he is stunned.

Unterhauten - Holding Down
The first hold

Ringeck writes:

"*Reach in while wrestling with your right hand at his arm behind his right hand, grabbing with your left hand at his elbow. [Illus. 26.1] And put his arm against yours, stepping behind him and holding him firmly. [Illus. 26.2] If you aren't satisfied with this, seize his right leg under the calf with your right hand and throw him on his nose. [Illus. 26.3] And hold him with both hands, [Illus. 26.4] or with one hand, as you want; you can also change the hand at his arm.*"

Christian writes:

The first hold begins with an arm lock behind the opponent's back. Pain compliance can end the fight right here - if he resists, apply more pressure.

In a more serious encounter, the same technique can be turned into a throw by again pulling one of his leg out from under him. This face-plants the opponent and gives you the option to finish with a ground-hold, using one or two hands to constrain him.

Illus. 26.1: *Christian catches hold of Ben's right arm, with the right hand grabbing near Ben's hand and the left hand behind his elbow.*

Illus. 26.2: *Stepping behind his adversary, Christian locks Ben's arm painfully behind him. This hold could be maintained in this position but....*

Illus. 26.3: *...instead, Christian releases his right hand from Ben's arm and seizes his right leg, forcing the hapless student to the ground.*

Illus. 26.4: *Christian takes hold of the right arm with his right hand. The original hold is once again in place, only now on the ground. From here Christian can hold Ben with only one hand and work other techniques with the free hand.*

Unterhauten - Holding Down

Ringeck writes:

"*If you throw him on his back, fall with your left knee onto his right arm, exactly on the joint. And then fall onto his neck with the left arm, pressing him hard. [Illus. 26.5] Seize his left hand with your right, [Illus. 26.6] taking hold of it with your left hand. You can then do whatever you want with your right. [Illus. 26.7] This can also be done on the left side.*"

Christian writes:

This hold would be a useful follow-up technique to many of the throws that appear in the rest of Ringeck's book - once the opponent has been knocked down, he can be restrained and injured further if necessary. The hold progresses in two phases: first the opponent's right arm is neutralized, ideally damaging, if not breaking his elbow in the process, while your left arm falls onto his throat. This causes pain, distraction, and if done properly, disrupts his breathing. At the same time it creates a pin against his throat. The second action ties up his remaining free hand, leaving *your* right free to "do whatever you want." In my interpretation, I've elected to strike my opponent once I've accounted for his arms.

Illus. 26.5: *Christian begins the second hold having thrown his opponent down. He has landed with his left knee hard upon Ben's right elbow joint, restraining him at the neck with the left arm.*

Illus. 26.7: *In the completion of the hold, Christian has transferred control of Ben's left arm from his right hand to his left. He now restrains Ben's neck and left arm, which frees Christian's right hand.*

Illus. 26.6: *Using his free right arm, Christian seizes Ben's left and begins to pull it towards his own left hand.*

Ringeck writes:

"If you want to throw him on his back, then grab his legs under the knees with both hands as he falls. [Illus. 26.8] And lift them as highly as you can, falling between his legs with both knees into the testicles. [Illus. 26.9] And bend so that you can hold both his legs with one hand, so you can then use the other hand as you wish." [Illus. 26.10]

Christian writes:

This is a particularly violent technique. Following a hard throw to his back, drop to your knees with your full weight into his groin. His pain and shock then allows you to pin his legs with one hand and continue to strike him with the other.

Illus. 26.8: *Christian has thrown Ben onto his back, this time by pulling both his legs out from under him. Christian retains control of the legs as Ben hits the ground, raising them high.*

Illus. 26.9: *Christian falls into the opening created by Ben's raised legs, landing hard upon the groin with his knees.*

Illus. 26.10: *Christian slides slightly off of his stricken opponent, and now uses a hand to constrain the legs. This leaves his other hand free to work other techniques, in this case, a strike.*

Chapter 27
Ston

The *Ston*--ground fighting techniques--comprise three methods for defeating your opponent once you are on the ground on your back, whether by design or happenstance. The term *ston* seems to refer to having come from a standing position and thence to the ground. In the first two techniques, you take your opponent to the ground by falling backwards and taking him along with you. You then must roll him off to the side so that his weight does not pin you down. In the third technique, your opponent is about to pin you down, so you must act quickly to roll him off before he can complete his hold. All three finish by restraining your adversary on the ground with a hold. In the previous chapter, we saw three such holds that can be put to good use at the conclusion of these techniques.

Ringeck writes:

"If you want to apply the first ground technique, let yourself fall down. Lift the knees as highly as possible and hold them to his back. [Illus. 27.1 & 27.2] Pull him against your knees, then stretch a leg so that he slides off. [Illus. 27.3] Follow after him with both hands and feet, holding him fast with a hold." [Illus. 27.4]

Christian writes:

To do this first technique, let yourself fall backwards, pulling your opponent's back onto your knees. Straighten one of your knees, causes him to fall towards that side. As he lands, face first, you roll onto him and restrain him with a hold.

Illus. 27.1: *Christian grabs Ben under the arms from behind.*

Illus. 27.2: *Christian lets himself fall down backwards while pushing his knees hard into Ben's back.*

Illus. 27.3: *Christian lets his right knee drop and straighten slightly so that Ben slides off to his right.*

Illus. 27.4: *With Ben face down on the ground, Christian begins to restrain his limbs with a hold.*

Ringeck writes:

"*hen your opponent applies a grip from above, bend your head till you're under his breast and pull him down with you.* [Illus. 27.5] *Bend the knee, seizing him with either hand between the legs and throwing him over you.* [Illus. 27.6] *Then throw yourself across him to make a hold.*" [Illus. 27.7]

Christian writes:

This is a variation on the first technique, but this time your opponent is facing you as you fall down. A hand between his legs helps to roll him over to one side, so that he isn't on top of you. As he lands on his back, move atop him to restrain him with a cross-body hold.

Illus. 27.5: *Christian falls backwards, taking Ben along with him. He has one hand between Ben's legs and the other grabbing him at his left arm.*

Illus. 27.6: *Using both hands, Christian throws Ben over to the ground.*

Illus. 27.7: *Christian moves quickly to restrain Ben's arms and legs with a hold.*

Ringeck writes:

"**W**hen a man has you under him, [Illus. 27.8] *look for which hand he has above. Grab the same to the side towards his arm* [Illus. 27.9] *– this is called a 'leg break' (Beinbruch)[1] and is often used in wrestling – and grapple strongly with hand and leg and with the entire body, till you bring the man under you.* [Illus. 27.10] *Then make a hold, as described before."* [Illus. 27.11]

Christian writes:

Should you find yourself about to pinned on the ground, you can use an arm lock to roll your opponent off of you. The motion of the legs and the rest of the body provide the power to roll him over so that you can in turn effect a counter-hold.

Illus. 27.8: *With Christian on the ground, Ben pins his opponent's right shoulder to the ground with his left hand.*

Illus. 27.9: *Christian locks Ben's left arm by driving his own right arm against it above the elbow. With his left hand, he pushes up against Ben's right shoulder.*

Illus. 27.10: *Christian uses his entire body, but especially his legs, to roll Ben over and off of him.*

Illus. 27.11: *Now that Ben is on his back, Christian begins to effect a hold, restraining Ben's arms and legs.*

---

[1] A *Beinbruch*, or "leg break," is a counter-technique involving the legs. These are described further later in this book.

Chapter 28
Mortstöße

The *Mortstöße*--"Murder Strikes"--are blows delivered with the hands that are designed to stun and distract your opponent so that you can more easily move to grapple. They represent some of the most directly offensive and punishing techniques in Ringeck's un-armed combat system. Various parts of the body are targeted: the chest, abdomen, face, temple, and groin. The last technique, which targets the navel, is interesting in that it explains some methods that may be used following the murder strike. Master Ringeck is, however, careful to tell us that every murder strike should be followed by additional grappling techniques.

Mortstöße - Murder Strikes
First, to the breast over the heart

Ringeck writes:

"*Seize the man with the left hand above the belt where you want. Push at the same time with your right fist with full strength against his heart. [Illus. 28.1] Then grapple on with the wrestling, as best as you can, following the struggle with both techniques and counters. You can apply the same techniques and counters in all situations: on horse, on foot, armed or unarmed, lying or standing.*"

Christian writes:

This first "murder strike" is a powerful blow with the fist over the opponent's heart. Like all of the murder strikes, it is a tactic designed to stun him before engaging in further grappling techniques. The master also admonishes us to use this tactic in all fighting situations.

Illus. 28.1: *Christian strikes Ben with his right fist over his heart. This is the first murder strike.*

Ringeck writes:

"Seize the man with the left hand above the belt and strike his testicles with your knee. [Illus. 28.2] Then start wrestling with strength.*

"In all wrestling use the holds, when necessary, and the ground fighting techniques. Afterwards also use murder strikes and throws over the leg."*

Christian writes:

Readers need no explanation of the efficacy of a knee strike to the groin. Again, we are told to use this as a prelude to other wrestling techniques.

Illus. 28.2: *Christian delivers the second murder strike by kneeing Ben in the groin.*

Mortstöße - Murder Strikes
Third, to the temple

Ringeck writes:

"*Grab the man with the left hand above the belt. With the right fist strike him as hard you can against the temple. [Illus. 28.3] Immediately after, start wrestling with strength.*"

Christian writes:

In this *mortstöße*, the opponent is restrained by the belt, providing no escape from the full brunt of a blow to the temple.

Illus. 28.3:*This is the third murder strike: a blow with the fist to the temple.*

Ringeck writes:

"Strike him with both fists against the neck as hard you can. [Illus. 28.4] *Afterwards wrestle.*"

Christian writes:

This is another technique, a blow with two fists to your opponent's neck, stunning and disorienting him.

Illus. 28.4: *Christian uses both fists to strike Ben's neck.*

Ringeck writes:

"Push both thumbs into his cheeks with the other fingers around his head, pushing with the right hand to complete the technique." [Illus. 28.5]

Christian writes:

Once again, both hands are employed in delivering the murder strike. With the thumbs against the cheeks and the other fingers of your hand restraining your opponent's head, you then use pressure from your right hand to push his head to the side, creating an opportunity to grapple.

Illus. 28.5: *In this, the fifth murder strike, Christian presses his thumbs hard into Ben's cheeks while his other fingers hold his opponent's head. He also pushes hard with his right hand, which twists Ben's head to the side.*

<u>Ringeck writes</u>:

"*Strike him with the right hand against the navel as hard as you can. [Illus. 28.6] Then, with your left hand, seize his right arm at the biceps. With your right arm, grasp him around his left side. [Illus. 28.7] Hold him fast by the jacket or hose, shift your behind before his hip, so that your right leg is in front of his right, throwing him in this way over the hip.*" [Illus. 28.8]

Illus. 28.6: *To begin the sixth murder strike technique, Christian punches Ben in the abdomen, at the navel.*

Illus. 28.7: *His opponent reeling from the blow to the navel, Christian steps in to grasp his right bicep and left mid-section.*

Illus. 28.8: *Christian now passes forward with his right foot, placing it behind Ben's right leg, throwing his opponent over his hip.*

A counter to the previous technique

Ringeck writes:

"*If he wants to throw you over the hip,* [Illus. 28.9] *put your left arm to his neck. Tear him to the rear on your left side, thus you throw him.*" [Illus. 28.10]

Illus. 28.9: *To start, Ben has already stepped in to throw Christian over his hip.*

Illus. 28.10: *To ecounter, Christian presses his left arm against Ben's neck, thereby throwing him backward over his hip.*

Ringeck writes:

"*If you want to counter the first technique, as described, then bend to the rear, as if you would fall to the rear,* [Illus. 28.11] *seize his left leg with your left hand* [Illus. 28.12] *and tear it upward: thus you throw him.*" [Illus. 28.13]

Illus. 28.11: *The counter to the counter-technique begins. Ben is trying to prevent Christian from throwing him and has raised his left arm to throw his assailant backwards.*

Illus. 28.12: *Christian ducks down and away from Ben's left arm. He grabs Ben's behind Ben's left knee with his left hand.*

Illus. 28.13: *Christian hoists Ben's left knee, throwing him backward.*

Ringeck writes:

"*ith the left hand, seize his right arm at the biceps. With your right grasp him around his left side.* [Illus. 28.14] *Put your right leg barely inside his right. At the same time turn to your right side and seize his right leg with your left hand just underneath the behind:* [Illus. 28.15] *thus you throw him.*" [Illus. 28.16]

Christian writes:

This is a series of techniques and their counters that begins with a murder strike, a powerful punch to his navel. This softens up the opponent and provides an opportunity to step in and throw him over your hip. If you find yourself on the receiving end of this technique, raise your left arm before your opponent's neck and throw him backward over your hip. Should you then have to fend off the counter-technique, there is also a counter to the counter: you drop back away from the hand at your neck and pull out your adversary's left leg, causing him to fall. The last technique simply offers an alternative strategy for throwing your opponent after delivering the strike to his navel.

Illus. 28.14: *In this variation on the murder strike to the navel, Christian has already softened up his opponent and seized him by the right biceps and left side.*

Illus. 28.16: *He then lifts Ben's right leg, depriving him of its support. He throws Ben with a push from his right hand against his left side.*

llus. 28.15: *Christian releases Ben's right biceps and bends to seize his right leg at the thigh.*

Chapter 29
Beinbrüche

The term *beinbrüche* has been a troublesome one for me to translate - as *bein* can mean either "leg" or "bone," it can be interpreted as "bone breaks" or as "leg breaks." To make matters worse, the word *bruch*, which today means "break" or "fracture," must be approached with caution as well: *bruch* means "break," but it also means "counter," as in a counter-technique. In the notes accompanying his 1965 transcription of the Ringeck manuscript, Martin Wierschin asserts that these techniques are "counter-techniques using the legs."[1] This seems too simple, for while each of these techniques does involve using one's own or one's opponent's legs, the same could be said for many other wrestling techniques that also appear in the manuscript.

Fortunately, understanding these techniques is nowhere near as difficult as understanding the word *beinbrüche*. The first three involve the use of your legs to provide the momentum for throwing your opponent as well as an obstacle for him to fall over; they have the added benefit of breaking or dislocating his arm. The fourth technique fells him by pulling his leg out from under him; this too breaks an arm. The last two techniques are grouped together as a pair. These come closest to being "leg breaks" in the literal sense, as each ends in the opponent's leg being broken or dislocated at the hip.

---

[1] Martin Wierschin, *Meister Liechtenauers kunst des fechtens*. Munich, 1965, p. 137.

Ringeck writes:

These are the common wrestlings at the arms that are called beinbrüche - move him with strength. Seize his right arm, [Illus. 29.1] *then step with the right leg to the rear and setting your left foot before his leg.* [Illus. 29.2] *Then push him before you over the hip."* [Illus. 29.3]

Christian writes:

The first technique begins with joint lock at the opponent's right elbow. You then step in with your left leg in front of his right. With his arm locked, he is easily thrown over your hip. If performed with vigor this technique could break the opponent's arm.

Illus. 29.1: *With his left leg leading, Christian seizes Ben's right arm just behind the hand.*

Illus. 29.2: *Christian steps to the rear with his right leg while placing his left leg in front of Ben's right.*

Illus. 29.3: *Christian pushes Ben over his left and down to the ground. In order to take Ben down while continuing the arm lock, Christian pulls up with his right hand and pushes down with his left hand.*

Ringeck writes:

"*Seize whatever hand he uses to grab at you. Grab the arm with both hands behind his hand* [Illus. 29.4] *and turn your back before his belly. In turning lift his arm on your shoulder and press it down.* [Illus. 29.5] *Thus you break his arm. If he tries a counter-grip, turn around and wrestle.*"

Christian writes:

This is another arm-breaking technique. Once you've grabbed your opponent's arm, turn and hyperextend his elbow over one of your shoulders.

Illus. 29.4: *Christian grabs Ben's outstretched arm with both of his hands.*

Illus. 29.5: *Turning his back against Ben's stomach, Christian pulls Ben's arm over his shoulder. As Christian pushes up with his body and pulls down with his arms he will break or dislocate Ben's arm.*

Beinbrüche – 'Leg Breaks'
Third leg break

Ringeck writes:

"*If he puts a hand forward and wants to attack you by grasping, pushing or wrestling, then seize that hand. [Illus. 29.6] Take it from below with the left hand. Run your right hand through under the same armpit by the left hand. Step with the right foot behind his right leg and push him to the rear over your hip, [Illus. 29.7] and hold him fast with the grip.*"

Christian writes:

In this technique you use both hands to lock your opponent's arm. Throwing him over your hip, you dislocate his shoulder.

Illus. 29.6: *Christian uses his left arm to grab Ben's right arm just behind the hand.*

Illus. 29.7: *Weaving his right hand beneath Ben' armpit, Christian passes forward with his right leg to place his right foot behind his opponent's right foot. As he throws Ben he dislocates his shoulder.*

Christian writes:

A variation on the *Throw Over the Shoulder From Under His Arm* demonstrated in the first chapter on wrestling, this technique is geared more towards breaking the opponent's arm than throwing him over. Duck under the arm that you seized so that the arm is pulled across your neck and upper back. As you pull out his adjacent leg, it will cause him to fall. His own weight provides the force that breaks the arm.

Ringeck writes:

"*Seize whatever hand he uses to grab at you, as in the previous technique. [Illus. 29.8] And drive through with your head and body under the same arm, and then push hard against his arm. Pull out his adjacent leg, so he then falls.*" [Illus. 29.9]

Illus. 29.8: *Christian again uses his left arm to seize Ben's right.*

Illus. 29.9: *Christian ducks under Ben's right arm while maintaining his grip on it. He pulls Ben's right leg out from under him so that his own weight brings him down. This breaks Ben's arm over Christian's upper back.*

Ringeck writes:

"*At the leg, two counters are possible:*

"*First*: *Seize his leg with both hands, one over the ankle, the other one at the knee. From this you can break the leg.* [Illus. 29.10]

"*Second*: *Seize his leg with both hands over the ankle and tear it over the shoulder, thus you break the leg.*" [Illus. 29.11]

Christian writes:

I've had to make some suppositions in interpreting these two "leg breaking" techniques. Few fighters will simply *let* you grab their leg, so these suppositions are with respect to how we would arrive in the situation that we've depicted. In the first, the opponent's leg must somehow have presented itself so that I could grab it to perform the break, which is a hyperextension of the knee. In the second, I have assumed that I must first have knocked my opponent to the ground. Essentially a hip dislocation, this would be quite horrific to behold if performed with speed and power.

Illus. 29.10: *Having seized Ben's left leg, Christian pushes down hard just above the knee with his right hand while pulling up hard at the ankle with his left hand. This creates a painful knee hyperextension.*

Illus. 29.11: *Ben is on the ground, having been thrown by Christian, who has seized one of his legs. Christian forces the leg up towards Ben's shoulder to dislocate his hip.*

Chapter 30
Other Wrestling Techniques

This section of the manuscript begins with the tell-tale words *"Hie heben an andere gutte ringen und brüch"* ("Here begins other good wrestling technique and counters") – a sign that we have forayed into a new major section. The manuscript wrestling passages have three such sections that begin with *"Hie heben…."* The first seven chapters of wrestling derive from the first of these three sections. This chapter comprises the second section. The third section comprises what we have gathered into Chapter 31; it deals with wrestling during the approach. Perhaps the three sections each correspond to the works of three different masters – this is a compelling idea given that there appears to be some degree of overlap in the techniques.

This section is a collection of various techniques. Unlike the previous wrestling material, they are not grouped by form or function; however, they are all throws or counter-techniques against holds. While some are very similar to ones we have seen previously, there are some unique entries – notably, the "back breaker," a particularly grim technique requiring the advantage of size and strength.

The author has recently discovered that this section of wrestling apparently derives from the second half of the techniques of the famous wrestling master Ott the Jew.

Other Wrestling Techniques
The first technique-- leg pull away

Ringeck writes:

"*If he seizes you at the arms and you are leading with the left foot, and he has his right leg outside of your left and wants to pull you over by the arms, [Illus. 30.1] withdraw your left leg rapidly behind you. At the same time, seize his right foot and push him against the chest; [Illus. 30.2] thus he falls.*"

Christian writes:

This technique is used to counter an opponent's attempt at a throw. Again, this is a basic use of a leg or knee lift to create a fall, which occurs repeatedly in all three of the major wrestling sections. The left leg is pulled away from his leg, which is then seized and pulled out from under him. Leverage is applied to his chest, facilitating his fall.

Illus. 30.1: *Ben seizes Christian's arms, who leads with his left leg.*

Illus. 30.2: *Christian passes back with his left foot while simultaneously pushing Ben's chest and pulling out his right foot, causing Ben to fall.*

Ringeck writes:

"*If he grabs you around your shoulders from the rear, [Illus. 30.3] then drive high with your arm into the bend of his elbow on the side where the foot is in front. Reach with the other hand to it and press above and outside on the opposite side. [Illus. 30.4] Stop his arm with a hand, with the other one grab his throat, [Illus. 30.5] and with your step into the knee of his forward leg, which turns the heel to you.*" [Illus. 30.6]

Christian writes:

One of the more complicated counter-techniques, this one starts by breaking a grab from behind. The strike is made to the side with the leading foot, to facilitate the follow-up grab - this will help pull him off balance. As the opponent's grasp is broken, his hand is stopped with your own, while he is felled with an open strike, grab to the throat and simultaneously stomp the back of the knee. This collapses his leg and drives him to the ground.

Illus. 30.3: *Ben seizes Christian about the shoulders from behind.*

Illus. 30.4: *Christian breaks Ben's hold by driving his left elbow into Ben's left arm and his right arm over Ben's right.*

Illus. 30.5: *Christian turns to push his left forearm into Ben's throat while seizing his opponent's left hand with his right.*

Illus. 30.6: *Christian steps into Ben's left knee with his left foot, collapsing the leg.*

Ringeck writes:

"*rab quickly with your right and seize the fingers of his right hand.* [Illus. 30.7] *With your left hand, hit his right arm, which you seized in front, upward. And throw him backward over your left leg.*" [Illus. 30.8]

Christian writes:

Here, both of your hands are used to grab his right arm to provide leverage for a throw. A step forward puts your left leg in position to throw him backward over it. Note that you begin by grabbing his fingers. While there is no express finger-locking technique, should he start to slip free before the arm strike, this puts you in position to prevent this with such techniques.

Illus. 30.7: *With his right hand, Christian grabs the fingers of Ben's right hand.*

Illus. 30.8: *Christian places his left foot behind Ben's right foot and grabs Ben's right elbow. He then pushes Ben's right arm up and back to force him to fall.*

Ringeck writes:

"*Strike his left hand outward with your right.* [Illus. 30.9] *Then with the right hand drive through between his legs and seize him in the back by the doublet or on your elbow. And strike him high with your left hand and push him,* [Illus. 30.10] *so that he falls backwards on his head.*"

Christian writes:

This is a throw using an arm thrust between the opponent's legs, as well as its counter-technique. The opponent's left hand is first moved aside to create an opening. Then drive the right arm between his legs. When doing the throw, you use this arm to lift him off of his feet, which unbalances him; a high strike with the other hand finishes the job.

Illus. 30.9: *With his right hand, Christian strikes Ben's right hand outward.*

Illus. 30.10: *Christian drives his right hand between Ben's legs and grabs ahold of Ben's doublet in the back. While lifting him between the legs, Christian strikes Ben in the upper chest, causing him to fall.*

A counter to the above

"*If he drives through with the right hand between your legs and seizes you in the back at the doublet,* [Illus. 30.11] *bend to him and drive from the outside down with both arms across his right arm, and raise it* [Illus. 30.12] - *then he cannot throw you.*"

The counter-technique focuses on preventing the arm from doing the lifting: you lock your assailant's arm by pulling up on it. I've shown in the photographs how this can also result in a throw of its own.

Illus. 30.11: *Ben tries to throw Christian by lifting him between the legs.*

Illus. 30.12: *Christian prevents Ben's lifting throw by pulling up on his upper arm, thereby locking the elbow joint.*

Ringeck writes:

"*If he has seized one of your hands with both of his and wants to pull you towards him: if he wants to pull you by the left hand on his right side, [Illus. 30.13] then move over his left arm and then under and through to his right side. And take hold of him with the right on the chest and with the left into the back of the knee.*" [Illus. 30.14]

Christian writes:

This counter is a fine example of regaining the initiative. Your opponent seizes a hand, so you step in towards him on the opposite side to throw him over with what is basically yet another application of the first of the *Drei Ringen.*

Illus. 30.13: *Ben grabs Christian's left hand with both of his hands and pulls his opponent toward him.*

Illus. 30.14: *Using momentum from Ben's pulling action, Christian rushes in upon his opponent and throws him with his right arm at the right side of the chest and the other at the left knee.*

Ringeck writes:

"*If he seizes you with both hands at the chest,* [Illus. 30.15] *drive through above with the right hand over his left and hold it fast. With the left, grab his elbow and interlock the right feet.*" [Illus. 30.16]

Christian writes:

This is another example of moving towards an attacker to regain the initiative. The opponent's grab to your chest is countered by stepping around his right foot with you own, while you seize his offending arms. This allows you to wrench him over your leg to the ground.

Illus. 30.15: *Ben grabs Christian at the chest with both hands.*

Illus. 30.16: *Seizing both of Ben's arms, Christian places his right foot behind Ben's right foot and throws him over his leg.*

Ringeck writes:

"*Defense against arm leverage: if he applies an arm lock for you with the right hand,* [Illus. 30.17] *set on with the left.*" [Illus. 30.18]

Christian writes:

In this counter to an arm lock, the free hand "comes to the rescue" of the other arm, essentially out-leveraging your opponent's.

Illus. 30.17: *Ben locks Christian's right arm with one hand behind the elbow and the other at the forearm.*

Illus. 30.18: *Christian defeats Ben's lock by bringing his left arm in to grasp his own arm, thereby strengthening it against the lock.*

Ringeck writes:

"*Grab quickly with both hands, seize him behind both knees, pull them to you, and push him with your head against his chest, thus throwing him backwards to the ground.*" [Illus. 30.19]

Christian writes:

Here is another set of a technique and its counter. The first is a simple matter of pulling both of your opponent's legs out while pushing his upper body backward with your head. In the counter, you prevent the pull away by refusing the attacker both legs, while pushing him earthward by the back of his shoulders.

Illus. 30.19:
Christian grabs both of Ben's legs and pushes his head against his adversary's chest, forcing him to fall backward.

A counter to the eighth technique

"*Grab him from above at the neck through the armpits and hold him fast. Step back with both feet, so that he cannot seize*

Illus. 30.20: *Ben attempts to push Christian backward by grabbing his legs and pushing with the head to his chest.*

Illus. 30.21: *Before Ben can get a good grip, Christian jumps backward with both legs and pushes Ben down by the shoulders. This breaks the technique and pushes his foe to the ground.*

Ringeck writes:

"*If he has his right foot forward, pull his right arm with your left hand* [Illus. 30.22] *and strike to his right ankle, and press it down.* [Illus. 30.23] *Or, move with the right hand to his throat and push him over backwards.*" [Illus. 30.24]

Christian writes:

An opponent's outstretched arm can be grabbed creating an opportunity to step inside and take him off balance. Two conclusions are presented here - in the first, the ankle is collapsed with a stomp of your foot; while in the second, a hand to his throat pushes him over.

Illus. 30.22: *With his left hand, Christian pulls Ben's right arm.*

Illus. 30.23: *Christian steps in with his right foot to stand on Ben's right ankle.*

Illus. 30.24: *Instead of stepping on Ben's ankle, Christian steps in to push against Ben's throat with his right hand.*

Ringeck writes:

"*If he holds you only at the arms, [Illus. 30.25] seize his right arm with your left hand and hold it with your hand inverted. Hold him fast, and strike high with your right. [Illus. 30.26] Then move it through under his right arm and grab him at the chest. With the left hand, grab behind a knee.*" [Illus. 30.27]

Christian writes:

In this counter to an arm grab, you restrain your opponent's right arm, which leaves your own right arm free to work against him. The opponent is then stunned with a strike to his face and grasped about the body. At this point, the left hand releases his right arm and seizes one of the opponent's legs behind the knee. Interestingly, Ringeck is not specific about which knee to use. If you grab the left knee, you can collapse the leg to aid in throwing him down; if you grab the right, you can do more of a hoisting throw. In the photographed technique, I've elected to show the hoist.

Illus. 30.25:
Ben seizes both of Christian's arms.

Illus. 30.26: *Christian grabs Ben's right arm with his left and strikes Ben high with his right hand.*

Illus. 30.27: *After stunning Ben with a strike, Christian releases Ben's right arm and grabs Ben's right leg instead. With his right hand beneath Ben's armpit, Christian hoists his opponent to throw him.*

Eleventh technique - belt grab

Ringeck writes:

"*If he seizes you in the back at the belt,* [Illus. 30.28] *let yourself sink down.* [Illus. 30.29] *If he then wants to pull you up, turn around against him, and throw him over a barrier.*" [Illus. 30.30]

Christian writes:

In response to a grab from behind you can drop and turn around to push your adversary over backwards. This technique calls for a barrier to throw him over. Our location wasn't so equipped, so we've done without.

Illus. 30.28: *Ben grabs Christian's belt from behind.*

Illus. 30.29: *Christian drops down. In response, Ben pulls up hard on Christian's belt.*

Illus. 30.30: *Christian turns Ben's energy against him by turning around quickly and lunging at his chest. This technique would work even better with the presence of a barrier to throw the opponent over, as the technique describes.*

Ringeck writes:

"*Go through with the right hand and seize him above the hip at the side. [Illus. 30.31] Move from above with the left hand through his right armpit and seize his right hand at the wrist. Hold it fast, and raise him high. [Illus. 30.32] And with your right hand lift his left knee, throwing him before you.*" [Illus. 30.33]

Christian writes:

This throw starts by locking the opponent's right arm behind his back. It is then used to throw him. The right hand pulls out the opponent's left leg, facilitating the fall.

Illus. 30.31: *Christian uses his right hand to grab Ben at the left side of his mid-section. This will keep Ben's left arm out of play for a moment.*

Illus. 30.32: *Christian keeps his right hand at Ben's side while grabbing Ben's right hand at the wrist with his left hand. He pushes Ben's arm high behind his back, locking the arm.*

Illus. 30.33: *Christian now moves his right arm down to Ben's left knee and pulls it out from under his foe. A hard push to the locked right arm will now topple Ben over.*

"*Seize his left hand with both hands and pull it to your right side.* [Illus. 30.34] *And step with your right foot behind his right, moving with the right arm to his left side and throwing him over your right leg.*" [Illus. 30.35]

In order to create an opening, the opponent's left hand is pulled hard in this throwing technique. Once his arm is extended, you step into the struggle and take hold of his left side so that you can throw him over your right leg.

Illus. 30.34: *Christian uses both hands to grab Ben's left arm and pull him toward him with it. This creates an opening whereby Christian can move to Ben's inside.*

Illus. 30.35: *Christian passes forward with his right foot, placing it behind Ben's right foot. He wraps his right arm around Ben's chest and throws him over the right leg.*

Ringeck writes:

"If he wants to seize you with both arms under your shoulders, [Illus. 30.36] move also with both arms from the outside down under his elbows, with the arms close. Then tear upward with strength, thus breaking his arms. [Illus. 30.37] You can also seize him by the throat and push him away." [Illus. 30.38]

Christian writes:

This is a very simple, but very nasty technique. Here, your opponent has grabbed you under the armpits, so you drive up from below with both of your arms and push up on his elbows, breaking his arms. The other (and probably less injurious) option is to instead apply pressure to his throat to drive him away.

Illus. **30.36**: *Ben grabs under Christian's armpits with both arms.*

Illus. **30.37**: *Christian drives up from under against the underside of Ben's upper arms, locking and breaking them.*

Illus. **30.38**: *An alternate outcome to the technique – Christian pushes from below against Ben's throat, forcing him away.*

Fifteenth technique - neck leverage

Ringeck writes:

"*If you have your arms above,* [Illus. 30.39] *you can seize him at the throat or at the jaw, breaking his neck over his back.* [Illus. 30.40] *Or, you must move your arms through under his arms.*" [Illus. 30.41]

Christian writes:

This technique describes two options for when you have seized your opponent with your arms above his. You can either force his head backward or drive your arms under his. The second option puts you into position to break his arms by driving up.

Illus. 30.39: *Christian and Ben each grab each other's arms, but Christian's are above Ben's.*

Illus. 30.40: *Christian grasps beneath Ben's jaw and pushes his head backward.*

Illus. 30.41: *In this alternate outcome, Christian drives his arms under Ben's from the outside and pushes up hard to break them.*

Christian writes:

This is a very simple throw over the leg. Step in with your left foot behind his right and push him over backward with a hand to his throat. You could also step with your left foot in front of his right, pulling him forward so that he falls. The availability of both options echoes that of the "wrestling at the sword" that appears in the long sword chapter on *Durchlaufen* – "running through."

Ringeck writes:

"*If you have your left arm down, move your right to his throat, stepping with the left foot behind him and pushing him at the neck over it.* [Illus. 30.42] *Note: You can throw him to both sides over the foot.*"

Illus. 30.42: *Christian places his left foot behind Ben's right and pushes him over with a shove from the right hand against his adversary's throat.*

Ringeck writes:

"*If you drove through with both arms under his arms and he is as large as you are or smaller, seize him around the middle.* [Illus. 30.43] *Close the hands together behind his back and lift him on the left side. And if you think you are capable of doing it, then push him down onto the knee, and so break his back towards you.*" [Illus. 30.44]

Christian writes:

This is a technique requiring you to have the advantage of size, as you lift your opponent bodily and then drop him onto your knee, breaking his back.

Illus. 30.43: *Christian seizes Ben by grabbing him through the armpits and clasping his hands behind Ben's back.*

Illus. 30.44: *Christian lifts Ben and then drops him backward onto his knee, breaking his back.*

A counter to the seventeenth technique

"*If he presses you to him,* [Illus. 30.45] *set your elbow to his throat or chest and press him quickly from you. And pass with the left foot to the rear.*" [Illus. 30.46]

In the counter-technique, you break your opponent's hold with a strong push of your elbow into his throat before he can drop you onto *his* knee.

Illus. 30.45: *Ben grabs Christian around the back.*

Illus. 30.46: *Christian slams his right forearm hard into Ben's throat, forcing Ben to release him.*

Ringeck writes:

"*If he wants to drive through with his head under your arm and throw you over his right shoulder,* [Illus. 30.47] *seize him with the arm at the neck and press him quickly to you. And put your chest on him from above, and push him down with your weight.*" [Illus. 30.48]

Christian writes:

In the chapter on "General Wrestling Techniques," we learned a technique for throwing someone by seizing their right arm and ducking under that arm with your head. Here, we learn a counter to that sort of technique, which is to simply drop with your chest against your opponent, which forces him down.

Illus. 30.47: *Ben seizes Christian's right arm and ducks under it to attempt a shoulder throw.*

Illus. 30.48: *Christian falls chest first onto his opponent, countering the shoulder throw.*

Other Wrestling Techniques

Nineteenth technique - throw from behind against a grab

Ringeck writes:

"*If one seizes you, [Illus. 30.49] and you turn your back to him and quickly raise your arms, bend quickly forward and throw him over you. [Illus. 30.50] Or take him down with a hand at the leg.*" [Illus. 30.51]

Christian writes:

If your opponent grabs you in front, turn around and throw him with a sudden forward bending of your body. Once turned around, you could also pull one of his legs out from under him, causing him to fall.

Illus. 30.49: *Ben grabs Christian, pinning his arms.*

Illus. 30.50: *Christian steps in with his left foot, turning himself around. He bends forward to throw Ben over.*

Illus. 30.51: *In this alternate conclusion to the technique, Christian turns around and lifts Ben's left leg, throwing him backward.*

Other Wrestling Techniques

Ringeck writes:

"*If he seized you from behind and has his arms under your arms* [Illus. 30.52] *and his hands are open, seize a finger (rotating it); then he must release you.*" [Illus. 30.53]

Christian writes:

Very nearly the same as one of the techniques from the chapter on "Counters to Grabs," this technique involves the grabbing of one of his fingers and bending it outward, thereby forcing him to release his hold on you.

Illus. 30.52: *Ben grabs Christian under the arms from behind.*

Illus. 30.53: *Christian grabs one of Ben's fingers and rotates is away, forcing his opponent to release him.*

Ringeck writes:

"*If he seizes and holds you with a hand at the collar,* [Illus. 30.54] *turn with your head under his arm; then he must release you.* [Illus. 30.55] *Or you can also hold him at the same time.*" [Illus. 30.56 & 30.57]

Christian writes:

The twenty-first technique comprises two variations on escaping from a hold at your collar. One is for when your adversary holds you from the front, the other when he holds you from behind. In both cases, duck under one of his arms and force him to release his grip.

Illus. 30.54: *Ben grabs Christian by the collar of the doublet.*

Illus. 30.55: *Christian ducks under and through Ben's arm, breaking the hold at the collar.*

Illus. 30.56: *In this variation on the collar grab counter-technique, Christian grabs the hand that is holding him at the collar.*

Illus. 30.57: *Christian maintains his grip on Ben's hand as he turns to free himself from the collar hold. From here he could break Ben's arm over his shoulder.*

Ringeck writes:

"*Even if he holds you from the rear at the collar, turn up under his arm, then he releases.*"
[Illus. 30.58 & 30.59]

Illus. 30.58: *Ben grabs Christian's collar from behind.*

Illus. 30.59: *Christian breaks the collar hold by ducking his head through under Ben's arm.*

Other Wrestling Techniques

Twenty-second technique - against a hold to the chest

Ringeck writes:

"*If he holds you with both hands at the chest,* [Illus. 30.60] *then push his right elbow upward,* [Illus. 30.61] *push through, and seize him around the waist.*" [Illus. 30.62]

Christian writes:

If your opponent grabs you at the chest, you can jam his right elbow to break his hold on that side. It also creates an opening through which you can grab him about the waist.

Illus. 30.60: *Ben grabs Christian's doublet at the chest.*

Illus. 30.61: *Christian breaks Ben's hold by pushing his right elbow up.*

Illus. 30.62: *After breaking Ben's hold, Christian moves his left hand over Ben's right arm and grabs his opponent about the waist.*

Ringeck writes:

"*If you seized him at the right arm at the biceps and pushed him to the rear,* [Illus. 30.63] *and he then strikes with the right arm over your left hand from the outside and presses his hand firmly to the chest,* [Illus. 30.64] *move with the same elbow into his right side* [Illus. 30.65] *and lower yourself down. Jump with your left foot behind his right, grabbing behind his knee with your right hand and throwing him.*" [Illus. 30.66]

Christian writes:

Use this technique should your opponent push you away with his hand as you try to grip his arm. Drive with your left elbow into his right arm pit and restrain his right leg against your left leg so that you can throw him over your leg.

Illus. 30.63: *Christian grabs Ben's right arm at the biceps.*

Illus. 30.64: *Ben pushes Christian away with a push of his right hand to Christian's chest.*

Illus. 30.65: *Christian jams his left elbow up into Ben's right armpit.*

Illus. 30.66: *Christian steps with his left foot to place it behind Ben's right foot. With his right hand, he restrains Ben's leg against his own while pushing Ben up and back with his left arm, thus throwing him backward.*

Chapter 31
Zulauffend Ringen

This chapter makes up the third and final section of the manuscript's wrestling techniques. As with the second section, the appearance of the words *"hie heben,"* "here begins," is a clue that we are in a new section. But this time there is a very clear reason for these techniques to be grouped together – each of them should be used when approaching your opponent. They are quick ways to take your opponent down as you come to grips. Some seem to require quite a bit of speed or power to make them work, as they throw your opponent backward by pushing his arms up and back, or slamming your head into his chest. Others will be familiar as they have direct analogues in the other wrestling chapters, particularly the three techniques that involve seizing an arm and then ducking beneath it.

We are not yet done with wrestling; *Ringen* is fundamental to all aspects of Liechtenauer's art and we will see *armoured* wrestling both on foot and on horseback in later chapters.

Ringeck writes:

"*Grab his right arm and his left* [Illus. 31.1] *and release the left. Loop your right arm around his left* [Illus. 31.2] *and throw him over his head.*" [Illus. 31.3]

Christian writes:

You can perform this throw by simply looping an arm around your opponent's arm, thus locking that arm.

Illus. 31.1: *While running towards Ben, Christian grabs both of his arms.*

Illus. 31.2: *Releasing his right hand's grip, Christian loops his right arm around Ben's left arm to lock the arm.*

Illus. 31.3: *Christian throws Ben over by his arms.*

Ringeck writes:

"*If he seized you under both arms,* [Illus. 31.4] *thrust your right arm under his left, setting your hand on his chest and throwing him from you.*" [Illus. 31.5]

Christian writes:

This technique should look familiar: the hand press that is used here to free you from your opponent's grip is the same one that your opponent uses at the beginning of the twenty-third "other wrestling technique" in chapter 29.

Illus. 31.4: *Ben grabs Christian under the arms.*

Illus. 31.5: *Christian press his right hand against Ben's chest, breaking his opponent's grip.*

Ringeck writes:

"*Loop your left arm around his neck, raising his left leg and throwing him on the right side.*" [Illus. 31.6]

Christian writes:

This too should be familiar, as it is very much like the first and second technique from the *Drei Ringen*, chapter 24. To perform the technique, you pull your opponent over by his neck while pulling out one of his legs. The only difference here is that the arm loops around the neck, as opposed to pressing straight against it.

Illus. 31.6: *Christian throws Ben by looping his left arm about Ben's neck and pulling out the right leg with his right hand.*

Ringeck writes:

"*Seize his right hand with your left,* [Illus. 31.7] *running through under his arm and grabbing him with the right hand at the right leg, throwing him over you.*" [Illus. 31.8]

Christian writes:

This is essentially the same technique as the "Throw Over the Shoulder" from chapter 23. After grabbing your foe's right arm, you duck under that arm and pull out his leg, while simultaneously jamming your shoulder hard into his side, thus throwing him.

Illus. 31.7: *Christian seizes Ben's right hand while approaching him.*

Illus. 31.8: *Passing quickly beneath Ben's right arm, Christian pulls out Ben's right leg and press his shoulder into his opponent's side to throw him.*

Ringeck writes:

"*Grab his right arm with both hands, passing through under his arm and throwing him over you.*" [Illus. 31.9]

Christian writes:

This is simply a variation on the previous technique. This time, you don't pull out his leg, but keep both hands on his arm as you effect the throw. If your opponent resists the throw, his arm breaks over your upper back.

Illus. 31.9: *Christian grabs Ben's right arm with both of his hands. Passing beneath the seized arm, he presses his shoulder into Ben's side to throw him.*

Ringeck writes:

"If you approach, then bend. Grab him at a leg, tearing it upward and striking him with your left hand, so that he falls." [Illus. 31.10]

Christian writes:

This is yet another variation on the *Drei Ringen* theme. The throw is accomplished by using a leg pull in conjunction with a high strike.

Illus. 31.10: *As Christian approaches Ben, he seizes and lifts his right leg while striking him high on the body, thus throwing him over.*

Zulauffend Ringen
Seventh wrestling while closing

Ringeck writes:

"*While approaching, seize both of his arms and strike him with your head against his chest* [Illus. 31.11] *so that he falls on his back.*"

Christian writes:

This not-so-subtle throw requires considerable force, so it's understandable that it appears in this section, whose techniques require forward momentum. By pushing your opponent's arms up and back while head-butting his chest, you can throw him backward.

Illus. 31.11: *Christian throws Ben backward by forcing his arms up and back while head-butting him.*

Ringeck writes:

"*If he seizes you at the shoulders,* [Illus. 31.12] *strike down at his arms with your hands and press them apart.* [Illus. 31.13] *And seize him to wrestle with whatever technique you like.*"

Christian writes:

This is a simple method for breaking your opponent's hold on your shoulders: strike down on his arms and he will release you. Your arms and hands are now "inside" of his own, which have been knocked down and wide, giving you an advantage in time and position to counter-grab him.

Illus. 31.12: *Ben grabs Christian at the shoulders.*

Illus. 31.13: *Christian breaks Ben's hold by striking his arms from above.*

Zulauffend Ringen
Ninth wrestling while closing

Ringeck writes:

"*Grab him with both hands from below* [Illus. 31.14] *and set both elbows into both his arms. Push your head against his chest, and seize him at both legs.*" [Illus. 31.15]

Christian writes:

Once again, the head is used to propel your adversary backward. You first create an opening by grabbing his arms and forcing them up. This also lifts his center of gravity up, and helps shift his balance backwards. This gives you te chance to drop and pull out his legs while smashing your head into his chest, causing him to fall.

Illus. 31.14: *Christian grabs and forces Ben's arms up.*

Illus. 31.15: *Christian ducks down, seizes both of Ben's legs and head-butts him in the chest, causing him to fall backward.*

Ringeck writes:

"*Grab both his hands and throw him on his back.*"
[Illus. 31.16]

Christian writes:

This technique would seem to require a lot of power, and the element of surprise. Grabbing both of your adversary's hands, you force his arms backward to topple him over.

Illus. 31.16: *Christian forces Ben to fall by rushing him and pushing his arms back.*

Ringeck writes:

"Watch how you approach him while running. Grab his right arm with both hands, passing through and breaking the arm." [Illus. 31.17]

Christian writes:

This is a less gentle version of the fifth technique. Rather than using the arm lock to facilitate the throw, the lock is continued until the opponent's arm breaks.

Illus. 31.17: *Christian grabs Ben's right arm with both hands and breaks the arm over his upper back.*

Ringeck writes:

"*If you approach and seize him at the chest and he does the same,* [Illus. 31.18] *strike his arms down* [Illus. 31.19] *and push behind his left arm with your left hand. Seize a leg with your right hand and throw him.*" [Illus. 31.20]

Christian writes:

When your opponent has met your grab to his chest with one of his own, break his hold by striking down onto his arms as in the eighth technique. You can then perform a hoisting throw by using one hand to grab his left arm and the other to grab the left leg.

Illus. 31.18: *Christian and Ben each grab the other at the chest.*

Illus. 31.19: *Christian breaks Ben's hold by striking down his arms.*

Illus. 31.20: *Christian throws Ben by grabbing at his left arm and leg and tossing him over.*

Ringeck writes:

"If he seizes you at the arms and you grab him also, [Illus. 31.21] *then release his right arm. Grab him at the left arm through between his legs* [Illus. 31.22] *and lift him on the shoulder. And throw him, as you wish."* [Illus. 31.23]

Christian writes:

This is another mutual grab scenario. When you and your opponent grab each other's arms, you can free up your left hand to grab between his legs. From this, you can do a lifting throw over your shoulder.

Illus. 31.21: *Christian and Ben grab each other at the arms.*

Illus. 31.22: *Christian releases his left hand's grip and drives that hand between Ben's legs.*

Illus. 31.23: *Christian throws Ben over by hoisting him between the legs.*

Ringeck writes:

"*If he grabs you under the armpit,* [Illus. 31.24 & Illus. 31.25] *push the arm with the right hand from you* [Illus. 31.26] *and then grab and wrestle.*"

Christian writes:

This technique is billed as a counter to the thirteenth technique, although it really seems to be more of a counter to a counter-technique. Assuming its relationship to the thirteenth technique isn't spurious, I've assumed that your opponent thwarts your attempt to throw him with a hand between his legs by grabbing you under the armpit. His counter can then be overcome by locking his offending arm. This sets up any number of other follow-on techniques.

Illus. 31.24: *Christian drives his left hand between Ben's legs to begin the throw.*

Illus. 31.26: *Christian in turn counters Ben's counter by locking Ben's left arm and driving him to the ground.*

Illus. 31.25: *Ben counters the throw by driving his left hand under Christian's armpit.*

Illus. 32.1: *The face is an excellent target should your opponent fight with his visor raised. Were the visor lowered, the eye slits would still present a target. The armour pictured here also ha*
two-piece defense for the head: the skull and upper half of the face are defended by the helmet, a long-tailed sallet, while the lower half of the face and neck are defended by a bevor. The intersec
of the sallet and bevor might present a gap through which you could also thrust.

Chapter 32
Vulnerabilities of a Man in Armour

Ringeck writes:

"*In St. George's name, here the art begins.*
"*Here the serious fighting begins on horse and on foot. Here is Master Johannes Liechtenauer's fencing in harness, which he wrote down in secret words. This is included in this book, laid out and explained, so that every fighter who already understands fencing can understand this art.*"

As in the beginning of the long sword section, Ringeck's presentation of Liechtenauer's *harnischfechten* ("armoured combat"), begins with the words "In Saint George's name," an invocation of one of the patron saints of warriors. Although this introductory passage is followed by the techniques for fighting with spears, I've elected to instead present the admonitions on how to target an armoured man first. This is a critical section of the armoured combat commentaries as it explains why all the techniques we are about to see deal with thrusting (and the occasional bludgeoning) rather than cutting. A working knowledge of the effective targets on a man in armour is essential for understanding how to use the techniques of spear and sword fighting that follow.

These two passages list the openings you should attack when facing a man wearing full armour and advocates using the point of the weapon in attacking those targets. By Ringeck's time--the mid-15th century--men-at-arms were wore substantial defensive armour. Almost the entire body was protected by plate, with the joints defended by sections of maille. A padded arming doublet served as a foundation garment for the armour and afforded additional protection. Against these three layers, a swinging blow from a long sword could do little. However, the point, especially on an acutely tapered long sword, could be used to exploit gaps in the armour, even where mail protected those gaps. Hence, Master Ringeck advocates those gaps as targets. Should the helmet's visor be raised for better vision and ventilation (and we see illustrations in various *fechtbücher* where this is so), the face becomes an obvious target. Even with the visor lowered, the *occularia*, or eye slits, present an entry point for a sword's point. The other areas--the groin, armpits, back of the knee and palms of the gauntlets--are all places where the motility of the armour requires that there be gaps. Ringeck advises to always use the point, regardless of the weapon being wielded, against these vulnerable targets on an armoured man.

Liechtenauer writes:

"*Leather and gauntlets and the eyes: the openings that you really should seek.*"

Ringeck writes:

This means: If you want to attack a man in harness, you must find his vulnerabilities quickly. At first try to strike him in the face, [Illustr. 32.1] and also in the armpits, [Illustr. 32.2] in his palms [Illustr. 32.3] or from the rear into the gauntlets, [Illustr. 32.4] or into the back of the knee, [Illustr. 32.5] between his legs [Illustr. 32.6] and at all limb joints, [Illustr. 32.7] inside where his harness has its' articulations. Because in these places it is best to strike. And you are to know exactly how you can strike these weaknesses so that you do not search for a farther one, when you could strike a closer one more easily. Practice with all of the weapons that are used in battle."

Illus. 32.2:
When a man-at-arms raises his arm to strike his armpit is vulnerable. Even very large besagews (the round plates defending the armpit) of this German harness allow some entry for a sword's point.

Illus. 32.3:
The palms of the hands are always a good target. It is impossible to defend this part of the hand because a combatant must have a good grip on his weapons.

Illus. 32.4:
You can cause grim injuries if you succeed in driving your point into your opponent's gauntlet through the back of the gauntlet's cuff.

Liechtenauer writes:

"*Remember, with all weapons: the point against the body's openings.*"

Ringeck writes:

"*That is, with all three weapons that are used in the fight, you should always thrust with the point to the openings, as has been previously mentioned. Otherwise, you will give yourself a disadvantage.*"

Illus. 32.5:
The back of the knee was usually unprotected in this period, so it is vulnerable. However, this is a hard to reach target.

Illus. 32.6:
The groin, although protected by maille, is vulnerable to strong blows and assaults with the sword's point.

Illus. 32.7:
A man wearing armour is vulnerable wherever there are articulations at the joints. Here, the inside of the elbow is shown.

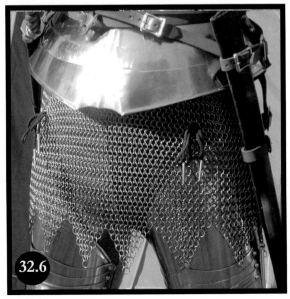

Illus. 33.1: *In the midst of a closing maneuver, Christian applies one of the Vier Leger, moving into Ochs for a thrust at Ben's face.*

Chapter 33
Combat with the Spear

In what seems to be a description of the weapons allowed or required in a judicial duel, Ringeck says that each armoured combatant should have a spear, a sword and a dagger. While this chapter describes the use of the spear and others will detail the use of the sword, no dagger work is included in the manuscript.[1]

The spear is the first of the three weapons that should be employed. It can be either thrown at your adversary or wielded with both hands to thrust to him. Ringeck therefore details two "positions" for use with the spear: standing at the ready to throw the weapon, and the other in preparation to thrust. For a throw, the weapon is held high in a position akin to *Ochs* from the long sword teachings. If you don't throw your spear, you can thrust with it from a "lower guard," which is like *Pflug*, or from the "upper guard," which is like *Ochs*. These two guards translate well to spear fencing - the spear is a thrusting weapon, and these are the long sword thrusting guards.

Other primary techniques from the long sword teachings are used with the spear such as *Zucken*, *Winden*, and *Durchlaufen*. We see the same tactical approach and the same mechanics of long sword fencing in action: use strength against weakness and weakness against strength, wind to find other targets if your first target is denied, and out-time your enemy with the traveling after. So there is much the same to fighting with the spear as with the long sword. The key differences are that the spear is an exclusively thrusting weapon, and that having your hands splayed makes fighting from guards only on the right side preferable.

---

[1] Well, *almost* no dagger work appears - there is one passage in the mounted combat techniques that advises you to take your opponent's dagger or other weapon and turn it against him.

Liechtenauer writes:

"When the fighting begins on foot, it starts with the spear. The two stand and raise to their right to defend.

"Spear and point thrust before. Thrust with strength, spring, wind, set truly on. If he defends, twitch: set it to his face."

Ringeck writes:

"If two fight together on foot in harness, each should have three weapons: a spear, a sword and a dagger. And the beginning of the fight should employ the spear. So you are to prepare for the first attack with two basic positions, as will be explained."

Christian writes:

This passage specifies the weapons that should be used in the fight - spear, sword, and dagger. Liechtenauer's verse says that the spear is the first weapon of the three to be used and suggests that both guards with the spear (essentially *Ochs* and *Pflug*).

Illus. 33.2: *Christian advances on his opponent with his left foot forward, his spear held at the ready for a throw.*

Ringeck writes:

"*hen you have both dismounted, stand with the left foot forward and hold the spear ready to throw.* [Illus. 33.2 p. 292] *And move closer to him in such a way that the left foot always remains in front. Wait until you can cast it before he can throw his.* [Illus. 33.3] *Follow the throw immediately with the sword, so that he cannot set a safe cast against you. Then grasp the sword.* [Illus. 33.4]

Christian writes:

This is the method for throwing the spear at your opponent.[2] Because the spear must be held at the right side of the body, it is important that you always keep your left foot forward as you advance upon your enemy.[3] Once you have cast your spear, rush in upon him with your sword drawn and held at the half-sword.[4] This is so you can catch your opponent off-guard should he deflect your thrown spear.

Illus. 33.3: *Christian casts his spear at Ben.*

Illus. 33.4: *Ben deflects Christian's spear cast while Christian sets upon him with his long sword held at the half-sword.*

[2] Readers may wonder at the likelihood of a cast spear penetrating heavy armour. The likelihood is virtually nil. However, a cast spear striking the visor could hit with considerable concussive force, and thus could not simply be ignored. Against an exposed face it could be lethal. Thus, the thrown spear serves as a useful distraction, while the attacker closes with his sword.

The judicial duel on foot was an ancient tradition amongst the Germans, extending at least into the "Barbarian Migration" era of the 5th and 6th century CE. It is possible that the cast spear was a ritualized, hold-over from an earlier period.

3 In the Liechtenauer tradition, *all* strikes from the right begin with the left foot forward, and are made with a passing step.

[4] It is interesting to note that some *fechtbücher* show the sword already drawn, and held *with* the spear. This is the case in at least four of Talhoffer's *fechtbücher* [Gotha, Forschungsbibliothek, Ms. Chart A558 1443; Berlin Kuperstchkabinett/ Preudischer Kulturebesitz 78A 15 1459; Copenhagen Det Kongelige Bibliotek Thott 290 2 1459; Muchen Cod. icon 394a 1467].

Ringeck writes:

"*If you do not want to throw your spear, then hold it apart from your right side in the lower guard and go in such a way to him.* [Illus. 33.5] *And thrust it courageously from below to his face, before he does the same.* [Illus. 33.6] *If he thrusts at the same time or displaces,* [Illus. 33.7] *then move high into the upper guard. Thus his point stays at your left arm.* [Illus. 33.8] *Thrust the point immediately over his arm and into his face.* [Illus. 33.9] *If he moves up then and displaces with the left arm,* [Illus. 33.10] *then jerk down and set the point into his left armpit.*" [Illus. 33.11]

Christian writes:

The second position shows the method for wielding the spear in hand-to-hand combat.[5] You can thrust from a lower guard, which corresponds to *Pflug*. If he displaces, simply wind to move into the upper guard, which is like the guard *Ochs*.[6] If that too is displaced, pull your spear out of the bind and thrust to his armpit. This is yet another application of the tactic of luring your opponent to over-commit to the defense of one target while exposing another.

Illus. 33.5: *Both men hold their spears in the lower guard, or Pflug.*

Illus. 33.6: *Christian thrusts his spear from the lower guard into Ben's face.*

5 Whereas the cast spear might be ineffective against an armoured man, when gripped in both hands, it becomes a real threat

[6] We have seen this simple transition from *Pflug* to *Ochs* many times before. For other examples of this same principle, look at the *absetzen*, chapter 12.

Illus. 33.7: *Christian thrusts at Ben, who displaces.*

Illus. 33.8: *Christian winds his spear up into the upper guard, or Ochs. Note how he keeps Ben's spear on his left hand as he raises his weapon.*

Illus. 33.9:
Christian attacks Ben's face.

Illus. 33.10: *Alternatively, Christian thrusts, but his spear is caught and displaced by Ben's left hand and spear.*

Illus. 33.11:
Christian jerks his spear out of the displacement to thrust to Ben's left armpit.

Liechtenauer writes:

"*When you thrust, the twitching learn against a counter.*"

Ringeck writes:

This means: If you thrust from the lower guard, and he displaces you with the spear, whose point passes laterally beside you, [Illus. 33.12] *then 'twitch through'* [Illus. 33.13] *and thrust him to the other side.* [Illus. 33.14] *Or remain in the second displacement with the point before his face and do not twitch.* [Illus. 33.15] *Remain with the spear at his and wind to the next opening which becomes exposed to you.*" [Illus. 33.16]

Christian writes:

This technique uses the concept of "twitching" (*Zucken*) from the long sword teachings but adapted to spear fencing. In this case, the *Zucken* is actually like a hybrid of two long sword concepts: "twitching" (*Zucken*) and "changing through" (*Durchwechseln*). With a long sword, you "twitch" when you strike from a bind to the other side of your opponent's body. Because the spear is not swung, it must be slid back out of the bind with your opponent's spear. In that respect it is somewhat like a "changing through," except that the point cannot disengage from the bind the way a long sword's point can; rather, it must be pulled straight back, or "twitched through."

Illus. 33.12: *Christian thrusts to Ben, but Ben displaces the thrust with his spear extended.*

Illus. 33.13: *Christian twitches out of the bind with Ben's spear.*

Illus. 33.14: *Christian follows the twitching with a thrust to Ben's right side.*

The technique also shows how one can wind at the spear to find another opening to attack. Rather than the eight windings of the long sword, a weapon like a spear has only four - two above, associated with the upper guard (*Ochs*), and two below, associated with the lower guard (*Pflug*). This is because Ringeck presents only right-side guards. In this way, he insures that the spear's point will always present a threat to the opponent. Another consequence of this bias that affects winding is that you can only change from an upper winding to a lower one on either side of the opponent's weapon; you can't switch from a left guard to a right one while binding as you can with the long sword.

Illus. 33.15: *Once more, Ben displaces a thrust from Christian's spear.*

Illus. 33.16: *Christian winds his spear in the bind to find another opening to attack.*

Liechtenauer writes:

"*If he moves to depart and will flee, so should you go after him. Stay surely on his trail.*"

Ringeck writes:

Note: this means: If you thrust and he displaces you [Illus. 33.17] and wants to free himself from the bind, [Illus. 33.18] follow immediately after him with the point. Hit him with it and so push him back. [Illus. 33.19] If he wants to flee backwards now before your thrust and thereby turns his side to you, run at this side and grab him using wrestling grapples and arm breaks, [Illus. 33.20] as you will find described in the following."

Christian writes:

This is another primary long sword technique adapted for fighting with the spear. If your opponent pulls back from a bind with your spear, travel after (*Nachreisen*) him with your point. Should he then retreat, this is an opportunity to *travel after* and use a wrestling technique.

Illus. 33.17: *Christian and Ben are once again in a bind.*

Illus. 33.18: *Ben moves his spear to his right to free it from the bind.*

Illus. 33.19: *Seizing an opportunity, Christian thrusts his spear to Ben and pushes him back.*

Illus. 33.20: *Ben moves to retreat from Christian's attack, so Christian drops his spear and seizes his opponent by the arm to begin grappling.*

Chapter 37
Sword against Spear

This short section of Ringeck's commentaries deals with a scenario where you have cast your spear at your opponent, but he retains his. The sword is used to get safely past his longer reaching weapon. In the first passage you do this by setting aside his spear's thrust with your sword held at the half-sword; that is, with your right hand holding your sword's grip and with your left hand grasping the blade in the middle. Once you have set aside his attack, you can then close to thrust to him with your sword's point. The other option, treated in the second passage, is to release your left hand from your sword and use it to either slap aside or grab his spear. Again, once this has been done, you "travel after" him with your sword to attack him with the point. As Ringeck admonishes us elsewhere,[1] all attacks against a man in full armour are with the point, regardless of whether the weapon is a sword or spear.

---

[1] See "Vulnerabilities of a Man in Armour," chapter 32.

Liechtenauer writes:

"*If he displaces it, the sword against the spear is drawn. The thrust is caught. Jump, move, grapple quickly with him.*"

Ringeck writes:

"*If you have cast your spear and he keeps his, put yourself into the following position: grab your sword with the left hand in the center of the blade and hold it before you at your left knee in the guard.* [Illus. 34.1] *Or, hold it next to your right side in the lower guard.* [Illus. 34.2]

"*If he thrusts then too above with the spear, then move up and parry the thrust in front of your left hand with the sword on your left side, and jump towards him, and attack with the point.* [Illus. 34.3] *If that is not possible, then let your sword fall and start wrestling.*"

Christian writes:

If you have chosen to throw your spear at your opponent and he deflects the throw with his own, you must now deal with the threat posed by his spear. The long sword can be held at the half-sword (*halbschwert*), with the right hand at the grip and the left holding the blade in the middle, to deflect any attacks from your adversary's spear. You can best do this by intercepting his thrust on the part of your blade that is in front of your left hand.

Illus. 34.1: *Christian stands on guard against Ben's spear with his sword held at the half-sword over his left knee. This is one of the primary half-sword guards.*

Illus. 34.2: *Christian passes forward with his right leg to displace Ben's spear-thrust on the sword blade ahead of his left hand.*

Illus. 34.3: *Christian now passes forward with his left leg. This pulls his sword clear from Ben's spear and allows him to thrust his point to Ben's face.*

Liechtenauer writes:

"The extended with the left hand hit. Jump deliberately, and this grasp. If he wants to jerk away and depart, grasp and press in, and to the opening with the sword point attack."

Ringeck writes:

"If you are in the lower guard and he thrusts from above at you, and he holds the spear in such a way that the point extends far in front of his hand, [Illus. 34.4] then strike his spear down with your left hand held laterally. [Illus. 34.5] Grab your sword again immediately with the left hand, jump towards him and attack him with the point." [Illus. 34.6]

Christian writes:

These are two ways to counter your opponent's spear thrust by using one of your hands. The first is a slapping action with the back of your left gauntlet that clears his spear of you so that you can advance and attack. The second is a grab to his spear – the opponent's natural reaction is to try and jerk his spear from your grasp, providing an opportunity to push his spear up and open your opponent up to the counterattack.

Illus. 34.4:
Christian stands in the half-sword guard at his right side as Ben begins to thrust his spear from above with his point extended far out in front of his hands. Note that Christian's guard with the half-sword looks like the long sword guard Pflug, while Ben's guard with the spear looks much like Ochs.

Illus. 34.5: *Ben thrusts at Christian, who deflects the thrust with the back of his gauntlet-clad left hand.*

Illus. 34.6: *With Ben's spear safely set aside, Christian passes forward with his right foot to thrust to the back of Ben's shoulder.*

Ringeck writes:

ℭote: If he thrusts down with the spear to the groin, then grab his spear with the left hand and hold it. At the same time thrust down at him with the right hand to the genitals.[2] [Illus. 34.7] *And if he then pulls his spear strongly and wants to tear it from your hand,* [Illus. 34.8] *press his spear high over him* [Illus. 34.9] *and release it: thus he opens himself up. Grab your sword immediately again with the left hand, follow him and attack him with the point."* [Illus. 34.10]

Illus. 34.7:
Ben thrusts down to Christian's groin. Christian grabs the point of Ben's spear to thwart Ben's attack and delivers his own attack to Ben's groin with the point of the sword.

Illus. 34.8 (left):
Here, Ben prevents the thrust to his groin by passing back with his right foot. He pulls his spear backward to try to break Christian's grasp.

Illus. 34.10 (below):
Christian grasps his sword blade with his left hand and thrusts behind Ben's shoulder defense.

Illus. 34.9:
Retaining his grip on Ben's spear, Christian passes forward with his right foot and presses the spear upward.

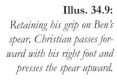

[2] Besides the obvious "flinch factor" of someone attacking your genitals, remember that there is no rigid protection for the groin - only a small flap of mail. Even a blow that did not penetrate the mail, would strike with a great deal of force...

#
Chapter 35
Kampfringen

Kampfringen--"combat wrestling"--is the art of wrestling in armour. The two techniques included in this section are more "muscular" versions of wrestling techniques that appear in the unarmoured wrestling chapters. They are two simple throws over the leg, one directed to your opponent's left, the other to his right. Each technique has the option of throwing him over your leg or of also bringing your other leg into play to clamp his leg in place, thereby limiting his escape options. This option also includes a blow to the opponent's head to unbalance and distract him.

The dynamic between the attack to your opponent's left leg and that directed against his right echoes the relationship between the first and second of the *Drei Ringen*--chapter 24--in the unarmoured wrestling section. When you can't throw your man to one side, keep closing with him by passing forward and try to throw him from the other side. That the throw over your right leg is the first option is easily explained: should you wish to switch to wrestling when wielding your spear or sword, you probably are in a left leg leading stance, which implies that your next step forward will be with your right leg. Thus, the right leg is the easier of the two to bring into play for grappling.

Illus. 35.1:
Christian and Ben begin grappling by seizing each other's arms.

Liechtenauer writes:

"*If you will wrestle, behind the leg to the right learn to jump, force a bar in place, which before the leg skillfully closes.*"

Ringeck writes:

This means: *If you approach him to wrestle, you are to know how you are to step in front or in back of his leg, and by taking only one step to do so.*

"*If you seize him and he you, pay attention to which foot he puts forward.* [Illus. 35.1 p. 304] *If he has the left foot forward, strike him on his left side with your right hand.* [Illus. 35.2] *As you strike him aside, jump with your right foot behind his left, and press your right knee to the back of his knee. And tear him backward over the knee with both hands.*" [Illus. 35.3]

Christian writes:

This passage details two methods for throwing an armoured man over your right leg. The first is to simply place your right leg behind his left leg and use both of your hands to wrench your opponent over it. The other is to put your right leg behind his left leg and then use your left leg to further constrain his left leg. A head strike is used with this variation to unbalance your foe before toppling him. It underlines the need to move quickly to the opponent's right, gettting into position behind his right knee for a throw.

Illus. 35.2: *Christian releases the grip of his right hand and strikes Ben's left arm from the outside with it.*

Illus. 35.3: *Christian passes forward to place his right leg behind Ben's left leg. With both hands, he tears Ben over his leg.*

<u>Ringeck writes</u>:

"⊙*r try the following: if you jump with your right foot behind his left, then go with the left to between his legs. Clamp his left knee between your legs and hold him.* [Illus. 35.4] *Strike him with the left hand in front against the forehead,* [Illus. 35.5] *and with the right pull him to the rear."* [Illus. 35.6]

Illus. 35.4: *Christian clamps Ben's left leg between his legs. The placement of Christian's left leg allow no avenue of escape for his left leg.*

Illus. 35.5: *Christian strikes Ben's head with his left hand while grasping his shoulder.*

Illus. 35.6: *Christian pulls Ben backward over his right leg with his hand.*

Liechtenauer writes:

"*From both hands, if you with art succeed to end.*"

Ringeck writes:

This means that you are to master all wrestling techniques from both sides, so that you can handle everything that he tries against you. If you jumped thus with the right leg behind his left and he back pedals then with his left foot, then follow immediately after him to the other side with your left foot behind his right. And throw him over the knee, [Illus. 35.7] or lock his knee with both legs, [Illus. 35.8] as was described before."

Christian writes:

Many of Liechtenauer's methods work from both the left and right sides. This is an example of that symmetry: if your adversary evades your attempt to throw him over your right leg, you follow him and throw him over your left leg instead. This is an armoured version of the second of the "Three Wrestlings" (*Drei Ringen*) that we saw in the unarmoured wrestling portion of this book.

Illus. 35.7: *Christian has passed forward to place his left leg behind Ben's right leg and throws his foe over it with both hands.*

Illus. 35.8: *Christian now performs the same throw over the left leg but with his right leg restraining Ben's leg from the front.*

Chapter 36
Verborgnen Ringen

Liechtenauer writes:

"The forbidden wrestling should you learn to use. To finish find: the strong thereby to overthrow."

Ringeck writes:

"This means: If he rushes in, then let your sword fall and work carefully the wrestling techniques that apply to combat fencing. One is not to teach or present these at publicly accessible fencing schools, as all wise masters of the sword have realized, because they are used for fighting in earnest. And those are arm breaks, leg breaks, groin strikes, murder strikes, knee strikes, finger breaks, eye gouges and others."

The *Verborgnen Ringen*--"Secret Wrestling"--comprises several methods for use against an armoured man. These methods are harsher than the throwing techniques of the last chapter. The first technique is a relatively simple throw, but the others employ pain compliance, the *Beinbruch* (leg breaks) and *Mortstöße* (murder strikes) presented in the unarmoured wrestling chapters. Any of these attacks or counters could be used to "soften up" or momentarily distract (with pain) an opponent so that you could finish him with a dagger.

Ringeck writes:

"*If he seizes you and you want to strongly pull or push him, then strike your right arm outside and over his left, a little behind his hand.* [Illus. 36.1] *Press his arm with both hands to the chest, jump with the right foot behind his left and throw him over the knee.*" [Illus. 36.2]

Christian writes:

This is a variation on a technique that appears frequently in Ringeck's work – the throw over the leg. Here, you break your adversary's hold on you and pin his left hand against his chest effecting the throw over your right leg.

Illus. 36.1: *In response to Ben's grab to his arms, Christian strikes aside his opponent's left arm with a blow of his right hand.*

Illus. 36.2: *A forward pass of his right leg brings his knee behind Ben's left. Christian seizes Ben's left hand with both of his and presses the hand to his foe's chest, throwing him over his right knee.*

Ringeck writes:

"*If he grabs you and does not hold firmly,* [Illus. 36.3] *seize his right hand with your right,* [Illus. 36.4] *and pull him with your left hand to you and grab his elbow.* [Illus. 36.5] *Step with the left foot in front of his right and pull him over it.* [Illus. 36.6] *Or fall with your chest against his arm and break it thus.*" [Illus. 36.7]

Christian writes:

This is another throw done in connection with an elbow lock. This time the left leg is placed before the opponent's right leg that you can throw him onto his face. Before you do this, lock the right elbow, enabling the option of breaking the right arm.

Illus. 36.3: *Ben grabs Christian's right arm with his left hand but fails to gain a good grasp on it.*

Illus. 36.4: *Christian breaks the grip and seizes Ben's right arm with his right hand.*

Illus. 36.5: *Christian places his left foot before Ben's right foot and throws Ben forward by pressing hard against the joint locked right arm.*

Illus. 36.6: *In this alternate conclusion, Christian brings his chest down hard upon Ben's locked right arm, breaking it.*

Illus. 36.7: *Christian grabs Ben's left arm with his right hand.*

Ringeck writes:

"*Grab his left arm with your left just above the hand and pull him to you.* [Illus. 36.8] *Strike your right arm with strength over his left into the crook of his arm,* [Illus. 36.9] *and using your left hand break his left hand over your right.* [Illus. 36.10] *Jump with the right foot behind his right and throw him over.*" [Illus. 36.11]

Christian writes:

Here is one more way to throw your opponent over your legs. First, you break his left hand (likely at the wrist) by immobilizing his arm with your right and then smashing his hand down with your left. By retaining the grip on the wounded arm and stepping the right leg behind your opponent's right, he can be thrown backward.

Illus. 36.8: *Christian grabs Ben's left arm with his right hand.*

Illus. 36.9: *Christian thrusts his right arm over Ben's left elbow joint.*

Illus. 36.10: *Enveloping and constraining Ben's left arm with his right, Christian strikes with his left hand to Ben's right to break the hand at the wrist.*

Illus. 36.11: *Pulling the injured hand towards Ben's right shoulder, Christian jumps with his right foot behind Ben's right and throws him.*

Ringeck writes:

"Ꝺꝺꝼen he moves his left arm under your right and wants to seize you around the body, [Illus. 36.12] strike with the right arm strongly from above and outside into his left elbow joint, turning from him." [Illus. 36.13]

Christian writes:

This counter-technique is a very simple arm lock. Your opponent invites the technique by putting his arm under yours.

Illus. 36.12: *Ben grabs Christian under the right arm with his left hand.*

Illus. 36.13: *Christian steps back with his left foot, pivoting sharply on his right. As he does so, he presses his right hand hard against Ben's left elbow. As Ben has his hand under Christian's right arm.*

<u>Ringeck writes</u>:

"*If he has seized you at the arms and you him, and he is standing with an outstretched leg, then step on that knee. Thus you break his leg.*" [Illus. 36.14]

<u>Christian writes</u>:

This is a hyperextension of your opponent's knee. While a plate armour leg defense offers some protection against such harmful motion, the weight of an armoured man's body would likely overcome it.

Illus. 36.14: *Both men have grabbed each other's arms. Christian steps on Ben's knee to hyperextend the knee joint backward.*

Ringeck writes:

"*Y*ou *can also strike with the knee or the foot into the genitals,* [Illus. 36.15] *if it is possible for you. But be sure that he cannot get a hold of your leg.*"

Christian writes:

Whether one is fighting in harness or without, a blow to the groin is always unpleasant. Techniques like this create a moment of sharp pain; the distraction creates a window of opportunity through which one can deliver a more devastating attacks.

Illus. 36.15: *Christian jams his knee vigorously into Ben's groin. The flexible maille defense there is insufficient to protect against the trauma and pain resulting from such a strike.*

<u>Ringeck writes</u>:

"*If he grabs with open hands or with outstretched fingers after you, then try to grab his fingers. Break them upward,* [Illus. 36.16] *and you can lead him to the edge of the list. You also weaken him in this way on that side and win a greater advantage.*"

<u>Christian writes</u>:

A finger bent backward is another source of pain and distraction. Note that the seizing of a single finger, as prescribed here, is only possible against someone wearing fingered gauntlets – a mitten gauntlet allows no such purchase, but alternatively the cuff can be grasped, which while not a lock does yield a measure of control.

Illus. 36.16: *Ben bends one of Christian's fingers backward, forcing the author to cooperatively move back.*

Chapter 37
Halbschwert

Ringeck's system of armoured swordsmanship deals exclusively with fighting at the *half-sword*. In half-sword fighting, the grip of the long sword is held in the right hand and the left hand grasps the center of the blade, turning the sword into a short thrusting spear. The sword's point is the most important part of the weapon when fighting an armoured man - by the late 14th century, plate armour defenses had mitigated most effects from a hacking blow delivered with a sword's edge. Because of this, the point is usually kept forward to menace the opponent and hence the usual left leg leads.

Half-sword techniques concentrate on finding gaps in the armour and occasionally using the sword as a lever for grappling with the opponent. There are four half-sword guards, corresponding to one degree or another with the four long sword positions: *Ochs*, *Pflug*, *Alber*, and *vom Tag*. The first two guards correspond to *Ochs* and *Pflug* – they are high and low thrusting guards respectively, are held in the same positions.

The connection between *Alber* and *vom Tag* and their half-sword counterparts is less obvious. As it is impractical to hold the sword at the half-sword in these positions, they have been adapted. The third guard is similar to *Alber* in that it is a low guard and that it is used to invite attack. However, the left leg leads in this case so that the point can come on line easily, and the sword is held over the left knee rather than pointing to the ground. The fourth position, similar *vom Tag*, is a powerfully offensive guard. However, *vom Tag* is a *cutting* guard, and there is little cutting against plate armour. Therefore, it has been adapted to be the most powerful *thrusting* position. The hilt is held at the right side of the chest, just below the shoulder, with the point facing the enemy. This guard is used to strengthen a thrust once your point has found purchase in one of your opponent's upper openings. In the the third and fourth half-sword guards we find that the function, if not the form, is the same as the third and fourth long sword positions.

The techniques of this chapter are divided into four sections, depending on which of the four guards they originate with. As with the unarmoured material, the techniques rely on the fundamental concepts of *Indes*, *Vor* and *Nach*, binding, winding, "traveling after," etc. It is interesting how much material Ringeck includes under just one line of Liechtenauer's verse! I am unaware, as of this writing, whether or not there are additional verses that apply to the half-sword guards in other German *fechtbücher*.

Liechtenauer writes:

"*Where one is seen to draw the sword from the scabbard into both, so shall he strengthen. The thrust now truly remember.*"

Ringeck writes:

"*If both have cast their spears and the sword fighting begins, then you must first pay attention to the four halbschwert guards. From these always thrust at him to the upper openings. If he thrusts then at the same time or binds against your sword then you are to notice immediately whether he is hard or soft at the sword. And if you notice this, use strength against him, as described in the following.*"

Christian writes:

We are about to explore the use of the four half-sword guards. These guards correspond to the four guards (*Vier Leger*) in order of presentation, form, and general function. Ringeck advises us to seek out the "upper openings," for several reasons. Firstly, it is easiest to strike forcefully to these targets. Secondly, and most importantly, the upper targets also include most of the primary weak points in plate armour - the visor, the armpit, the small articulation points, etc., all of which can lead to immediate death or incapacitation if the armour is breached (see chapter 32). We are also reminded to be aware of whether and opponent binds hard or soft, for just as it was with the long sword techniques, blade pressure at the half-sword is the arbiter of your actions.

---

[1] At the end of the mounted combat material in the manuscript are several pages of additional techniques for fighting from the second and third half-sword guards. I have included them here for the sake of logical order.

Ringeck writes:

"*Hold your sword with the right hand at the grip and with the left in the center of the blade. Hold it at your right side over your head and let the point hang downward, towards the man's face.*" [Illus. 37.1 & 37.2]

Christian writes:

The first half-sword guard is like the *Ochs* from the long sword teachings. Like *Ochs*, it is held high at the right side of the head with the point menacing your opponent, enabling powerful thrusts from above. The only two differences between this one and *Ochs* are that the left hand holds the blade rather than the grip and, in half-sword fighting, there are no left side versions of this or any of the other three guards.

Illus. 37.1: *This is the first half-sword guard, which corresponds in both form and function to the long sword guard Ochs.*

Illus. 37.2: *The first half-sword guard from the front.*

Ringeck writes:

"*If he is in the lower guard and wants to thrust at you from below, thrust from above down between the sword and his forward hand. [Illus. 37.3] Press the pommel downward, [Illus. 37.4] wind the point at the sword through from below to his right side and set the point at him.*" [Illus. 37.5]

Christian writes:

You can stop your opponent's thrust from below by from the first half-sword guard. You do this by pushing your point into the gap created by your opponent's sword blade and his left arm. Once the attack is jammed, press your pommel down, putting you into the second guard, the equivalent of *Pflug*, and thrust to an opening on his right side. This opening is likely to be the gap in the armour at the right armpit. The beauty of this technique is that in transitioning from one guard to another, you move from defense to offense — or, from the *After* into the *Before* which is in itself, an application of *Indes*.

Illus. 37.3: *Ben thrusts from below to Christian, who jams his attack by thrusting down from the first guard in between Ben's left hand and blade.*

Illus. 37.5: *Christian thrusts his point into Ben's right armpit.*

Illus. 37.4: *Christian winds his hilt downward, putting himself into the lower guard, and presses Ben's sword down. This type of pressing action immobilizes not only the opponent's sword but also the opponent himself as both his hands are on his weapon and spread apart.*

Ringeck writes:

Thrust from the first guard to his face. [Illus. 37.6] *If he repels the thrust,* [Illus. 37.7] *then 'twitch'* [Illus. 37.8] *or go through with the thrust to the other side,* [Illus. 37.9] *like before. If you set the point to him,* [Illus. 37.10] *put your sword under your right shoulder with the hilt at your chest and push him in this way from you."* [Illus. 37.11]

Christian writes:

As we saw in the spear combat, "twitching" (*Zucken*) is a very important skill when armed with a thrusting weapon, especially against an armoured opponent. In this technique, *zucken* is used to slip the sword out of a bind and thrust to another opening; it is repeated until the opponent's defense fails. Once your point finds purchase in one of the openings, raise the hilt to your chest to apply a forceful thrust against your opponent's vulnerable spot.[2] This position, with the hilt tucked against the right side of the chest and the point directed to your opponent, frames the fourth half-sword guard.

Illus. 37.6: *Christian thrusts from the first guard to Ben's face.*

Illus. 37.7: *Ben displaces Christian's thrust by pushing it to his right with his sword's tip.*

[2] Although not specifically called out in the text, the target if most likely the armpit, where there is only a mail defense. Fifteenth century long swords, such has those shown here, were often wickedly pointed, and the braced thrust Ringeck advises could drive the point through the riveted links of maille. Should the thrust miss and snag on the armour, this braced thrust would still set up a strong push against the opponent, maintaining initiative for a follow-on attack.

Illus. 37.8: *Christian 'twitches' out of the bind by jerking his own point back.*

Illus. 37.9: *Christian thrusts to Ben's face on the other side of Ben's blade.*

Illus. 37.10: *Alternately, Christian thrusts to Ben's armpit after twitching to the other side of Ben's blade.*

Illus. 37.11: *Christian places his hilt at the right side of his chest to strengthen his thrust into Ben's armpit. This position is the fourth half-sword guard.*

Ringeck writes:

Thrust from the first guard to his face, like before. [Illus. 37.12] *If he displaces you in front of his left hand with the sword and remains with his point before your face,* [Illus. 37.13] *in order to set it at you, grab the point of his sword with your left hand and hold it firmly.* [Illus. 37.14] *With the right hand thrust strongly to his groin.* [Illus. 37.15] *If he pulls the sword back to free it, release it suddenly, which will create an opening.* [Illus. 37.16] *Grab the middle of your sword blade again with the left hand and follow him."* [Illus. 37.17]

Christian writes:

This technique is much like the "*Absetzen* with the Open Hand" as seen in chapter 34, above. Rather than twitching out of the bind, you seize the opponent's blade at the point with your left hand. With only your right hand holding your sword, thrust down to your foe's groin. Should your opponent try to wrest his sword point free of your grasp, you suddenly release it. His own momentum unbalances him, creating an opportunity for you to "travel after" (*Nachreisen*) him with a thrust. This allows you to remain in the "Before" (*Vor*), and force him into a completely defensive fight.

Illus. 37.12: *Christian thrusts from the first guard to Ben's face.*

Illus. 37.13: *With a hooking motion, Ben displaces Christian's thrust to his left side. This action also brings his own point into position to thrust against Christian.*

Illus. 37.14: *Christian grabs Ben's point with his left hand and forces it to his left.*

Illus. 37.15: *Christian passes forward with his right foot and thrusts down to Ben's groin while holding his foe's point with his left hand.*

Illus. 37.16: *In an effort to escape the thrust to groin, Ben pulls back hard on his own sword. Christian releases the point from his grip, which sends his opponent reeling backward.*

Illus. 37.17: *Christian "travels after" his opponent, setting his point into the gap at the back of the spaulder, or shoulder plate armour.*

Ringeck writes:

"*If you seize his sword and he yours,* [Illus. 37.18] *release his sword and grab yours again with the left hand at the center of the blade.* [Illus. 37.19] *Wind the point outside over the left hand and set it to him there.* [Illus. 37.20]

"*Or throw your sword to your feet, seize his left hand with your left and use an arm break or other wrestling technique.*"

Christian writes:

Of course, your opponent can also grab *your* point. If such a stalemate occurs, suddenly release your grasp on his point and grab your own blade again in the middle. Wind your sword then out of your opponent's grasp. By winding "outside over the left hand," you can free your weapon without resorting to a strength match - you have superior leverage, and, winding in this direction naturally causes his wrist to be turned, opening his grip. The finish to this wind puts you in position for an immediate thrust to the nearest available opening.

A second option is to catch your opponent unawares by relinquishing your weapon, and stepping in to grapple. Once you've cleared his sword's point, you needn't fear his weapon, so long as you maintain control of his arm.

Illus. 37.18:
Following a thwarted attempt by Christian to thrust from the first guard, both combatants grab each other's sword points with their left hands.

Illus. 37.19: *Christian releases Ben's point and grabs the center of his own blade anew.*

Illus. 37.20: *Christian winds his point over Ben's left hand. This frees his sword from Ben's grip and allows him to thrust to his adversary in one motion.*

Ringeck writes:

"*If you thrust from the upper guard to his face and he seizes your sword between your two hands with his left hand,* [Illus. 37.21] *move your pommel to him outside or inside over his left hand.* [Illus. 37.22] *Tear to your right side, and attack him.* [Illus. 37.23] *You can strike him from the upper guard with the pommel as well, if you can.*" [Illus. 37.24]

Christian writes:

When your opponent grabs your blade *between* your hands, he has made your choices much simpler, since gripping between your hands makes his hand the fulcrum on a lever. Drive your pommel over or under the left hand and wrench your sword free of his grip, using the same joint turning principles we saw in the previous technique. This sets up an immediate thrust. Another option is to not resist his strength; instead close in striking with the pommel, rotating around the fulcrum of his hand. Although he does not specifically mention so in his text, the fact that Ringeck does not tell the student what to do when making this grip, combined with the obvious weakness of the grip itself, makes it fairly clear that it is not advisable to grasp the opponent's sword *between* his hands.

Illus. 37.21: *Christian attempts to thrust to Ben, who seizes Christian's blade between the hands with his left hand.*

Illus. 37.22: *Christian drives his pommel forward and over Ben's left hand, bringing the tip quickly back on-line.*

Illus. 37.23: *Christian breaks Ben's grasp on his sword and thrusts to his opponent's armpit.*

Illus. 37.24: *In an alternate counter to Ben's grip on his sword, Christian steps in to strike his pommel to Ben's head.*

Ringeck writes:

"*Hold your sword with both hands, next to your right side, with the grip beside the knee. Your left foot should be forward and the point should be directed against your opponent's face.*" [Illus. 37.25 & 37.26]

Christian writes:

The second guard is the half-sword cousin to the long sword guard *Pflug*. It is held at the side with the point threatening the opponent's face and is the point of origin for thrusts from below.

Illus. 37.25: *This is the second half-sword guard, which corresponds to the long sword guard Pflug in both form and function.*

Illus. 37.26: *The second half-sword guard from the front.*

Ringeck writes:

"*When you stand in this guard and he faces you in the upper guard wanting to attack you from above,* [Illus. 37.27] *thrust first and aim your point at his forward hand into the opening at the palm.* [Illus. 37.28] *Or thrust it over his forward hand through with your sword,* [Illus. 37.29] *push your pommel down, and aim it at the other side.*" [Illus. 37.30]

Christian writes:

We learned in the exposition on "Vulnerabilities of a Man in Armour" (chapter 32) that the palm of the hand is an excellent target as it is protected only by glove leather. You can thrust to this opening from the second guard as the opponent thrusts at you from above. Such a counterattack prevents his assault and greivously injures his hand, weakening any further attack. The other options in this technique is to go over his forward hand and press it, and thereby his sword, down so that you can thrust safely at another opening. This second option again reinforces the idea of "feeling" (*fühlen*) and fighting "on the sword" (*am schwert*). Strike into his attack, and immediately bind strongly against his weapon, pulling it down and setting up a follow-up attack.

Illus. 37.27: *Ben prepares to thrust from the first guard. Christian faces him in the second.*

Illus. 37.28: *Christian prevents Ben's attack by thrusting up from the second guard into the palm of Ben's hand.*

Illus. 37.29: *In this variation, Christian prevents the thrust by thrusting over Ben's left hand.*

Illus. 37.30: *Christian presses with his sword to force Ben's left hand down and force his own point into Ben's right armpit.*

Ringeck writes:

"*If he thrusts from above at you,* [Illus. 37.31] *grab his sword in front of his left hand with your left.* [Illus. 37.32] *With your right hand, bring the hilt to your chest and set the point at him.*" [Illus. 37.33]

Christian writes:

This is another technique that works much like the "*Absetzen* with the Open Hand" from chapter 24. Release the left hand from your blade and grab your opponent's sword near the point. (Again, note that you grab in *front* of his hands, not *between* them.) Once you've secured his sword, you're free to thrust using your right hand, while retaining the grip of your sword. Bringing the hilt up to your chest puts your sword in the third guard, strengthening the thrust.

Illus. 37.31: *Ben thrusts from the first guard to Christian's face.*

Illus. 37.32: *Christian grabs Ben's sword at the point, preventing the thrust.*

Illus. 37.33: *Christian thrusts his point behind Ben's spaulder and raises his hilt to his chest to strengthen his attack.*

A counter against the "setting through" (Durchsetzen)

Ringeck writes:

"*If you thrust from the lower guard and he thrusts at you from the upper guard between your forward hand and the sword,* [Illus. 37.34] *push his pommel down,* [Illus. 37.35] *going immediately into the upper guard and attacking.*" [Illus. 37.36]

Christian writes:

This is a counter to a technique that was presented in the passages on fighting from the first half-sword position - "A Defense from the First Guard," and again uses the concepts of *Indes* and remaining on the opponent's sword. If your opponent "sets through" his point after pushing his pommel down in the bind, break the technique by changing from the second, or lower, guard to the first, or upper, position. This action also brings the point back in line for a counterattack, putting you back in the "Before"--the coveted *Vor*.

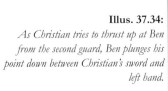

Illus. 37.34:
As Christian tries to thrust up at Ben from the second guard, Ben plunges his point down between Christian's sword and left hand.

Illus. 37.35: *Ben winds his pommel downward and moves to thrust to Christian's right side.*

Illus. 37.36: *Christian rises up into the first guard, an action that in one motion stops Ben's attack and brings him back on the offensive. From here Christian can thrust with power.*

Ringeck writes:

"*If you thrust from the lower guard at him and he moves through with the pommel under your sword to displace,* [Illus. 37.37] *remain strong with the point before his face and so press his right hand downward.* [Illus. 37.38] *Then attack him.* [Illus. 37.39]

"*You can also change through with the pommel and set aside his thrust.*" [Illus. 37.40 & 37.41 p. 334]

Christian writes:

You can displace a thrust by bringing the pommel forward and catching the thrust between your hands. If your opponent uses this tactic against one of your thrusts, push down on his blade such that you press down his right hand. As you press his sword down find an opening to thrust at.

Illus. 37.37:
Ben displaces Christian's upward thrust to his face by moving forward with his pommel and passing forward with his right foot.

Illus. 37.38: *Christian presses down with his sword, focussing his pressure on the part of Ben's sword nearest his right hand.*

Illus. 37.39: *Christian thrusts to Ben's face while constraining the latter's sword.*

Illus. 37.40: *Ben thrusts to Christian's face from the second guard.*

Illus. 37.41: *Christian passes forward with his right foot and drives his pommel forward and up to displace Ben's thrust.*

Ringeck writes:

Note: thrust to him strongly from the lower guard to the face. If he thrusts the same way to you, [Illus. 37.42] *grasp his sword in the center to yours with your left hand inverted and hold the two swords fast together.* [Illus. 37.43] *And go through with the pommel under his sword,* [Illus. 37.44] *with the right arm jerking it over to your right side, so that you take his sword."* [Illus. 37.45]

Christian writes:

If you and your opponent each thrust from below and bind, you can break this stalemate by grabbing both blades together with your left hand and hooking his sword from below with your pommel to jerk his sword away from him. This disarm is the half-sword analogue of the "Sword Taking" from chapter 15 on *Durchlaufen* ("Running Through").[3]

Illus. 37.42: *Christian and Ben each thrust up from the second guard and bind their swords.*

Illus. 37.43: *Christian grasps both swords together at the point where they bind.*

Illus. 37.44: *He passes forward with his right foot and drives his pommel under Ben's sword.*

Illus. 37.45: *Christian hooks Ben's sword with his pommel and yanks his right hand back thus him of his weapon.*

---

[3] This techniques uses a simple wrist turning--and leverage; this time to affect a complete disarm. Note how many techniques derive from, learning one simple form of wrist locking.

Ringeck writes:

Note: this is the counter: when he grabs your sword in the center and wants to take it away from you, [Illus. 37.46] *note: when he has your sword held fast in his left hand, drive up into the upper guard and set upon him."* [Illus. 37.47]

Christian writes:

The "Sword Taking" of the previous technique can be easily countered by moving up into the first guard. This not only breaks your opponent's hold but also brings your point back on to the offensive.

Illus. 37.46: *Ben grasps both swords together with his left hand at the point where they bind.*

Illus. 37.47: *Christian rises up into the first guard, breaking his sword free from Ben's grasp and bringing it into position to thrust.*

Ringeck writes:

Note: Thrust to his face from the lower guard while turning. If he displaces, [Illus. 37.48] zucken [Illus. 37.49] and thrust to his face. If he displaces, [Illus. 37.50] move your pommel over his right shoulder and around his neck, jumping with your right foot behind his left, [Illus. 37.51] and tearing him over your leg with the pommel so that he falls." [Illus. 37.52]

Christian writes:

In this technique you *Zucken* twice trying to break the opponent's defenses. If you can't get through after the second twitch, step in, hooking the pommel around his neck and throwing him over your right leg.

Illus. 37.48: *Ben displaces Christian's thrust from below to his left side using the forward part of his blade.*

Illus. 37.49: *Christian jerks backward to 'twitch' out of the bind.*

Illus. 37.50: *Christian thrusts again to Ben, but is displaced again, this time toward Ben's right.*

Illus. 37.51: *Christian passes forward to place his right foot behind Ben's left foot and hooks his pommel around the right side of Ben's neck.*

Illus. 37.52: *Using his pommel, Christian pulls Ben over his right leg.*

Half-Swording
Counter to the previous technique

Ringeck writes:

Note: this is the counter: when he moves his pommel over your right shoulder and around your neck jumps with his right foot behind your left, [Illus. 37.53] *grasp his left hand.* [Illus. 37.54] *And press it toward your breast, and turn from him to the right side; and throw him over your left hip.* [Illus. 37.55]

"Note, you will also want to strike him from the lower guard, when he likewise has you." [Illus. 37.56]

Christian writes:

This is a counter-technique that you can use should your opponent hook *you* around the neck with his pommel, as in the previous technique. When your opponent wants to throw you backward over his leg, there's often an opportunity for you to throw *him* over your leg. You should release your left hand's grip on your blade and use it to grab your opponent's left hand, pulling him over your leg. An alternate counter to his attempt to throw you is to back out from his hooking action and thrusting from the second guard.

Illus. 37.53: *After being displaced, Ben steps with his right foot behind Christian's left foot and hooks his pommel around the right side of Christian's neck in an attempt to throw his opponent.*

Illus. 37.54: *Christian's releases his left hand's grasping his sword blade and uses it to grab Ben's left hand.*

Illus. 37.55: *Christian pulls Ben's left hand toward him and pivots back with his right foot to throw Ben forward over his left leg.*

Illus. 37.56: *In this alternate counter to Ben's attempt, Christian pivots back to escape the pommel hook and thrust from the second guard to Ben's right armpit.*

<u>**Ringeck writes**</u>:

"*Hold your sword with both hands, as described before, over the left knee. And from it, break all his techniques by displacing.*" [Illus. 37.57 & 37.58]

<u>**Christian writes**</u>:

While it may look quite different, the role of the third half-sword guard is the same as that of the third long sword guard *Alber*. Both are low guards that invite an attack. Unlike *Alber*, the third half-sword guard is done with the left leg leading. The other major difference is that this guard doesn't point toward the ground.

Illus. 37.57: *This is third guard with the half-sword. While it looks different than the third long sword guard, Alber, it's function is similar: to invite and intercept attacks.*

Illus. 37.58: *The third half-sword guard from the front.*

Ringeck writes:

"*If he thrusts to your face from the upper guard,* [Illus. 37.59] *set the thrust aside to his right side with your sword in front of your left hand* [Illus. 37.60] *driving into the upper guard and setting the point upon him.*" [Illus. 37.61]

Christian writes:

Should your opponent accept your invitation to attack while you are in the third guard, raise your sword to deflect the attack off of the forward part of your b;ade and move to the upper guard in preparation for an attack. This is another technique that reiterates the idea that many of the half-sword techniques come from understanding how and when to transition from one guard to another.

Illus. 37.59: *Ben passes forward with his right foot while thrusting from the first guard to Christian. Christian awaits the attack in the third guard.*

Illus. 37.60: *Christian drives up from the third guard to displace Ben's thrust with his sword in front of his left hand.*

Illus. 37.61: *Christian remains in motion after deflecting Ben's thrust and moves into the first position to thrust.*

Ringeck writes:

"☉*r drive up with the sword, displacing the thrust from above between your two hands.* [Illus. 37.62] *And drive with the pommel over his forward hand* [Illus. 37.63] *and with it jerk down;* [Illus. 37.64] *setting the point upon him.* [Illus. 37.65] [Repetition] *Move the pommel over his forward hand and then back through, and jerk him down with it. Later, you'll find written how you can displace the blows with the pommel from the third guard.*"

Christian writes:

This is a variant of the previous technique. Displace his attack on the part of your blade that is between you hands.[4] While in the bind, hook your pommel around his left hand and wrench it down, breaking his grip on his sword's blade and creating an opportunity for a thrust.

Illus. 37.62: *Ben thrusts from the first guard. Christian counters the thrust by driving up from the third position to catch it on his sword between his hands.*

Illus. 37.63: *Christian drives his pommel forward over Ben's left hand.*

Illus. 37.64: *Christian hooks Ben's left hand with his pommel.*

Illus. 37.65: *Christian jerks his pommel down to his right side, breaking Ben's hold on the blade. This brings Christian's sword into the second guard, from which he can thrust up at Ben.*

---

[4] It is worth noting that this displacement is similar to the Crown (*Kron*) displacement that we studied in the chapter on the Scheitelhau in the long sword section. The *Kron* appears to be best performed by starting in *Alber*, just as this displacement starts in the *Alber*-like half-sword guard.

Christian writes:

The fourth guard is the half-sword analogue to the long sword guard *vom Tag*. Like the third guard, its relationship to its long sword counterpart isn't immediately obvious. It is held with the hilt at the right side of the chest and the point aimed at your opponent, so it's very much like the version of *vom Tag* where the sword is over the right shoulder, only here the point has been dropped into your left hand. However, it is the guard's function that makes its kinship with *vom Tag* most apparent. *Vom Tag* is the primary striking guard in the long sword teachings and has the most obvious offensive potential. The fourth half-sword guard should be used once the point has found purchase in a gap in the opponent's armour; hence, it also has the most offensive potential. Moving into this guard turns it into a short spear, as it allows your weight to contribute to the thrust's power. This is why Ringeck tells us to come into this guard whenever the point finds its mark, for putting the hilt to the chest makes for the most powerful thrust.

Ringeck writes:

"*Hold your sword with both hands as described above. Hold it with the grip under the right shoulder and put the hilt in front on the right of your chest, so that the point rises up to your opponent. [Illus. 37.66 & 37.67] You should come into this guard from all three of the aforementioned guards. If you thrust to an opening and your point gets stuck in his armour, [Illus. 37.68] always wind your hilt before your chest and push him away from you. [Illus. 37.69] Do not permit him to free himself from your point, because in that way he can neither thrust nor strike.*"

Illus. 37.68: *Christian thrusts from the second guard into Ben's armpit.*

Illus. 37.69: *Christian moves up into the fourth guard to strengthen his attack into Ben's armpit.*

Illus. 37.66 & 37.67 (opposite):*This is the fourth guard with the half-sword. It corresponds to the fourth long sword position, vom Tag, although it looks a bit different. As vom Tag allows the whole body to be brought to bear for powerful cutting strokes, the fourth half-sword guard allows the whole body to empower a thrust into the gaps in an opponent's armour.*

Half-Sword

Ringeck writes:

"*If you face him and he is taller than you, push your point up well into the rings [of the maille].* [Illus. 37.70] *If he is shorter, let the pommel of your sword drop to your right hip, and the point should rise upward and be set well into the rings, like above.* [Illus. 37.71] *So you push him from you, and don't let him leave your sword.*"

Christian writes:

This passage explains some subtleties of using the fourth guard to thrust in between armour defenses. These gaps in the plate armour are usually defended by mail. However maille an acutely tapered sword point can penetrate between the links with a strong thrust. Ringeck explains that once you've got the point in, you can adjust for your opponent's height by how high on your body you hold the hilt. If your opponent is as tall or taller than you, you should hold the hilt high to create a powerful thrust; if he is shorter, you should drop your hilt, perhaps into the lower guard, so that you can work your way into the gap in the armour to thrust. Working the point into the gap in the armour is important – as long as you are applying a powerful thrust, your opponent can not move to attack you.

Illus. 37.70: *Christian uses a thrust with the fourth guard to keep Ben out of range thus preventing a counterattack. This would be the ideal position to use if Ben were as tall or taller than Christian...*

Illus. 37.71: *However, Ben is shorter than Christian, so moving into the second guard is better for working the point deeply into the armpit.*

Chapter 38
More Half-Swording

I've combined three short passages in this chapter, two of which are "old friends" from our study of the umarmoured long sword techniques. The "Before and After" is a review of the importance of initiative in Liechtenauer's method, which was hinted at in the first series of techniques and is now explicitly reiterated. This time it is approached from an armoured combat perspective, where the use of the sword's point is paramount and the footwork must be done in such a way that the point can be oriented to attack. The "traveling after" is another familiar concept from the long sword teachings. While the idea is still to out-time the foe, it is specifically applied here against opponents who employ swinging blows against an armoured opponent. The nimbleness of thrusts from the half-sword can be put to good use against the relatively slower movement of a fully armoured man drawing back to strike with both hands on the grip of his long sword.

The newcomer in this chapter is the passage on the attack with the point, a series of options for counterattacking an opponent once he has set his sword's point at one of your openings. Like all counter-techniques in Liechtenauer's system, these are designed to remove the threat while attacking and recovering the initiative. Hence we find an attack against the opponent's leading hand, a technique for pushing his sword down, and a bit of evasive footwork that removes you from harm's way without interrupting your offensive.

<u>**Liechtenauer writes**</u>:

"*Before and After, of these two things know. Learn to jump suddenly.*"

<u>**Ringeck writes**</u>:

This means: You are of all things to know the 'before' and the 'after', because from this the whole art of combat proceeds. Remember to always forestall him, with strike or thrust, for then he must displace. And if he binds against your sword, immediately use your technique. Thus he cannot use his techniques because of your attack. That is the meaning of 'before'.

"The 'after' - these are all counters against the techniques that he uses against you. If it occurs thus that you must displace, from the displacement immediately find the next available opening with the point. Thus you come from the defensive again into the offensive. That is the meaning of 'after'.

"You are to make certain that you do not take more than one step to him or away from him in combat fencing. If he is faster than you are and you can't displace him any more, go back with the left foot only one step. And make sure that you can move to him with a step of the left foot to attack him again or seize him for wrestling."

<u>**Christian writes**</u>:

It is just as important to maintain the initiative in armoured combat as it is in unarmoured fencing. Master Ringeck reminds us in the first two paragraphs to be mindful of the *Vor* and the *Nach*--"Before" and "After"--the offensive and defensive principles. The third paragraph however, is information specific to fighting in armour. It's important in any strategic retreat to only step back with the left foot, for the left foot must be forward to threaten an enemy with your point. You can step back one pace with the left foot, but must be able to step back quickly with a single step into the fray in order to attack anew.

The ability to move quickly in and out of the fray is what Master Liechtenauer is alluding to in his admonition to "Learn to jump suddenly." In any of the cases where Ringeck or Liechtenauer uses the term *jump*, they are describing footwork that involves keeping one foot planted while the other suddenly springs forward or backward and, almost invariably, outward. When fighting with the half sword, the left foot is kept forward in all of the guards because this is the orientation that allows you to thrust from the right side of your body. Therefore, you should *jump* in and out of range as necessary with the left foot - it is the farthest forward and should you need to deny your enemy a target, you must pass back with the left foot to do so.

Liechtenauer writes:

"*H*ollows all blows, the strong want to strike. If he defends, then
twitch. Thrust - if he defends, to him jerk. If he is seen extended,
then the thrust you skillfully direct.*"

Ringeck writes:

"*Y*ou are to use the Traveling After (Nachreisen) against a
strong man who fights with outstretched arms and otherwise knows nothing of the true art.*

If he faces you in a guard, assume also one against him. [Illus.
38.1] *Pay attention to when he actually pulls back his sword. If
he wants to thrust or he lifts the sword for a strike,* [Ilus. 38.2]
*attack his next opening with your point before he can complete
the thrust or strike.*" [Illus. 38.3]

Illus. 38.1:
*Ben stands in the long sword guard vom Tag with both of his
hands on his sword's grip. Christian faces him in the second
half-sword guard.*

Illus. 38.2: *Ben begins pulling back his sword to strike at Christian.*

Illus. 38.3: *Christian passes forward and to the right to thrust up into
the gap behind Ben's spaulder (shoulder defense) before his opponent can
strike.*

Ringeck writes:

"*If however he detects your attack and displaces in time with the sword,* [Illus. 38.4] *then without exposing any of your openings, 'twitch through'.* [Illus. 38.5 & 38.6] *And always use the twitching, if he displaces only to strike the sword. Thus you come to the arm breaks and other counter techniques. And this is used against those who forget the art and strike to the sword and not the man.*"

Christian writes:

In the long sword teachings we learned that *Nachreisen*-- "traveling after"--encompasses technique for out-timing your opponent in order to re-seize the initiative. Ringeck tells us to use timing against an opponent who uses swinging blows with the sword. Such an opponent "knows nothing of the true art" because this is not an efficient way to fight a man in armour. This is not to say that such a strike is harmless – a powerful blow can stun even a fully armoured man. However, thrusting attacks with the half-sword are very fast and have the advantage in time over a swordsman swinging his sword with both hands on the grip. They are also more likely to be lethal, so an armoured man is less likely to be willing to just accept a blow on his harness to gain an advantage. You should immediately attack such a fighter when he raises his sword to strike. If he strikes in time to displace your attack, Rely on the "twitching" to clear the bind and attack again.

Illus. 38.4:
Ben strikes to Christian's thrusting sword, displacing it.

Illus. 38.5: *Christian "twitches" out of the bind by jerking his sword back.*

Illus. 38.6: *Christian thrusts again, this time to Ben's right armpit.*

Liechtenauer writes:

"When he also with strength sets upon, set the thrust upon him."

Ringeck writes:

"If he sets upon you and pushes you back then thrust at him into the palm of the hand that holds the sword in the center of the blade. [Illus. 38.7] If he has the hand reversed, thrust down from above, but from the same guard."[5] [Illus. 38.8]

Christian writes:

This passage describes what to do if your opponent sets his point against you. He can be countered by an attack to his gauntleted hand, either at the palm or behind and into the cuff. If you find yourself in a situation where both points have found purchase, maintain your attack while negating his by stepping back with your left foot. Your hilt should then be positioned at the right side of your chest for a thrust against his left side. Since your opponent is likely doing the same thing, refuse the opening on your left with the step back while keeping your right side in position to maintain an offensive.

Illus. 38.7: Ben thrusts to Christian's left armpit from the fourth half-sword guard. Christian counters the attack by thrusting in to the palm of Ben's left hand.

Illus. 38.8: Ben thrusts to Christian's armpit but this time with his left hand cradling the blade. Christian counters the thrust by working his point into Ben's palm.

[5] Ringeck's instruction to thrust from the same guard regardless of whether the opponent's left hand is upright or inverted is enigmatic – one would expect that you'd thrust from a high guard in one case and a low guard in to the other. I've therefore had to 'make some allowances' in my photographic interpretation of this technique.

More Half-Swording

More Ansetzen - "attacking with the point"

Ringeck writes:

"O*r thrust at his arm from behind and into the gauntlet.* [Illus. 38.9] *And if the thrust sticks, follow him, and you have crippled this side and therefore win another advantage.* [Illus. 38.10] *Or thrust through over his forward hand* [Illus. 38.11] *and press your sword low from above,* [Illus. 38.12] *setting your hilt to your chest and attacking him.* [Illus. 38.13] *If he sets his point to your left armpit,* [Illus. 38.14] *withdraw with the left foot and thus his point drops, but yours holds fast.* [Illus. 38.15] *You can also increase the range of your sword, if you set your pommel in front of your chest."* [Illus. 38.16]

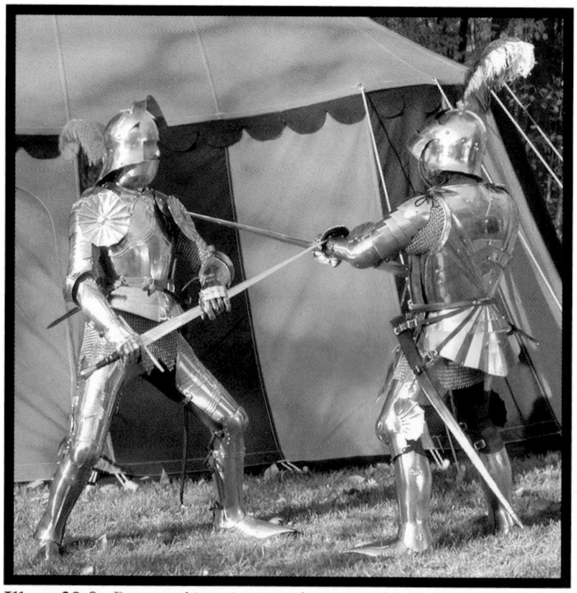

Illus. 38.9: *Ben sets his point into the gap in the armour at Christian's left armpit. In response Christian inserts the point of his sword behind Ben's left gauntlet cuff.*

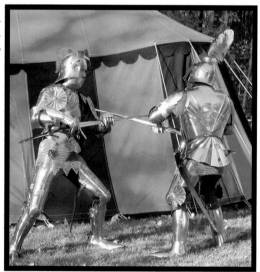

Illus. 38.10: *Christian drives his point deep into the cuff of Ben's left gauntlet.*

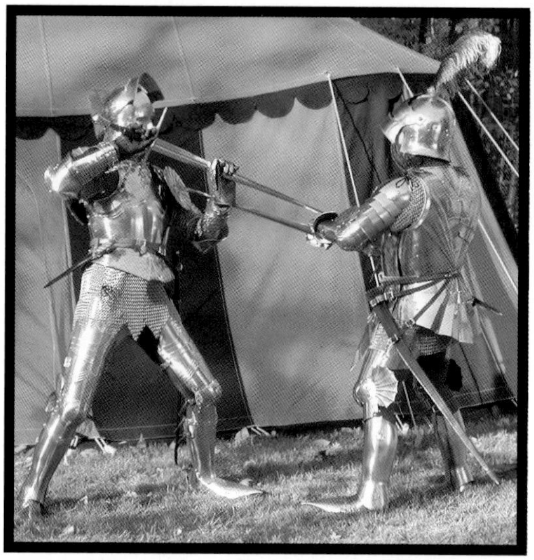

Illus. 38.11: *Ben thrusts to Christian's left armpit. Christian thrusts his point over Ben's left hand.*

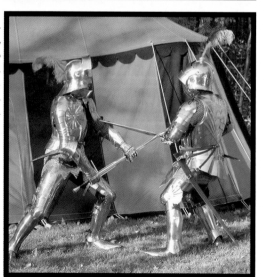

Illus. 38.12: *Christian drives his pommel below to press Ben's left hand, and therefore his sword, down. In doing so he thrusts his point into Ben's right armpit.*

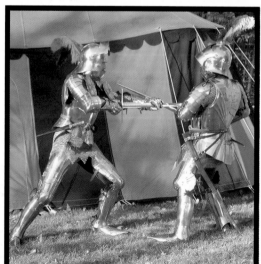

Illus. 38.13: *Christian strengthens his thrust to Ben's armpit by driving up into the fourth guard.*

Illus. 38.14:
Christian and Ben have each thrust into each other's left armpits. They both strengthen their thrusts by pushing forward from the fourth guard.

Illus. 38.15: *Christian breaks the stalemate by passing back with his left foot, which leaves his point in place against Ben while freeing himself from Ben's point.*

Illus. 38.16: *Christian gains further safety by moving his hilt to the center of his chest, which extends his sword's reach.*

Chapter 39
Schlachenden Ort

The *Schlachenden Ort*,[1] --"Battering Point"--is the name Liech-tenauer gave to strikes with the sword's pommel. These are delivered with both hands on the blade of the sword so that the pommel or hilt strikes with an impact like that of a pollaxe. Ideally, these should be aimed at the forward extremeties of an adversary's body, the lead leg or lead hand. I expect that this is so that you don't get into trouble with your opponent's point as you execute such a relatively slow technique. This chapter focuses on several means for defending against pommel strikes and on the proper way to execute them from the first and second half-sword guards.

---

[1] Talhoffer's 1467 *fechtbüch* calls the strike with the pommel the *Mortschlag*--"Murder stroke"--and the *Tunrschlag* -- "Thunder stroke." *Medieval Combat*, trans. and ed. Mark Rector, Greenhill Books, 2000. Plates 33, 34, 37, 47, 52, 53 and 73.

<u>**Liechtenauer writes**</u>:

"*With the battering point he protects himself. He strikes without fear with both hands. Learn to turn the point to the eyes.*"

<u>**Ringeck writes**</u>:

The 'battering point' is the strike with the pommel. When he wants to overrun (Überlaufen) you with a strong strike, hold your sword over your left knee in the lower guard. [Illus 39.1] *If he strikes then to your head, and he is a strong man, strike at his blow with the sword in front of your left hand to his right side.* [Illus. 39.2] *And move up high into the upper guard.*" [Illus. 39.3]

<u>**Christian writes**</u>:

The third half-sword guard is a good starting point when you need to displace your opponent's strike with the pommel. These pommel strikes are delivered by swinging the sword with both hands on the blade so that the long sword functions like a pollaxe or war-hammer. In this technique displace the pommel strike on the part of your sword in front of your left hand and move in one smooth movement into the upper, or first, half-sword guard threatening your opponent's face.

Illus. 39.1:
Christian stands in the third guard with the half-sword as Ben begins to swing a pommel strike at him.

Illus. 39.2:
Christian deflects Ben's pommel strike on his blade in front of his left hand.

Illus. 39.3:
Christian moves through into the first half-sword guard to threaten Ben's face.

Ringeck writes:

"*If he is weaker than you, step to him, catch the blow between your hands on the sword* [Illus. 39.4] *and set the point into his face.*" [Illus. 39.5]

Christian writes:

This time, the pommel strike is caught between the hands on your blade. If your opponent is soft in the bind, push his sword to your right side as your bring your point on line to thrust. If he binds hard against your sword, drive over his to hook his hilt with yours and relieve him of the weapon.

Illus. 39.4: *Closing the distance, Christian passes forward with his right foot and intercepts Ben's pommel strike on his blade between his two hands.*

Illus. 39.5: *As Ben is soft in the bind, Christian pushes his foe's sword to the right and brings his point in position to thrust to Ben's face. Note Christian's pass forward with the left foot to bring his point forward.*

Ringeck writes:

"*If you catch the blow with the pommel in the center of the sword,* [Illus. 39.6] *move with the pommel over his sword in front at the hilt,* [Illus. 39.7] *tearing upward to your right side, so that you take his sword with it.*" [Illus. 39.8]

Illus. 39.6: *Christian catches Ben's pommel strike between his hands on the blade.*

Illus. 39.7: *Christian drives his pommel over Ben's sword to hook his hilt on his opponent's.*

Illus. 39.8: *Christian turns to his right to jerk Ben's sword out of his hands.*

Ringeck writes:

"*If he strikes at your left knee, catch the blow between the hands on your sword so that your pommel rises up from below.* [Illus. 39.9] *And drive through with the pommel under his sword,* [Illus. 39.10] *in front at the hilt, and tear upward to your right side, thus forcing the sword from his hands.*" [Illus. 39.11]

Christian writes:

In this sequence the opponent strikes with his pommel at your left knee. Displacing the blow between your hands from the third guard, you hook your pommel on his hilt by driving under his sword. Disarm him with a powerful pull to your right.

Illus. 39.9: *Christian catches Ben's pommel strike between his hands on his blade.*

Illus. 39.10: *Christian passes forward with his right foot and drives under Ben's sword to hook his pommel around his adversary's hilt.*

Illus. 39.11: *Christian jerks his pommel to his right and relieves Ben of his sword.*

Ringeck writes:

"*If he strikes down with the pommel at your foot, strike with your pommel downward against his blow.* [Illus. 39.12] *Then jump towards him and wrestle.*" [Illus. 39.13]

Christian writes:

Should he strike to your left foot, knock the blow aside with your pommel and then close to grapple.

Illus. 39.12: *Ben swings his pommel to Christian's left knee. Christian passes forward with his right foot and knocks Ben's strike aside with his pommel.*

Illus. 39.13: *Dropping his sword, Christian advances on his opponent to grapple.*

Ringeck writes:

"*If you hold your sword at your side in the lower guard and he strikes with the pommel at your tip, knocking it aside,* [Illus. 39.14] *jump immediately close to him, so that he strikes with the pommel past you* [Illus. 39.15] *- nothing can happen to you - and set the point at him.* [Illus. 39.16] *You can always 'travel after' and attack while he draws the pommel back.*" [Illus. 39.17]

Christian writes:

A strike with the pommel can be used to knock an enemy's point off-line. That's what happens in this technique as you stand in the second half-sword: the opponent knocks your point towards your right side. In response, rather than fighting to recover your weapon, move with his displacement by stepping toward him with your left foot and thrusting in one continuous motion. Another option is to follow him as he raises his sword for another assault and attack him with the point.

Illus. 39.14: *As Christian stands in the second guard, Ben forces his point aside with a pommel strike.*

Illus. 39.15: *Christian takes a small step forward with his left foot toward Ben, freeing his sword from the bind.*

Illus. 39.16: *Christian sets his point into the gap between Ben's right spaulder and backplate.*

Illus. 39.17: *As Ben raises up his sword for another strike with the pommel, Christian travels after him and attacks his right armpit with a powerful thrust.*

<u>Liechtenauer writes</u>:

he forward foot you must hit with the strike."

Ringeck writes:

"If you want to strike with the pommel, you are to direct it particularly to his forward extremities. If you want to strike, hold your sword in the guard over the head and do it in such a way as if you want to thrust him in the face. [Illus. 39.18] Then release the sword with your right hand and seize the blade with it beside the left. [Illus. 39.19] Strike with the pommel to his lead foot or his forward hand, where he holds the sword at the blade. [Illus. 39.20] You can also strike from the lower guard from the right side. [Illus. 39.21 & 39.22]

"Pay attention to whether he strikes with the pommel to your forward knee or forward hand and displace him with the previously described counter techniques so that he cannot harm you."

Christian writes:

In this passage, Master Ringeck describes how one should strike a blow with the pommel. Begin in either the first or second half-sword guard and removing your right hand from the grip so that it can hold the blade alongside the left. The best targets for such at strike are the left leg or left hand as they are the closest parts of your opponent's body and may be struck with less worry. (It should also be noted that the hand target breaks the opponent's connection with his weapon, and, even in gauntlets, can do serious damage to his hands as a benefit. The attack to the left foot or knee can be used as a hook to sweep him off of his feet.[2]

Illus. 39.18: *Christian stands in the first half-sword guard while Ben stands in the second position.*

Illus. 39.19: *Christian releases his right hand from the sword's grip to grasp the blade.*

---

[2] see Talhoffer 1459, 1467 (plate 47) and the Copenhagen Codex, for comparable examples.

Illus. 39.20: *Christian passes forward with his right foot to smash Ben's left hand with a pommel strike.*

Illus. 39.21: *From the second half-sword guard, Christian has placed his right hand upon his blade to deliver a pommel strike.*

Illus. 39.22: *From the second position Christian strikes upward with the pommel against the left side of Ben's head.*

Illus. 40.1: *Andrew sits on his mount in the first lance guard, his lance under his right arm with the point hanging at the left side. From this position Andrew can lift his lance against an adversary's, forcing it aside while striking.*

Chapter 70
Roßfechten

Ringeck writes:

"*H*ere begins the knightly art: fighting from horseback.

"*Here begins Master Johannes Liechtenauer's fighting from horseback, which he wrote down in secret words. This is included laid out and explained, so that every fighter who already understands fencing can understand this art.*"

This chapter comprises of Master Liechtenauer's techniques for fighting on horseback--*Roßfechten*--which starts with the use of the lance. Unlike the jousting seen in today's movies, where the riders seemingly aim their lances at each other and hope for the best, the techniques here are designed to safely deflect an opponent's lance while striking with one's own. The method is the same as that of the *Absetzen* (setting aside) from the long sword teachings – they are thrusts made while deflecting the opponent's weapon in a single-time action. We can also see the familiar Liechtenauer tactics here: lure the opponent into attacking a seemingly unprotected opening to counter him while attacking.

Liechtenauer didn't set down any instructions on basic equitation. The skills of horsemanship would surely have made up the better part of what it would take to successfully perform one of these techniques, but I don't think that should be viewed as an omission--after all, he doesn't teach us how to settle our weight, develop power for a strike, or avoid striking flat in the long sword teachings and these elements are necessary basics. There is a presumption of basic skill in all parts of this, or any other, *fechtbüch*. He does say that it is important to have good control of the mount and to ride well-seated if we are to perform the actions that make up this section. Those who ride at a full gallop will be met by their opponent *"before the eyes."*

Liechtenauer writes:

"Your spear direct, riding against comes to naught."

Ringeck writes:

That is: when you have a lance and another also has one, wanting to ride at you, you shall know how to aim your lance so that you deflect his lance and strike with the thrust while he does not. And you should know how to use the techniques from both guards that you will find described."

Christian writes:

The techniques for fighting with the lance against another lance-wielding rider are based on *Absetzen*, or "setting aside." *Absetzen* is a primary technique from the long sword teachings (chapter 12); it is the simultaneous deflection of an attack with a thrusting counterattack. In the mounted techniques the idea is to set aside your opponent's thrust while successfully striking him. The same technique will be described twice below, from two different guards.[1]

Liechtenauer writes:

"If it drops, the end undoes him."

Ringeck writes:

"When you ride at each other, hold your lance under your arm for the thrust. When he comes to strike, let yourself appear burdened and let your point sink low on your left side. [Illus. 40.1 p. 363] As he rides to thrust, lift your lance with strength across his so that you hit and he does not, when his lance is beaten off next to you."

Christian writes:

In this technique, your lance falls to the left side of your horse into the first lance guard. This guard is analogous with the third half-sword guard for fighting in harness on foot and with *Alber* from the long sword teachings, and with the third half-sword guard for fighting in harness on foot. Each is a guard of invitation or provocation. With your lance down along the side of your horse, you appear to be unable to hold it up. As your opponent approaches, suddenly jerk the lance into position so that it is couched in your right armpit. This sudden and forceful motion knocks your adversary's lance aside as your own lance point hits him.

Illus. 40.2: *This is the second lance guard. Andrew holds the lance in the middle with both hands. This guard can also be used to launch strong setting aside (Absetzen) movements that simultaneously defend against an oncoming opponent's lance and strike him.*

[1] In the early 16th century *fechtbüch* "Goliath," much of which is based on Peter von Danzig's 1452 *fechtbüch*, the position with the lance couched beneath the right armpit and the point directed against the foe is labeled as the first of *three* lance guards. It's peculiar that Ringeck doesn't include the position with the lance aimed at the opponent as a guard, as one of his techniques uses the position exclusively: "A Technique Using a Short Lance against a Long One from Horseback."

Ringeck writes:

Note, when you ride at each other, hold your lance with both hands in the middle. [Illus. 40.2 p.] When he rides at you to thrust, hit his lance with the front part of your lance to your right side away from you, winding your lance under your right arm so you hit and he does not.

Christian writes:

This is essentially the same technique as its predecessor, only this time you begin the technique in a "half-lance" guard – that is, with both hands holding the lance in the middle. The result is the same: use a forceful motion to set aside your adversary's lance and in doing so strike him with your lance's point.

Ringeck writes:

Note, when you have a short lance and he has a long one, ride calmly with your point against his face. And when he comes to strike, let loose the reins and, with your left hand, drive his lance above and to your left side. Then ride on, setting your point to him.

Christian writes:

This technique has much in common with the "*Absetzen* with the Open Hand" from chapter 34. In that technique, the opponent's superior range is dealt with (he has a spear, while you have a sword) by forcing his spear aside before counter-thrusting. Much the same thing happens here: if you wield a shorter lance than your opponent, strike aside his incoming lance with the back of your gauntlet-clad left hand and safely strike as you close.

Liechtenauer writes:

The lance thrusts, fights: learn to counter it well seated on guard.

Ringeck writes:

Note, when he rides to you with a lance, you will then want to work with skill against him on horse. You should ride with a good seat against him and will want to set aside his lance with yours and otherwise gain advantages with the sword and also with wrestling. If you hurry or race to him, you can not do any technique correctly; you are not secure on the horse.

"Note, this teaches the seventeenth figure,[2] which says: 'Who runs now with the spear, the other meets with under the eyes.'"

Deo Gratias

Christian writes:

This very interesting passage instructs us to not gallop pell-mell against the opponent. While Ringeck does not teach horsemanship, he certainly acknowledges the importance of controlling the mount. If you ride at a full gallop toward your opponent it will be hard to target his openings or set aside his attacks. One must also have a good seat to be sufficiently secure in the saddle. Otherwise, the techniques of this chapter and those that follow would be impossible.

This passage is followed by the words "Deo Gratias" – "Thanks to God," which is curious as this is not the end of the manuscript or even of a major section.

---

[2] This our first exposure to a type of verse for mounted combat that are called *figures*. Peter von Danzig's 1452 *fechtbüch* includes twenty-six of these figures, but Ringeck only quotes a handful of them. They appear to be statements that summarize certain concepts in the teachings.

Illus. 40.3: *The first sword guard for mounted combat, the sword is angled across the saddle, blade resting upon the left arm. This guard is the point of origin for the Taschenhau, or "pouch strike," a powerful upward blow against the opponent.*

Illus. 40.4: *The second sword guard for mounted combat, similar to Ochs. The sword is held with the hilt next to the right side of the head, with the point hanging to menace an opponent's face.*

Illus. 40.5: *The third sword guard for mounted combat is similar to Pflug. The sword is held at the right side with the point rising up to menace an adversary's face.*

Illus. 40.6: *The fourth sword guard for mounted combat. The sword is held with the pommel resting upon his saddle-bow, the point aimed at an adversary. Some of the techniques for taking an opponent's sword terminate here.*

Illus. 40.7: *The fifth sword guard for mounted combat is a half-sword position.*

Illus. 40.8: *This is the mounted combat version of the Nebenhut. It is so named because the sword is held near the leg. This guard is used when riding "at ease" against an opponent against whom you intend to thrust with the Langen Ort.*

Christian writes:

Here we find a fighting scenario quite different from the unarmoured long sword combat of the earliest chapters. We've come a long way from the art of the long sword: the fight is on horseback, the combatants are clad in armour and, as if those didn't make things different enough, the long sword is now wielded with one hand. Despite these differences, the same tactical and bio-mechanical principle apply. We still find techniques employing binding, winding, striking, thrusting, and setting aside; there are grappling methods and sword disarms; and controlling the initiative of the fight remains as important as ever.

Ringeck writes:

"Here begins the art of the sword on horseback.

"Note, when you fight on horseback with the sword, you should know the five guards:

"When you sit on the horse, hold your sword with the right hand at the grip and place the left blade[3] of your blade upon your left arm. [Illus. 40.3]

"Note, hold your sword with the right hand to your right side high over your head; and let the point hang against his face. [Illus. 40.4]

"Hold your sword beside your right leg with the point towards him. [Illus. 40.5]

"Hold your sword in your right hand, and set the pommel on your saddlebow, with the point facing him. [Illus. 40.6]

"Hold your sword with the right hand by the grip, and hold the middle of the blade with the left hand, and hold it across your saddle. [Illus. 40.7]

Christian writes:

The first guard is the primary offensive guard in Liechtenauer's mounted combat system. Most of the strikes described in this section originate from this position, but there is no obvious correspondence between this one and any of the *Vier Leger*--although its offensive potential suggests kinship with *vom Tag*.

The second is a mounted version of *Ochs*. It is a thrusting guard used to menace an opponent from above. It also corresponds to the upper *absetzen* and upper hanger, used in binding and winding against an opponent's sword.

Guard three, similar to *Pflug*, is also a thrusting position threatening with the point from below. It corresponds to the lower *absetzen* and lower hanger and is used in binding and winding against an opponent's sword.

Position four is a specialized guard used primarily in disarming. Hooking the pommel over your opponent's sword hand you can come into this guard to pull his sword away. The instruction to orient the point so that it faces toward the opponent implies that it must have some direct offensive application, though no such technique appears in the manual.

The last is a half-sword guard for mounted combat. Although it is not featured in any of Ringeck's techniques, other German *fechtbücher* of the 15th and 16th centuries employ this guard to hook an adversary's neck with the point as he rides by.

---

[3] *Lincken clingen*--"left blade"--is a term that appears only in the mounted sword techniques. It might be another term for the short edge or it might be the flat of the blade that faces to your left as you hold the sword in your right hand with the point up.

Liechtenauer writes:

"*If he changed it, so that the sword against the sword is put up, truly seize the strong: the Taschenhau ('pouch strike') you search for and remember.*"

Ringeck writes:

"*If you are both coming from the lance and are to fight now with swords, then note: When you ride at him, place your sword on your left arm in guard, riding straight before his eyes to his right side. If he strikes or thrusts to your face, move up and displace with the long edge at the strong of the sword, so that your point stands against his right side. And thrust from below to his face. If he displaces your thrust by moving high up, strike with the long edge to his reins or his left hand. Or, if you want to distress his horse, then strike his right leg and thereby send it running.*

"Note, this teaches the seventh figure, which says: 'Now raises to, the one the Taschenhau seeks.'"

Christian writes:

The *Taschenhau*-- "pouch strike"--is an attack that originates from the first guard. I believe it is so named because it strikes out of the "pouch" created by the bent left arm as it cradles the blade in the first guard. The *Taschenhau* is used to strike aside an opponent's incoming blow and either strike him in the process or putting one's sword in position to thrust. The strike counterattacks while defending, just as the five strikes of the long sword teachings do; a *meisterhau* on horseback.

Strike so that the strong of the sword is brought against the opponent's sword. The strike terminates in the third guard, *Pflug*, where it threatens the opponent's face from below. If your opponent escapes by driving his sword up to displace your thrust, you can strike down onto either his left hand or reins or to his right leg. A rider gives commands to his mount by varying the pressure from his legs against his horse's body, so the strike to the leg will drive a rider's leg against his horse thus giving it a queue to run.

Liechtenauer writes:

"*Learn to bind strongly before all counters. With it force him, set on before. Who grazes, hang to him at the hair.*"

Ringeck writes:

"*Note, you should with all strikes and in all defense always bind with the strong of your sword to his. At the sword constrain and coerce, with the point skillfully displace. If you want, you should attack him. If he displaces and rides along by you, so go on with the pommel, under through his sword, over his left shoulder around the throat. And come with the left hand behind to help hold the pommel, jerking him by you to the side.*

"Note, this teaches the fifth figure, which says: 'Bind before working all striking, hewing, and thrusting.'"

Christian writes:

In this variation on the *Taschenhau*, your opponent begins to ride along past after displacing your strike - that is, he *grazes* your sword. In response to this, drive through to hook your pommel around the left side of his neck. You then grab your pommel with the left hand around the back of your adversary's neck to secure your hold on him and pull him from his saddle.

The fifth figure verse summarizes the concepts at work here, reminding us of the importance of binding in working these techniques.

Ringeck writes:

Note, when you strike at him as he displaces and rides approaching you, grab his right hand with your left. And with your right, set the point to his face.

"Note, this teaches the eighth figure, which says: 'Take the right hand, set the point to his eyes.'"

Christian writes:

Here is another variation on the *Taschenhau*. If your strike is displaced, use your left hand to grab your opponent's sword hand and restrain it while you thrust from the third mounted sword guard at his face. The eighth figure summarizes the action.

Ringeck writes:

When you strike an Oberhau and he displaces, in so doing approaching you, drive your hilt under his jaw. And with the left hand grasp yours behind on your left side by the helmet. And pull him with it to you, and with the hilt push him from you so that he falls."

Christian writes:

This technique also involves a strong bind but does not originate with the *Taschenhau*, but with an *Oberhau* delivered from the right side. In what amounts to a "changing through" (*Durchwechseln*), drive the pommel to the opponent's jaw. You also wrench his head around with a grab to his helmet with your left hand. The combined action of pulling the back of his helmet toward you and pushing with your hilt against his jaw twists him around and out of the saddle.

Ringeck writes:

Note, when you have struck at him and he moves up high to displace, then drive your hilt under his elbow and push him up from you. And go with your right foot under his right, lifting him up with it so that he falls."

Christian writes:

If your opponent counters your *Oberhau* by displacing with his sword held high, he exposes the underside of his arm. This creates an opportunity to use one of the wrestling techniques from the last chapter. This time, your right hand is busy holding your sword, so instead of grabbing with your hand behind his elbow and push there with your hilt. You should then raise your right foot beneath *his* right foot to assist in throwing him from of his horse.

Ringeck writes:

Note, when you strike an Oberhau, and he displaces the strike with a Zwerchhau, move up high with your sword and hang the point to his face, thrusting at him. Or, when you have the point hanging over his sword and he then comes up close to you, move your right arm through his right and press the arm close to you so that you take his sword.

"This teaches the fourth figure, which says: 'Set upon high, swing, go through or the sword break.'"

Christian writes:

Here's another familiar technique from the long sword teachings: the *Zwerchhau*. Your opponent can displace your *Oberhau* with a *Zwerch* from his left. If he does, wind your sword over his blade so that your point hangs down to his face. If your he rides past you, move through his sword arm with your own to take his sword away.

Ringeck writes:

Note, when you ride at him, place your sword on your left arm in guard. If he strikes then to your head, drive up and displace with the long edge so that your point is against his right side. And quickly wind the pommel over his right hand in front of the hilt, press his hand near your chest with your arm, and ride on: thus you take his sword."

Christian writes:

In this sword taking technique, start from the *Taschenhau*, the strike from the "pouch" originating from the first guard. If your opponent strikes defend against the blow by displacing it with the *Taschenhau*. From the bind, immediately drive your pommel inside and over his sword hand, pulling it to your chest. As you continue riding, his sword will be pulled from his hand. This is much like the sword taking techniques of the last chapter - the only difference is that you now have a sword in your hand.

Ringeck writes:

Note, when you have struck an Oberhau at him and he displaces it and in doing so approaches you, move your pommel outside over his right hand. Push it with the hilt to your saddle-bow, grabbing his pommel with your left hand, and riding on, thus taking his sword.

Christian writes:

This sword taking occurs after you strike an *Oberhau* and your opponent displaces it. Drive then over his sword hand from the outside and hook his hand with your pommel. As you pull his hand to your saddlebow, relieve him of the sword by grasping his pommel with your left hand.

Liechtenauer writes:

"*If you want to take a wide approach: this troubles greatly whoever it fends, so wind and the attack the eyes first. If he displaces it onward, to the reins and dagger not allow.*"

Ringeck writes:

Note, if you want to fight while riding at ease, this you should do from the Nebenhut from your right leg [Illus. 40.8 p. 364] with an attack with the Long Point (Langen Ort). And note: when he displaces the thrust, that you wind the point to the face. Then as you force your way in, you will want to use other techniques. And you will find how you shall wind written down in the next techniques.

"This teaches the nineteenth figure: 'Set on the point to the face.'"

Christian writes:

In addition to his commentaries on Liechtenauer's long sword verse, Master Ringeck included his own extrapolations from them, methods that derived from Liechtenauer's teachings but were not found in them. The techniques for fighting from the *Nebenhut*, or "near guard" were included in these additional instructions. In long sword combat, the *Nebenhut* is a guard in which the sword is held near the trailing leg. Therefore, on horseback, the sword hangs down along the right leg. This is a comfortable way to hold the sword if you need to ride "at ease." From this guard, you can quickly raise your sword arm to extend it forward into the guard of the "Long Point." This is another familiar position from the long sword techniques, one where the sword's point is extended toward an opponent's face.

Ringeck writes:

The first technique[4] of the Nebenhut from the right leg, do like this: When you ride to him, hold your sword near your right leg in guard. And thrust long at him with your arm straight to the face. If he then displaces the thrust, go on with the right hand into the upper guard and hang the point at his face. If he remains at the sword and rides towards you, then drive up so that he will wind through, and set the point to him."

Christian writes:

In this technique, ride toward your opponent with your sword at your right leg in the *Nebenhut*. As you approach, you raise your arm and extend it forward into the *Langen Ort* (Long Point) to thrust to your adversary's face. If he displaces this thrust, drive into the second mounted sword guard and thrust to his face from above. If your opponent keeps riding toward you while displacing, raise your hilt even higher and let him ride right into your point as his sword passes by yours.

---

[4] Ringeck calls this the first technique from the *Nebenhut*, but no others follow. In fact, the mounted combat in the manuscript ends abruptly with this technique, giving way to additional half-sword techniques for foot combat without the appearance of a new section heading.

Christian writes:

Wrestling figures in all aspects of Liechtenauer's fighting art and mounted combat is no exception. The techniques of this chapter are similar to those we studied in the long sword chapter on *Durchlaufen*--"running through." In mounted combat, the mechanism for running through an opponent's attack is not *stepping* under and through it, but *riding* through it. As in the teachings on *Durchlaufen*, we find methods here for throwing an opponent – this time, from his saddle – and the disarming techniques of *Schwert Nehmen*, or 'sword-taking'. In either case the motion of the horse, whether in driving forward or wheeling away to the side, provides the impulse that accomplishes the technique. In *Roßfechten*, the motion can't come from your feet, it must come from the horse.

Ringeck writes:

Note, when you both ride towards each other with lances such that you both miss each other, then you will want to rely upon all other fighting skills. Let your lance fall from your hand and draw neither sword nor dagger. And turn to bring your left side onto his right, staying on his right arm and using the wrestling techniques that will be described."

Christian writes:

Master Ringeck tells us we should use other fighting skills if the encounter with lances has come to naught. Part of this arsenal of other skills is wrestling. The first group of wrestling techniques apply for when you've turned your horse about and ridden up so that your left side is alongside your opponent's right side.

Ringeck writes:

Note, do the first wrestling thus:

"When you come with your left side to his right side, throw him with the unnamed or with the hidden grip. And you will find described how you shall use these two wrestling techniques.

"Note, when you come with your left side to his right, if he has his sword drawn and moves forth to strike, grab his right arm behind the elbow with your left hand. And push him upward while raising your left foot up under his right beneath the stirrup leather, so that he falls.

"Or, when you have grabbed with your left hand behind his right elbow, hold the arm fast; and grab the pommel of his sword with you right hand and so take his sword:

"This teaches the third figure, which says: 'With a straight saddle wrestle and catch one.'"

Christian writes:

These passages describe two ways to counter your opponent's attempt to strike at you with his sword when you have ridden up with your left side alongside his right. You can jam his elbow upward while raising his right foot with upward pressure from your own, thus throwing him out of his saddle towards his left. Again, this is an example of defensive and offensive actions taking place in one motion – his sword strike is prevented and he is dashed to the ground.

In the second technique, you still prevent his sword strike by grabbing behind his right elbow, but instead of throwing him from the saddle, you disarm him by grabbing his sword by the pommel.

Also note Liechtenauer's third figure, quoted above, which is another reminder that a rider must be securely seated in the saddle to work these techniques or any of the others of the *Roßfechten* teachings.

Ringeck writes:

"*If you come to his right side with your right side, use the following described wrestling techniques.*

"*Note, when you both have missed with your lances, and you don't want to come with your left side to his right, then keep your right side to his right side. And if he has his sword drawn and wants to strike you, then grasp with the left hand to his right arm behind the elbow. And with the right hand grasp his sword by the pommel, and pull it out of his hand. Or with your right hand take his dagger or some other weapon and use it against him.*"

Christian writes:

Here are two wrestling techniques used on the approach with your opponent on your right side against his right. In one, you stop his sword attack with your left hand behind his elbow and relieve him of the sword by grabbing his pommel with your right hand. The second technique here also involves jamming his elbow to prevent the sword attack. However, instead of disarming him, the right hand draws your foe's dagger and attacks him with it. This is the *only* technique in Ringeck's *fechtbüch* involving the use of a dagger.

Ringeck writes:

Note, when you come with your right side to his right side, and he has his sword drawn and raised up to strike at you, drive with your right arm outside over his right arm. And press under it into your right side, and ride on, so taking his sword

"*Or, drive with the right arm inside and over his right arm. And press it to the front of your chest, and ride on, again taking the sword.*"

Christian writes:

In these two "sword taking" (*Schwert Nehmen*) techniques, you use the forward motion of your horse to pull the sword from his hand after wrapping your right arm around his. This can be done by driving your hand over or under his arm, as the two variations here show.

Ringeck writes:

Note, when you come with your right side to his right side, and he has his sword drawn and raised up to strike, grab his right arm behind the elbow with your right hand, and push him upward while raising your right foot up under his right beneath the stirrup leather so that he falls."

Christian writes:

This technique is the same throw from the saddle that we saw earlier; it employs a hand against your opponent's sword arm and a foot beneath his right foot to help him from the saddle. This time, you have ridden with your right side to his right, so it is your *right* hand that pushes his elbow upward and your right foot that forces his foot up and out of the stirrup.

Ringeck writes:

Note, when you come with your right side to his right side, then grab his right hand with your left, and pull it to your chest; and turn your horse from his, thus dragging him off of his horse:

"*This teaches the second figure, which says: 'To overturn him from his horse, pull his right with your left.'*"

Christian writes:

This is an action that pulls your opponent off of his mount. By grabbing his right hand with your left, pull him off by wheeling your horse to the left, away from his.

finis

Epilogue

This ends our study of Master Ringeck's work. I hope that I have presented his system as the integrated and sophisticated martial art that it deserves to be recognized as. I also hope the reader has been moved to study this material in earnest, to add to our understanding of this manuscript and to do whatever they can to support the resurgence of our Western martial traditions.

In this book I've focussed exclusively on this one manuscript despite the temptation to draw from other German *fechtbücher* to fill in the gaps in Ringeck's commentaries. In some of the other 14th and 15th century works there are additional and/or different commentaries on Liechtenauer's verse and techniques that Ringeck neglects For instance, the 1452 fechtbuch attributed to Peter von Danzig has much more complete merkeverse and glosa for the armoured foot combat teachings, and includes the teachings of several other German masters as well.

There are more more techniques from horseback than we saw in this work and there are strikes and counter-techniques with exotic names like the "Viper's Tongue," "Peacock's Tail," and "Turkish Strike" that Master Ringeck is silent on.

At this time, we can't have too many dedicated people working their way through these ancient treatises. There are manuscripts yet to be explored and more secrets of German medieval swordsmanship yet to be revealed.

Further Commentary on the Zornhau and Krumphau
55v – 59v

<u>Ringeck Writes</u>:

Of the Zornhau

"*When you strike from above, with the point of the Zornhau threaten. When he becomes aware of it, take it above and move it away.*

"*Understand this also:*

"*When one strikes at you from above, strike a Zornhau with the long edge, so that his strike is repelled by your sword's long edge. And wind your point so that it stands against his face with strength, that is with force. And when he then becomes aware - that is, of the point - and clearly displaces it, then take off above from it, as if in the taking off you have been repelled, just as whenever he clearly displaces you, you should take off. Or otherwise catch the strike on his sword to work as I have taught you. What goes first to you, then from that take off. As he displaces you and that strike becomes displaced so do the same by standing thereupon, or if it gives way wind with a thrust or strike. Also know, that when one strikes at you, that you can use the Zornort[1] (Point of Wrath) alone. And you are also not to displace, when you really should attack - as you have been taught, it is bad to displace. When you want to harm him, then drive in to one who wants to strike or thrust to you so that he must displace that: thus you come to the previously described techniques.*

Of the Krumphau

"*Note, when you fight someone: whenever he strikes at you, and you really can't determine that it is coming down upon you from above, you should displace this with the Krumphau. The teachings say: 'Who Krumps to displace, with the step will strike last.' This means: as one strikes to you, move with the Krumphau thereupon: and strike before it comes to you. But work and wind your point to him or strike, so that he must displace. So you come again to more strikes, that you then want to use: feinting, thrusting, winding, striking, or overrunning, when you displace him low or go against with a displacement.*

"*Note, also shall you set aside high strikes using strikes or thrusts - as you have been told - so that you do not have to drive hard thereafter and that your point at all times stands ready to thrust against his face. If he strikes to the other side from your Absetzen, then do not move to him, but wind to the other side to set him aside. And stay and thrust: so you displace and so must he receive your thrust. So you come again to your work.*

"*Note, if one knows something of the Teachings and displaces your technique with the Krumphau, thus he will also wind the thrust to you. So pay attention, and set his thrust or strike thoroughly away. And with that hit him with your point or a strike: so that you always work in such a way that as he cuts to you, he must displace. And when you have practiced this, so that you are ready when you displace him, as you work with a thrust or strike, then you will confuse and break him, so that he must keep on displacing you.*"

<u>Christian Writes</u>:

This curious group of passages appears in the manuscript between the sword and buckler techniques and the beginning of the wrestling section. It begins with an incomplete repetition of Liechtenauer's long sword *merkeverse*, which goes only as far as the verses for *Abschneiden*; I have not included this repetition here. The passages go on the comment on two couplets from the *Zornhau* verse and a single couplet from the *Krumphau*.

There are several interesting things about these passages, not the least of which is their existence in the manual. The inclusion of an "alternate glosa" for the *Zornhau* and *Krumphau* is certainly curious. These passages read quite differently than Ringeck's other commentaries: they appear to be written in a different style and their approach to the material is completely different. Where the earlier commentaries are practical in their approach, these are more conceptual - they tell us little about how to step, what side to strike to, or how the opponent is attacking. Lastly, the lack of completeness in the verse and commentaries is also curious. Perhaps we are looking at a fragment of another master's work? Without knowing the detailed history of the manuscript itself - who wrote it and whether or not it is a copy - the open questions about these fragmentary passages will likely never be answered.

Nevertheless, these include useful comments that reveal some of the mindset behind the techniques. In the *Zornhau* passages, the author describes the act of "taking off" from a bind as being done in a way that makes it appear as if you have been repelled. He also stresses the importance of the "point of wrath" - the position you thrust from after winding the hilt high after binding to your opponent's sword. Also valuable is the observation that one should rely on the *Krumphau* in countering blows whose origin, from above or below, is difficult to determine. Lastly, the passages are reminders of the need to couple your defense with a counterattack so that your opponent must focus all his attention on protecting himself rather than on defeating you.

---

[1] Ringeck uses the term *Zornort* only in this passage. I have assumed from the other commentaries that this is the position one is in when you wind your hilt up from a bind to thrust from what is basically the left side *Ochs*. This is supported by Plate 3 of Hans Talhoffer's 1467 fechtbuch. Source: *Medieval Combat*, trans. and ed. Rector, Greenhill Books, 2000.

Appendix 2

The interpretation of the *Krumphau*--"crooked strike"--posed one of the greatest challenges in my study of the long sword teachings presented in Sigmund Ringeck's book. This is a confusing part of the work for several reasons:

1. Ringeck doesn't specify whether one should strike with the long or short edge of the sword.
2. It isn't clear from Ringeck's text whether the *Krumphau* is an *Oberhau* (a strike from above) or an *Unterhau* (a strike from below).
3. Ringeck's description of the primary technique advises that you should use it to counter a strike "from your right side" by stepping clear of the strike with a step to your right.

The third point was certainly the more troubling of the three. If one is to strike the opponent's hands with the point, this seemed awkward if not improbable – if you step right towards someone swinging from their left side, you'll likely walk into their strike. I began to feel certain that Ringeck actually meant that to say "von *seiner* rechten sytten" rather than "von *deiner* rechten sytten" as the manuscript has it written – that is, that your opponent is striking from *his* right side, not from *your* right side. After all, striking "*from* your right side" is rather strange phraseology, and is quite inconsistent in its wording from the remainder of the manuscript. However, I wanted to seek out something to corroborate my hunch.

The earliest commentary on the *Krumphau* available to us is in Hanko Döbringer's 1389 *fechtbüch*,[1] the earliest surviving manuscript treating Liechtenauer's teachings. On page 25v, we have:[2]

> "*Hie merke und wisse das der Krumphau ist ein ober haue der damit eine guten aus schreiten / krump dar geht / zum noch einer Seite…*"

> "Now note and know that the *Krumphau* is an *Oberhau* with which one steps well out / The *Krump* there goes / to the other side…"

This passage clearly indicates that the *Krumphau* is, without a doubt, an *Oberhau*. It also seems to indicate that the strike attacks the side opposite that to which one steps. However, Döbringer's work tends to be more conceptual and less of a how-to, so I searched further.

This led me to Peter von Danzig's 1452 fechtbuch[3]. The glosa for Liechtenauer's long sword teachings is very similar (and perhaps related to?) the commentary in Ringeck's work. While there is a passage where that master advocates stepping to the right to counter a left side *Ochs* guard assumed by your opponent, that doesn't really match the situation of being struck at from the opponent's left side. The technique that *most* closely resembles the first technique of the *Krumphau* as described by Master Ringeck appears on page 17r of the Danzig manuscript:

---

[1] Hanko Döbringer, *Fechtbuch*, Nürnberg, Germanisches Nationalmuseum - Cod.ms.3227a 1389.
2 Transcription by Grzegorz Zabinsky.
[3] Peter von Danzig, *Fechtbuch*, Rom, Bibliotheca dell´Academica Nazionale dei Lincei e Corsiniana - Cod.44 A 8 (Cod. 1449) 1452.

"Merck den krump haw magstu auch treiben aus der schranck hut von paiden seitten und in die hut schick dich also wenn du mit dem zu vechten zu ym kumpst. So ste mit dem lincken fuess vor und halt dein swert mit dem ort neben deiner rechten seitten auff der erden das die lang schneid oben sey und gib dich plöss mit der lincken seitten haut er dir denn zu der plöss. So spring aus dem haw gegen ym mit dem rechten fuess wol auff dein rechte seitten und slach yn mit gekräuczten henden aus der langen schneid mit dem ort auff sein hend."

"Note, the *Krumphau* can be done from the *Schranckhut* from both sides and in that guard should you do thus: when you come to him in the *Zufechten*, then stand with your left foot forward and hold you sword with the point beside your right side to the earth with the long edge up and provide and opening with your left side. When he strikes to that opening, then spring out of the strike with your right foot well to your right side and strike him with crossed hands with the long edge with the point to his hands."

This version clears up some ambiguities left by Ringeck's glosa. It is described as starting from the *Schranckhut* on the right side, but could easily be struck from *vom Tag*, as I have depicted it. This technique not only indicates which edge to use, it also infers that when you step "out of the strike" to your right, that you are countering a blow from *your opponent's right side*, not "from your right side" as the Ringeck manuscript says. After all, if your enemy is striking your left side, it's pretty likely that he has swung from his right side. Interestingly, in the subsequent passage, the von Danzig manuscript advocates striking from the *left side Schranckhut* with the short edge when attacked from your opponent's left. The blow is a *Krumphau* not because the strike *ends* with the hands crossed, but because they *begin* crossed.

Further confirmation can be garnered elsewhere. Much later, Joachim Meyer would write this of the *Krumphau* in Folio XII of his 1570 opus:[4,5]

"Diser Hauw wirt also volbracht / stehe in der Zornhut mit dem Lincken fuß vor / Hauwet dein gegen Man auff dich / so trit mit deinem Rechten fuß wol auß seinem streich gegen seiner Lincken seiten / Hauwe mit Langer schneid unnd geschrenckten henden seinem hauw entgegen / oder zwischen seinen Kopff und Klingen / uberzwerch auff seine hendt / und laß die Kling wol uber seinen Arm uberschiessen…"

"This strike is thus done – stand in the *Zornhut*[6] with the left foot forward. If your man strikes against you then step with the right foot well from his strike toward his left side. Strike with the long edge and outstretched hands against his strike or between his head and blade against his hands and let the blade shoot well over his arms…"

Once again, we see the use of the long edge called out explicitly, as well as the manner in which the strike should counter the opponent's attack.

From this evidence, it becomes clear that the primary idea behind the *Krumphau* is to evade the opponent's attack while counterstriking. If your opponent strikes from his right, step away from the strike by stepping to his left and striking across yourself to hit his hands or sword - if he attacks from his left, step to his right. We also know that the *Krumphau* is an *Oberhau* and that, at least from the right, it is delivered with the long edge.

The *Krumphau* problem and its solution, show the benefit of having not just a single manuscript, but an entire tradition to draw upon. My interpretation has therefore been informed not only by Ringeck's somewhat unclear words, but by those of his predecessors, contemporaries and successors.

---

[4] Meyer, Joachim, *Grundtliche beschreibung der freyen ritterlichen und adelichen kunst des fechtens*, Strasbourg, 1570.
5 Transcription by Marlon Hoess-Boettger.
[6] The *Zornhut* is the "guard of wrath" and is a variant of the guard *vom Tag*. In the *Zornhut*, the blade actually hangs behind the back so that a very powerful stroke can be delivered.

Glossary

Abnahmen - (Taking off) A sudden departure from a bind whereby one's sword is freed to strike to the other side. Similar in meaning to *Zucken*.

Abschneiden - (Cutting off) Slicing cuts, delivered from above or below. One of the *Drei Wunder* ('Three Wounders').

Absetzen - (Setting aside) To deflect a thrust or strike at the same time as thrusting. The word can also denote a type of parry wherein the opponent's blade slides off of one's own.

Alber - (The Fool) One of the four primary guards in Liechtenauer's long sword fighting system. In it the sword is held with the hilt low and the blading angled 45 degrees with the point to the ground. It is a guard that invites an opponent's attack.

After - see *Nach*.

Am Schwert - (At the Sword) Techniques performed while remaining in a bind with an opponent's sword.

Ansetzen - (Setting Upon) To attack with the point.

Ausser Abnahmen - (Outer taking) A type of Nachreisen ('traveling after') that is done by keeping your blade on the outside of the opponent's blade.

Beinbruch - (Leg break) A type of wrestling counter-technique (bruch) that involves using one's own or one's opponent's legs to effect resulting in a throw, joint lock, or dislocation.

Before - see *Vor*.

Binden - (Binding) The act of making contact between two swords or other weapons.

Blosse - an 'opening' or target area. In unarmoured combat (Blossfechten), there are four openings: two (left and right) above the belt, and two below it.

Bloßfechten - (Exposed Fighting) unarmoured combat.

Bruch - (Break) A counter-technique, something that 'breaks' an attack.

Buckler - A small, usually round, shield used for foot combat.

Buffalo - see *Buffel*.

Buffel - (Buffalo) Period slang term for a cloddish fighter who relies on only strength.

Crown - see *Kron*.

Displacement - see *Versetzen*.

Drei Wunder - (Three Wounders) The three ways of injuring an opponent with a long sword: thrusting, slicing, or striking. All three may be performed from each of the eight windings (*Acht Winden*).

Duplieren - An attack made from a bind wherein one winds the sword behind the opponent's blade to strike or slice him in the face.

Durchlaufen - (Running through) Wrestling technique performed in long sword fighting in which one 'runs through' the enemy's attack to grapple with him.

Durchsetzen - (Setting through) Technique performed in half-sword fighting where one thrusts down between the opponent's sword and his body.

Durchwechseln - (Changing through) Techniques for escaping from a bind by sliding one's point out from under an opponent's blade to thrust to another opening.

Edel Krieg - (Noble War) A close-combat technique in which one winds one's hilt high to escape a bind an then proceeds to thrust repeatedly until an opening is hit.

Fechten - fencing or fighting

Feler - (Feint) A deception with the sword that causes an opponent to commit to the defense of one opening while one's intent is to actually attack another opening.

Fencing - Specifically, fighting with swords. However, in the 15th century, the word fencing had a broader connotation than it does today, including all the arts of defence.

Fühlen - (Feeling) The skill of sensing the degree of pressure exerted by one's opponent in a bind. One should determine how to react to an opponent by sensing whether he is 'hard' or 'soft' at the sword.

Glosa - Commentaries made by Sigmund Ringeck (and other masters, in different fechtbucher) that explain the meaning of Johannes Liechtenauer's cryptic verses (*Merkeverse*).

Halbschwert - (Half-Sword) Method of wielding a long sword where the right hand holds the grip of the sword while the left grasps the mid-point of the blade. In this method, the sword can be wielded as a short thrusting spear or, with the pommel forward, as an implement with which to hook your opponent and throw him down. Also appears in Ringeck's manuscript as Kurtzen Schwert, or 'shortened sword'.

Half-Sword - see *Halb Schwert*.

Hard - see *Hert*.

Harnischfechten - (Harness fighting) Armoured combat, usually implying foot combat in harness.

Hau - (Hew or Strike) A strike or hewing blow with a sword.

Hende Trucken - (Pressing of the Hands) Slicing technique where one slices under an opponent's hands as he attacks from above and then winds the sword's edge so as to slice down onto his hands, thereby pushing the opponent aside.

Hengen - see *Zwei Hengen*.

Hert - (Hard) Condition in a bind where one is pressing strongly against an opponent's blade.

Hut - See *Leger*.

Indes - (During, or Meanwhile) Term describing the act of responding almost simultaneously to an opponent's actions, whether using one of the 'Five Strikes' to counter a strike or reacting in a bind based on the degree of blade pressure being exerted by the opponent. This quick reaction allows one to go from a defensive response (Nach) into an offensive one (Vor).

Krieg - (War) The second phase of a fighting encounter, when the combatants have moved to close combat range. The techniques used in this close combat are limited to those associated with winding (Winden) and wrestling at the sword (Ringen am Schwert).

Kron - (the Crown) A defensive position wherein one raises the long sword, point upward, to intercept a downward blow on the hilt. Once the attack has been caught, one can rush in to grapple with the opponent.

Krumphau - One of Liechtenauer's five strikes, directed diagonally downward from one's right side to the opponent's right side, such that the hands are crossed. It is usually directed against an opponent's hands or the flat of his sword. Also, in the general sense, any strike delivered with the hands crossed. The name derives from the crossing of the hands, i.e., *krump* means twisted. The Krumphau counters the guard *Ochs*, as it closes off that guard's line of attack.

Kurzen Schneide - (Short Edge) The back edge of a long sword. When a sword is held out with the point facing an opponent, this edge is the one that is facing up.

Langenort - (the Long Point) A secondary guard described by Ringeck. It is much like the guard Pflug (the Plow) except that the hands are extended forward so as to menace an opponent's face at longer range.

Langen Schneide - (Long Edge) The true edge of a long sword. When a sword is held out with the point facing an opponent, this edge is the one that is facing down.

Langen Schwert - (Long Sword) A late medieval hand-and-a-half sword, usually with a sharply tapering point that is suited to thrusting attacks. The long sword is the weapon that Liechtenauer's teachings focus most on.

Liechtenauer, Johannes - German fight master who flourished in the 14th Century. After studying with other masters throughout Europe, Liechtenauer synthesized his own system of fighting which he ensconced in cryptic verse (*Merkverse*). These teachings were included in the works of many subsequent masters and informed German swordsmanship for over 200 years.

Long Edge - see *Langen Schneide*.

Long Sword - see *Langen Schwert*.

Leger - A guard or fighting stance. Liechtenauer's system specifies the use of four guards (see also Vier Leger), but other masters, including Sigmund Ringeck, later added other positions to the system.

Meisterhau - (Master Strikes) Name for the five secret strikes of Johannes Liechtenauer's system of long sword fighting. The word does not appear in Ringeck's manuscript however. These strikes are designed to defend against an opponent's attack while counterattacking him.

Merkeverse - (Teaching Verse) The cryptic verses of Master Johannes Liechtenauer, which were written to obscure their meaning to the uninitiated and serve as a series of mnemonics to those schooled in his fighting system.

Mittelhau - (Middle Strike) Any horizontal blow, usually directed to an opponent's mid-section.

Mortstöße - (Murder Strikes) Blows with hand used to stun an opponent as a prelude to grappling with him.

Mutieren - A long sword technique, employed from a bind, whereby one winds the sword so that one's point comes down on the opposite side on the opponent's blade to thrust to a lower opening.

Nach - (After) The defensive principle in Liechtenauer's system. When one is forced to respond to an adversary's attack, one is fighting in the After. As it is imperative that one regain the initiative, one employs techniques from the After to get back to fighting in the Before - that is, on the offensive.

Nachreisen - (Traveling After) Methods for out-timing your adversary's attack so that you can return to fighting offensively. One can strike right after a missed strike by your opponent, or right before he strikes, for instance.

Nebenhut - (Near Guard) Secondary guard position where one holds the sword at either side of the body with the point trailing slightly backward. The name derives from the sword being near the leg. Similar to the 'Tail Guard' of other Medieval systems.

Oberhau - (Over Strike) A strike directed downward from above, either diagonally or vertically.

Ochs - (the Ox) One of Liechtenauer's four primary guards. The sword is held with the hands crossed high at the right side of the head, with the point directed down towards the opponent's face and the left leg leading. There is also left side version of this guard where the sword is held with the hands uncrossed, with the right leg leading.

Play - A sequence of techniques, with actions and responses, comprising a set

Pflug - (the Plow) One of Liechtenauer's four primary guards. The sword is held with the hands crossed at the right side, the hilt at the right hip, with the point directed up towards the opponent's face and the left leg leading. There is also left side version of this guard where the sword is held with the hands uncrossed, with the right leg leading.

Redel - (Wheel) A blow with the long sword in which one strikes from below on the right side with outstretched arms, swinging the sword in a wide horizontal arc.

Ringeck, Sigmund - A German fight master of the early to mid-15ᵗʰ Century who interpreted the cryptic writings of Master Johannes Liechtenauer. Ringeck was fight master to Albrecht, Count Palatine of the Rhine and Duke of Bavaria.

Ringen am Schwert - (Wrestling at the Sword) Techniques for grappling in a bind in long sword combat. These are grouped under *Durchlaufen*, one of Liechtenauer's primary techniques.

Roßfechten - (Horse Combat) Liechtenauer's mounted combat in armour.

Scheitelhau - (Scalp or Parting Strike) One of Liechtenauer's five strikes, a vertical strike from above with the long edge aimed at the opponent's head or upper chest. It counters the guard *Alber* by means of superior range. The name derives from the primary target of this strike, the scalp.

Schielhau - (Squinting Strike) One of Liechtenauer's five strikes, a vertical strike from above with the sword edge aimed at the opponent's right shoulder. It counters the guard Pflug by closing of its line of attack. The name derives from the position of the person striking - one turns such that one is 'squinting' at the opponent with only one eye.

Schlachent Ort - (Battering Point) Strikes with the pommel, delivered against an armoured opponent with both hands on the blade.

Schnitt - (Cut) Slicing cuts made with either edge of the long sword. One of the 'Three Wounders' (*Drei Wunder*). There are four basic cuts: two directed from above, using a position corresponding to the guard Pflug, and two directed from below, from a position like the guard Ochs.

Schranckhut - (Barrier Guard) A secondary guard that figures in Ringeck's commentaries but not in Liechtenauer's verse. To stand in the guard you either lead with your right leg with your sword hanging diagonally down almost to the ground on your left side, or lead with your left leg with your sword hanging diagonally down on your right side.

Schwech - (Weak) The part of a long sword blade extending from the middle of the blade to the point. You can not bind strongly on this part of the sword.

Schwert Nehmen - (Sword Taking) Binding and grappling techniques designed to disarm the opponent swordsman.

Setting Aside - see *Absetzen*.

Short Edge - see *Kurzen Schneide*.

Sprechfenster - (Speech Window) One of the techniques of *Zwei Hengen* (Two Hangers). After binding with an opponent's sword, you remain in the bind with your arms extended. From this position you wait and sense his actions through changes in blade pressure (*Fühlen*). Thus, your adversary's intent is 'spoken' through the 'window' created by the bind.

Ston - (Ground Techniques) Wrestling techniques used to take the fight to the ground where a hold may be effected.

Störck - (Strong) The part of a long sword blade that extends from the crossguard to the middle of the blade. One can bind with strength on this part of the blade.

Strong - see *Störck*.

Stuck - (Piece) A technique or series of techniques strung together.

Sturzhau - (Plunging Strike) A strike from above in which the sword is turned while striking so that the short, or back, edge plunges down over an opponent's defense.

Taschenhau - (Pouch Strike) A strike used in mounted combat in which one begins with the blade resting on the left arm, which holds the reins. With the right hand on the grip, one strikes from the 'pouch' created by the slight bend of the left arm.

Überlaufen - (Overrunning) Techniques whereby one out-reaches an opponent's low strike or thrust with a high strike or thrust. One of Liechtenauer's primary techniques, it also includes methods for reaching over and pulling down an opponent's blade as he attacks high.

Unterhalten - (Holding Down) Wrestling techniques used for holding an opponent once he has been thrown to the ground.

Unterhau - (Under Strike) A strike directed upward from below, either diagonally or vertically.

Verborgen Ringen - (Forbidden or Secret Wrestling) Wrestling techniques intended only for deadly fighting encounters. It was deemed unwise to teach them in public.

Verkehrer - (Inverter) A technique performed while in a bind by inverting the position of the hilt so that the right thumb is situated beneath the sword. This brings the hilt high while the point menaces the opponent's face.

Versetzen - (Displacement) To parry or block. Liechtenauer's teachings advise against using purely defensive displacements, as they allow one's opponent to maintain the initiative. A proper displacement must contain an offensive component.

Vom Tag - (From the Roof) One of Liechtenauer's four primary guards, designed primarily as starting position for strong strikes. One stands leading with the left leg, with the sword held at either the right shoulder or over the head.

Vom Schwert - (From the Sword) Term describing actions that involve removing one's sword from a bind.

Vor - (Before) The offensive principle in Liechtenauer's system. As the control of initiative in the fight is all-important, one should seek to strike before an opponent does, so that the opponent is forced to remain on the defensive. Many of Liechtenauer's teachings describe methods for regaining the initiative if it has been lost momentarily.

Weak - see *Schwech*.

Wechselhau - (Change Strike) A strike that is initially aimed at one opening, but then 'changes' during its execution to strike another. This can be a change from a left side opening to a right side opening, or from an upper or opening to a lower one, or vice-versa.

Weich - (Soft) Condition in a bind where one is exerting little pressure against an opponent's blade.

Wierschin, Martin - German author who published a transcription of the Ringeck manuscript in 1965.

Winden - (Winding) A hallmark of Liechtenauer's fighting system, these are techniques where the sword or spear winds or turns about it long axis while binding an opponent's weapon. Winding is used to regain leverage in the bind and to seek out targets by changing the angle of attack without exposing a weakness in one's defense. There are eight basic windings, four performed while binding in the guard *Ochs* and four while binding in the guard *Pflug*. *Duplieren* and *Mutieren* are also types of winding.

Zornhau - (Strike of Wrath) One of Liechtenauer's five strikes, a diagonal strike from above. It is so named because it is a powerful strike that an enraged man would instinctively employ.

Zucken - (Twitching) The act of jerking one's blade out of a bind to strike around to another opening. In spear and half-sword fighting, this also means to jerk the weapon backward out of a bind to thrust to another opening.

Zufechten - (Coming to the Fight) The first phase of combat, where one closes with the opponent.

Zulauffend Ringen - (Wrestling While Closing) Grappling techniques applied while approaching an opponent.

Zwerchhau - (Cross Strike) One of Liechtenauer's five strikes, struck horizontally to the left side of the opponent's head using the short edge. If struck to an opponent's right side, the long edge is used. The Zwerchhau counters the guard *vom Tag*, as it closes off the line of attack of strikes from above.

Zwei Hengen - (Two Hangers) Positions in which the swords bind. One is where one's sword is held in the bind so that the pommel hangs down with the point menacing the opponent's face. This corresponds with the guard *Pflug*. The other is where the point hangs down from above to threaten the face, which corresponds with the guard *Ochs*.

Bibliography

Primary Sources

Döbringer, Hanko, *Fechtbuch* (1389). n.p. Codex Ms. 3227a, German National Museum, Nuremburg.

von Danzig, Peter, *Fechtbuch* (1452). n.p. Codex 44 A 8, Library of the National Academy, Rome, Italy.

Dei Liberi, Fiore, *Flos Duellatorum in arnis, sine arnis, equester, pedester.* Italy, 1409 (MS Ludwig XV.13, Getty Museum, Los Angeles).

Meyer, Joachim, *Grundtliche beschreibung der freyen ritterlichen und adelichen kunst des fechtens* (A Thorough Description of the Free, Knightly and Noble Art of Fencing). Strasbourg, 1570.

Ringeck, Sigmund, *Fechtbuch* (c.1440). Dresden, State Library of Saxony, Ms. Dresd. C 487.

Secondary Sources

Anglo, Sydney, *The Martial Arts of Renaissance Europe.* London and New Haven, Yale, 2000.

Galas, S. Matthew, "Kindred spirits: The art of the sword in Germany and Japan," published in the *Journal of Asian Martial Arts*, VI (1997), pp. 20 - 46.

Hils, Hans-Peter, *Master Johann Liechtenauer's kunst des langen schwerts.* Frankfurt am Main, 1985.

Oakeshott, R. Ewart, *The Sword in the Age of Chivalry.* Woodbridge, UK, 1964.

Talhoffer, Hans, *Medieval Combat: A Fifteenth-Century Illustrated Manual of Swordfighting and Close-Quarter Combat.* edited Mark Rector, London, Greenhill Books, 2000.

Wierschin, Martin, *Meister Johann Liechtenauers kunst des fechtens.* Munich, Muenchener Text und Untersuchungen zur deutschen Literatur des Mittelalters, 1965.